Inclusive Aims

Studies in Rhetorics and Feminisms
Series Editors: Cheryl Glenn and Shirley Wilson Logan

The series promotes and amplifies the interdisciplinarity of rhetorics and feminisms, connecting rhetorical inquiry with contemporary academic, sociopolitical, and economic concerns. Books in the series explore such enduring questions of rhetoric's rich and complex histories (globally and locally) as well as rhetoric's relevance to current public exigencies of social justice, power, opportunity, inclusion, equity, and diversity. This attention to interdisciplinarity has already transformed the rhetorical tradition as we have known it (upper-class, public, powerful, mostly political, antagonistic, and delivered by men) into regendered, inclusionary rhetorics (democratic, deliberative, diverse, collaborative, private, intersectional, and delivered by all people). Our cultural, political, and intellectual advancements will be enriched by exploring the varied ways rhetorics and feminisms intersect and animate one another (and take us in new political, cultural, scientific, communicative, and pedagogical directions).

Books in the Series

Not Playing Around: Feminist and Queer Rhetorics in Videogames by Rebecca S. Richards (2024)
Inclusive Aims: Rhetoric's Role in Reproductive Justice edited by Heather Brook Adams and Nancy Myers (2024)
A Rhetoric of Becoming: USAmerican Women in Qatar by Nancy Small (2022)
Rhetorical Listening in Action: A Concept-Tactic Approach by Krista Ratcliffe and Kyle Jensen (2022)

INCLUSIVE AIMS

Rhetoric's Role in Reproductive Justice

Edited by
Heather Brook Adams and Nancy Myers

Parlor Press
Anderson, South Carolina
www.parlorpress.com

Parlor Press LLC, Anderson, South Carolina, USA

Printed in the United States of America on acid-free paper.

S A N: 2 5 4 - 8 8 7 9

Library of Congress Cataloging-in-Publication Data on File

1 2 3 4 5

978-1-64317-424-2 (paperback)
978-1-64317-425-9 (PDF)
978-1-64317-426-6 (EPUB)

Cover design by David Blakesley.
Cover image: "Justice" by Francesco Ferrucci del Tadda (1497–1585). Metropolitan Museum of Art (New York City). The Friedsam Collection, Bequest of Michael Friedsam, 1931. Used by permission.

Parlor Press, LLC is an independent publisher of scholarly and trade titles in print and multimedia formats. This book is available in paper and ebook formats from Parlor Press on the World Wide Web at www.parlorpress.com or through online and brick-and-mortar bookstores. For submission information or to find out about Parlor Press publications, write to Parlor Press, 3015 Brackenberry Drive, Anderson, South Carolina, 29621, or email editor@parlorpress.com.

Contents

Rhetorics of Practice

Preface

This collection engages with reproductive politics at a time marked by unparalleled anti-racist activist protest and movement, renewed labor activism, the COVID-19 pandemic, increasing projections about climate-related change, the so-called "great resignation," and—last but surely not least—the United States Supreme Court's overturn of *Roe v. Wade.* Doing so necessitates an endlessly recursive process of assessing dire events and rhetorical situations. The reversal of *Roe,* the 1973 legal decision that has garnered substantive and long-standing political attention, reflects more than implications, however significant, for people seeking and obtaining a safe and legal abortion. Rather, public commentary, personal introspection, and shared discussions of imagined futures have revealed the current, lamentable state of reproductive politics—the term we as editors of this collection use to refer to the landscape of reproductive policy, reproductive health and wellness, birthing, parenting, and elective or compulsory non-parenting.

For those who legitimately value the needs, desires, and safety of reproducing people, recent years have demonstrated that in the United States especially, reproductive matters represent not only contestation but extreme precarity. Such precarity results from, among other things, key rhetorical problems: how and by whom reproductive issues are discussed, what topics and rhetors are excluded from public discussion, and how public discourse flattens complex issues of the reproductive realm. Reproductive politics necessarily warrants the following actions and, of course, many more not present on this short list:

- being knowledgeable about bodies' reproductive capabilities and using this knowledge to make informed decisions about one's fertility management;
- making such decisions in non-moralizing, shame- and stigma-free contexts;
- valuing the ability to safely and legally obtain an abortion in an affirming and supportive facility;
- being realistic about the looming and potentially draconian ripple effects of an anti-abortion agenda;

- respecting the individual right to reproductive autonomy as one aspect of a more holistic approach to reproductive health and dignity;
- desiring that other people have avenues to safely and legally manage their own fertility and supporting such management as a matter of public concern;
- recognizing the dire need for basic items (such as baby formula) and services (like healthcare) that are needed to raise a child in safe and healthy ways; and
- demanding leadership and public policy that concretely support safe, non-life-threatening, and enriching environments for all people, including children.

Reproductive politics can and should also be understood as a contemporary realm that has been shaped by historical injustices differentially experienced across communities. In the past and now in the present, those supporting reproductive freedoms have too often forwarded ideological commitments that uphold white, patriarchal, heteronormative, and ableist values. Even in this moment, though, some people who support "women's"[1] reproductive autonomy do so in harmful ways that perpetuate injustice and demonstrate the ongoing deflation of dynamic political possibilities. A poignant example in 2022 was the call by some (allegedly "journalists" and "activists" responding especially to comments made by Oklahoma Governor Kevin Stitt that set off much speculation) for tribal lands in the US to be safe havens for abortion care because of the legal sovereignty of such lands (Hilleary). Some Indigenous people speaking out about this idea have explained how offensive, uninformed, and "tone-deaf" the proposal was based on realities that they know particularly well. For instance, limitations on publicly funded abortion care services based on the long-standing Hyde Amendment—passed by Congress in the wake of the original *Roe* ruling and upheld in decades since—result in the denial of abortion access on tribal lands, where health care is provided by the federal government (Maher). The proposal also fla-

1. We invite readers to engage with this term in its expansiveness rather than as a way to reassert a rigid gender binary. We further support understanding reproductive politics as a realm that directly implicates people who may not use the term "woman."

grantly demonstrates a lack of awareness of the long and unjust history of reproductive violences experienced by Indigenous people because of US policy that sponsored compulsory sterilization and family separation and that failed to mitigate many instances of sexual and gender violence related to such policies. Not least important, the sanctuary idea demonstrates nonnative people speaking over instead of with Indigenous people, advocating for desires that do not take into consideration what these people themselves think and want. Significantly, this rhetorical response to a material reproductive injustice perpetuates further injustice and deepens, rather than alleviates, precarity. For all these reasons, the sanctuary response demonstrates the need for more strategic, inclusive, and coalitional efforts. The possibility of a more capacious and equitable reproductive politics exists, but only if more people open themselves to the breadth of this realm and if they listen and learn across experiences in order to challenge their own understandings and collaboratively reframe the stakes and aims of reproductive change.

The arguably stressed and potentially fractured state of feminist coalitional resistance to the curtailment of rights, freedoms, and support for reproducing people adds additional urgency to the pursuit of such inclusive aims. While calls for coalitional solidarity exist and are surely being enacted in many places and in various ways, mainstream progressive responses to reproductive exigences have too often perpetuated a distinct lack of coalition. Elsewhere among feminists, division threatens to break down coalitional possibility rather than encourage strategically collaborative paths of rhetorical action. Activists, advocates, and academics alike have the opportunity to use the current toxic state of reproductive politics as motivation for rethinking broader strategies as we move forward, together. Despite, indeed because of, our varied experiences, we have the opportunity to recognize how many people might be fueled by the same fire and to use our range of reactions and responses as additional fuel for acting boldly, coalitionally, and in broad, unprecedented, and long overdue ways.

With such pressing exigencies in mind, the premise of the collection, as exemplified in our title, *Inclusive Aims: Rhetoric's Role in Reproductive Justice*, is that those who desire justice in the realm of reproductive politics can benefit from thinking about such events and actions rhetorically, and not in isolation but as interconnected and connected to larger webs of action. These chapters offer paths for yoking two dynamic thought traditions: rhetorical theoretical approaches that have been honed in the academy and reproductive justice theory and practice, which has been developed across activist and scholarly sites. Rhetoric, long the study of persuasion, identification, discursive power, and pathways for seeking social change, is the intellectual tradition that we, as editors, work within. Our specialty in feminist rhetorics enables us to consider the broad realm of rhetorical possibility through a lens especially attuned to intersectional feminist concerns and methods—all the while being compelled to "*do something*" with our feminist rhetorical scholarship in light of "contemporary and global politics" (Enoch, Jack, and Glenn 7). Rhetoric provides conceptual and pragmatic approaches to engaging across difference, opening ourselves to unfamiliar futures, listening more carefully, and articulating injustices and the just worlds toward which we can strive.

Alongside this rhetorical insight, this collection makes an explicit commitment to engaging concerns of reproductive politics through the lens of reproductive justice, an inclusive framework and methodology that has emerged from the partiality and lack of coalition that has been a hallmark of most mainstream feminist organizing. Given the complexity of this moment, the Reproductive Justice Movement and its framework—focused on the three principles of the right to have a child, the right to not have a child, and the right to raise a child in a safe and healthy environment—is needed now more than ever. As two white people who care about reproductive issues and who are laboring to heed the call of people of color who have created this activist theory of change, we consider our move to glean insights from reproductive justice thought leaders to be non-negotiable. We make such a move not only with a disposition of respect, a sense of ethical urgency, and a desire for strategic coalition, but with the true belief that the framework and associated methods offer the *best* way forward (in so many senses of the word). In our introduction, we provide a brief history of the Reproductive Justice Movement and articulate our understanding of the movement's theory and our orientation, as white scholars, to learn from such work. Our introduction also locates the collection within the movement's framework and demonstrates rhetoric's role in critiquing exclusionary reproductive politics and in supporting and promoting reproductive justice for all.

The collection coheres to the broad premise that all peoples deserve rights and dignity in relation to concerns of sexuality, reproduction, and family. In content, methods, and form, the collection enacts our commitments to coalition and rhetorical possibility—through time and place and from the local to the global. We explicitly anchor the rhetorical work of the collection in storytelling, a vital route, as reproductive justice work demonstrates—to the rhetorical worldbuilding that this collection's afterword writers call for. The collection models how storytelling functions to bring together varied and disparate narratives that, collectively, demonstrate the complexity of rhetorical contexts that may not be apparent in the tidiness of a single story or the contours of controlling narratives. We invite readers to reshuffle and reconsider the chapters as possibilities for additional insights, oversights, and questions—to reflect coalitionally not just within a chapter but in dialogue across them. This storytelling emphasis echoes the goal of reproductive justice to create meaningful apertures and meaningful linkages—epistemological ruptures that render tacit understandings apparent and foreground overlooked or suppressed knowledges. As Loretta J. Ross and Rickie Solinger maintain, reproductive justice "is neither an oppositional nor a peacemaking framework" but rather is "an emergent radical theory that reframes" injustices, always in pursuit of ways of knowing and doing that promote human rights for all persons (113).

To that activist aim, the collection's organization urges readers—whether academics, practitioners, or policy makers—to consider to what additional ends a rhetorical mindset, rhetorical practices, and an explicit commitment to purposeful storying can be engaged. We arranged these collection chapters so that the two sections, "Rhetorics of Alliance" and "Rhetorics of Practice," begin with scholars who work primarily outside of our academic discipline and who investigate race, rhetoric, and reproductive justice. Opening with these chapters enacts the Reproductive Justice Movement's commitment to listening coalitionally and centering the perspectives of those who are otherwise marginalized. The second chapters investigate histories that shed light on the complicated uptake and extensions of reproductive justice theory in our contemporary rhetorical moment. The following three chapters in each section provide illustrations of various alliances and practices invoking the reproductive justice framework as an "open-source code"—one that is expanding, inclusive, and evolving (Ross et al. 19). The afterword, written by Shui-yin Sharon Yam and Natalie Fixmer-Oraiz, reflects on the chapters as a whole and responds with a call for ongoing and especially transnational "world-making" for reproductive justice. Whether engaging in questions of historical or contemporary importance, each chapter of this collection poses, with hope and intellectual rigor, specific possibilities for our collective futures. In the wake of the *Dobbs* ruling, these reproductive political futures are primarily imagined, but, we contend, the durable responses in this collection will remain relevant as reproducing people experience additional and varied political, social, and material realities.

Overview of Chapters

The five chapters in "Rhetorics of Alliance" illustrate the importance of storytelling as both individual and communal acts in making visible the injustices and possibilities of reproductive politics. Sharing stories can lead to identifying with others, to recognizing common issues and goals as well as compelling differences across experience, and to creating and sustaining coalitional partnerships for engendering reproductive justice. As one strategy for making the "invisible" apparent, storytelling toward coalitional inclusivity becomes vital to understanding the possible means for responding to reproductive injustices both social and institutional. Karma R. Chávez refers to these alliances however brief or long-lived as a "coalitional moment" in which "political issues coincide or merge in the public sphere in ways that create space to re-envision and potentially reconstruct rhetorical imaginaries" (8).

Offering stories of rhetorical possibilities, the chapters in this section draw from history, personal story sharing, personal experience, and feminist theory to consider alliances past and future and to analyze examples of alliance that provide cautionary tales and models to replicate. In each case, the authors consider such associations in light of reproductive justice goals. Fabiola Carrión's chapter amplifies the often surprisingly parallel and substantively overlapping experiences of women of the Global Souths—Black activists in the southern US and Latine activists in the Americas south of the Mexico-US border. Carrión's lived experience, meticulous textual research, and personal interviews with activist leaders from these locations enable her to tell a compelling—and sorely needed—activist story. Her contribution details international reproductive activists' historical collaboration toward a human rights framework, explains why this united "reproductive liberation" story deserves attention, and points to emerging sites of renewed solidarity among advocates of the Global Souths who are reengaging and extending such activist traditions. In her exploration of the exclusionary logics of some self-help clinics, Hannah Dudley-Shotwell imagines how these spaces of care might take up the rhetorical expansiveness of reproductive justice investments in queer inclusivity and broad-based human rights. Doing so, Dudley-Shotwell argues, necessitates new and more gender-affirming language practices, an attunement to the implications of clinic spaces as rhetorical, and a reckoning with lingering essentialist logics that suggest that self-help feminist care is for some bodies and not for others.

James D. Warwood's focus on the exclusions and traumas experienced by pregnant and birthing people who are masculine-of-center sheds light on how the perceived juxtaposition of pregnancy and assumed masculinity translates to such people's emotional turmoil as well as unreasonable material experiences before, during, and after birthing. Warwood listens attentively and systematically to stories of masculine-of-center birth experiences as invited by the podcast *Masculine Birth Ritual* and inductively extracts three countertactics that can help activists, healthcare providers, masculine-of-center pregnant people, and those who care for them understand one another and interact in more harmonious and just ways. Making visible the negative outcomes of the "curated" story in alliance building, Meta Henty recovers and bears witness to the recent rhetorical efforts of the #NoTeenShame movement, drawing implications for ongoing sites of advocacy. Henty tracks the multimodal rhetorics of young women of color who formed the #NoTeenShame movement and makes a compelling case for recognizing how these activists have been unrecognized despite having encouraged discursive reframings of the so-called teen pregnancy issue. In her chapter on the complex rhetorical context of State Senator Wendy Davis's efforts to maintain reproductive access in Texas from the floor of the state capital, Jill Swiencicki theorizes rhetorical brokering as a promising enterprise for navigating the constraints of rhetorical situations that, by design, delimit the number and range of perspectives available for consideration. Examining the affordances and constraints of this moment of distributed rhetorical action, Swiencicki anticipates future misuses of rhetoric and offers useful considerations for the wider uptake of reproductive justice in legislative and other advocacy spaces.

The chapters in "Rhetorics of Practice" use storytelling to highlight sites of power and to explore how that power operates, how it circulates, and how it can be resisted. Without doubt, in the realm of reproductive politics both institutional and non-institutional power exists. Institutional power becomes manifest through a range of policies and practices such as those currently upheld by the healthcare profession and pharmaceutical interests that are oppressive and that too frequently place harmful constraints on material bodies. In relation to this collection, non-institutional power refers to varied forms of agency—the often emergent, sometimes successful, sometimes unsuccessful, and disparate efforts among individuals and groups of people responding to constraining situations. These five chapters identify the power limitations and exclusions that block a foundational reproductive justice goal: the safety and dignity of every individual. Further, each offers strategies and suggestions for changes needed to offset specific oppressions.

The section opens with Adele N. Nichols's unwavering call for an end to euphemisms that obscure the fact that Black women giving birth have died and continue to die because of systemic abuse that is operationalized through language, action, and medical neglect. To do so, she poignantly centers and amplifies the stories of Black women experiencing what she terms systemic racialized maternal abuse across three centuries. Michelle C. Smith's archival research into the nineteenth-century intentional settlement of Oneida reveals how one community's goal for radical equity—enacted through decisions to have children (or not) and intentional plans for how to responsibly raise them—cannot rise above the biopolitical control exerted by those holding the most power within the community. This historical case offers a unique and eerily useful meditation on the rhetorical limits of notions of choice, a concept that erroneously upholds the myth of pure autonomy and unfettered agency. Through her inventive application of the three tenets of reproductive justice to a historical case study, Smith also enables readers to grapple with the possibilities (and limitations) of widening the uptake of the more contemporary justice framework. How might we best gauge the ethical uses of the reproductive justice theory of change when encountering histories of all-white communities given that the paradigm's development, as Carrión explains in her chapter, has prioritized injustices experienced by non-white people and others "who have been historically oppressed"?

Considering how companies exploit women's reproductive anxieties, Melissa Stone and Zachary Beare next provide an incisive critique of Nurx, a web-based fertility management company that, while premising the value of their product on its ability to uphold privacy and reduce embarrassment, reinforces scripts of sexual shame in order to sell its service. Nurx's paradoxical story illustrates the slipperiness of what should and can matter when entities mired in capitalist imperatives attempt to pursue justice-oriented goals. Focusing on vasectomy, a material procedure of fertility management that has generally garnered limited public attention but that might be of increasing interest within the realm of reproductive justice, Jenna Vinson closely reads television and film representations of this elective surgery. Vinson analyzes how, through story, viewers are dissuaded from considering vasectomy as an equitable, safe, and dignified alternative to tubal ligation, thus extrapolating assumptions about which bodies are perceived as holding greater responsibility for reproductive control and deemed capable of enduring such measures. Turning to yet another service—one that many birthing people do not have access to—Sheri Rysdam's explores the rhetorical possibilities of birth doulas (non-medical support people who advocate for birthing people's desires, especially while they are in labor). The chapter not only teaches readers about what services doulas provide but leverages this exposition in order to articulate the issues of birthing people's compromised rhetorical agency in many medicalized interactions and to call for wider doula access. Rysdam's story explains her own experiences as a volunteer who draws upon her rhetorical training to be a birth doula-rhetor: a person who listens, who speaks, who touches, and who interjects in timely and appropriate ways, given the specific birthing context and people with whom she is engaging. Significantly, Rysdam considers how inclusive and accessible care at the individual level, when considered as a matter of reproductive justice, prompts thinking about these same concerns in structural ways and on institutional levels—even when doing so leads to complex questions rather than easy strategies for implementation.

The entire set of chapters, with their predominantly US-focused lens, are brought in conversation with global, transnational concerns in the afterword. A collaborative response to the collection by Yam and Fixmer-Oraiz, two rhetorical scholars of reproductive justice, the final chapter extends this storied conversation in ways that have fostered both dialogue across the bookends of the collection and accountability through the alliances enacted in this project. Yam and Fixmer-Oraiz name four "key moves" by which such imagining is operationalized in the collection's chapters: by pursuing "a deep understanding of critical histories," by engaging in "a politics of refusal" that rejects the status quo, by writing from "an eagerness to identify and cultivate coalitions with different stakeholders and communities," and by seriously analyzing "hegemonic discourse and institutions." Drawing on their attunements to the need for transnational and cross-border reproductive justice activism, the afterword writers remind readers that reproductive justice activists "have long articulated an intersectional and transnational orientation towards organizing across borders." They deepen this claim by offering two specific cautions—the dangers of working (1) at scale and (2) with potential preconceptions in mind as we act coalitionally—as well as a motivating possibility: that "we can co-produce a body of knowledge that reflects the diverse but intersecting experiences of marginalization and resistance."

This collection of ten chapters, introduction, and afterword reflects both individual perspectives as well as a community of activist-scholars and scholar-activists committed to enacting reproductive justice through their analysis and writing—through the stories they reveal. This collection draws on various types of stories to practice the power of storytelling—what Ross and Solinger argue can be "an act of subversion and resistance" (59). As the chapter previews suggest, stories can do numerous types of rhetorical work that can aid alliance-based efforts through various forms of practice, such as informing, offering perspective, and providing the basis for reflection on what one does know, what one does not know, and why that is the case. The perspective-building that comes with storytelling across experiences also contributes to opportunities for more critically considering systems and activities that may not be intended as overtly and egregiously harmful but that nevertheless contribute to regimes of injustice. In each chapter, authors employ rhetoric, while the collection as a whole spans multiple academic and activist realms. To wit, contributors are academics drawing from many fields such as rhetoric, feminist and gender studies, history, law, critical race studies, and communication. In multiple cases, contributors extrapolate, explicitly or implicitly, from their experiences as reproductive justice activists.

Because such varied perspectives animate and inform the chapters that follow, the collection offers a range of considerations: theoretical, pragmatic or practitioner-oriented, historical, and activist. Nevertheless, each of the collection's chapters include specific stories that, collectively, address the three foundational rights of reproductive justice—to have a child, to not have a child, and to parent with dignity. Centering such human rights requires, among other things, understanding and empathy that enables structural critique and prompts coalitional possibility. As Clare Hemmings suggests: "[G]ood empathy will emphasize the independent life of the other subject; bad empathy will project one's image, and always subsequently" (201). In this way, we build on existing and emerging work across rhetorical studies and rhetorical feminism (Glenn), in particular. Reading the subsequent chapters together and noting their foundational similarity and divergent aims and methods has the potential to provoke new insights and paradoxes. As an experience of "jarring disruption" and as a form of rhetorical feminist practice, paradox can, according to Nancy Small, inspire "re-viewing from a liminal location" and can sponsor "inventive, generative thinking and potential new rhetorical feminist tactics" (9). As rhetoric, this collection works to recognize and support "the independent life of the other subject" as well as the interdependences, paradoxes, and productive disruptions that underpin the goal of reproductive justice for all.

Works Cited

Chávez, Karma R. *Queer Migration Politics: Activist Rhetoric and Coalitional Possibilities.* U of Illinois P, 2013.

Enoch, Jessica, Jordynn Jack, and Cheryl Glenn. "Introduction: The Endless Opportunities for Feminist Research." *Retellings: Opportunities for Feminist Research in Rhetoric and Composition Studies,* edited by Jessica Enoch and Jordynn Jack. Parlor P, 2019, pp. 3–15.

Glenn, Cheryl. *Rhetorical Feminism and This Thing Called Hope.* Southern Illinois UP, 2018.

Hemmings, Clare. *Why Stories Matter: The Political Grammar of Feminist Theory.* Duke UP, 2011.

Hilleary, Cecily. "Native Americans Bristle at Suggestions They Offer Abortions on Tribal Land." *Voice of America.* voanews.com/a/native-americans-bristle-at-suggestions-they-offer-abortions-on-tribal-land-/6639480.html. Accessed 30 June 2022.

Maher, Savannah. "How Tribal Lands Became Abortion-Care Deserts, and Why They Won't Fill New Gaps in Access." *Marketplace.* marketplace.org/2022/06/30/why-tribal-lands-wont-fill-new-gaps-in-abortion-access/. Accessed 30 June 2022.

Ross, Loretta J., and Rickie Solinger. *Reproductive Justice: An Introduction.* U of California P, 2017.

Ross, Loretta J., Lynn Roberts, Erika Derkas, Whitney Peoples, and Pamela Bridgewater Toure. Introduction. *Radical Reproductive Justice: Foundations, Theory, Practice, Critique,* edited by Loretta J. Ross, Lynn Roberts, Erika Derkas, Whitney Peoples, and Pamela Bridgewater Toure. Feminist P, 2017, pp. 11–31.

Small, Nancy. *A Rhetoric of Becoming: USAmerican Women in Qatar.* Parlor P, 2022.

Introduction: Rhetorical Movement and the Pursuit of Reproductive Justice

Heather Brook Adams and Nancy Myers

Arguably, reproduction is increasingly political in the US. Reproduction is politicized through regulation at state and national levels, and it is also experienced as a personal or community-oriented matter in which autonomy is inhibited by powerful social and institutional forces. A reference to "reproductive politics" likely calls to mind those aspects of reproduction that most fully connect to sweeping public policy, such as the 1973 *Roe v. Wade* ruling that functionally decriminalized abortion, the 1977 Hyde Amendment that restricted abortion care for Medicare recipients, and the 2022 *Dobbs v. Jackson Women's Health* decision that overturned *Roe*. Such decisions are "landmark" because they are perceived as distinguishing a clear boundary— a change in law that enables or denies a reproducing person's access to, in these cases, abortion care. These narratives, however, fail to account for the ripple effects of decisions made by those in power, and they fall short in addressing reproductive realities in their numerous, varied, and everyday—if still often life-altering—instantiations. As reproduction continues to animate public discussion and variously unite and divide those who care about it, more perspectives—more stories—must be shared, listened to, and considered.

Indeed, additional perspectives on the wider sweep of reproductive concerns abound. For instance, in 2020, numerous fertility and reproductive healthcare centers independently determined how to follow Centers for Disease Control mandates during the COVID-19 pandemic. Some closed for as many as fifteen weeks, interrupting, at minimum, an estimated 100,000 "assisted reproductive technology cycles" and "leaving treatment plans in disarray" (Greenberg). At the same time, people[1] who were pregnant may have experienced hospital policies that, for example, disallowed birth doulas, partners, or family members to accompany them while birthing (Searcy and Castañeda). Non-pandemic situations illustrate other concerns. When considering the looming threats of climate crisis, some people—typically from the US or other wealthy nations— choose not to have children. Such decisions are complex and can be based on a variety of concerns not limited to the potential carbon impact of such a decision and the ethics of parenting a child into unknown, potentially dangerous and painful, futures (Green; Osaka). Issues of reproductive concern for those who already have children are different, if not less weighty. For example, across recent years and in relation to various policy decisions, migrant children have been separated from their parents and guardians along the US-Mexico border. This practice escalated in 2018 with the US Department of Justice's announcement of a "zero tolerance" immigration enforcement policy, even for those migrants seeking asylum. At the time of this writing, new iterations of such family separation policies are emerging.[2] These events, all differently political, illustrate contemporary reproductive politics and also insufficiently stand in for additional stories that trace the deep negative effects of oppressive politics on material bodies and communities.

Reproductive politics—the wide realm of reproductive health and wellness, birthing, and parenting as well as the related personal and public implications of this realm—is, of course, not a recent phenomenon. Rather, such politics persist through time and will endure into the future. As these stories illustrate, attending to reproductive politics is not only a matter of addressing the who, what, and when of reproduction. As matters of politics, such stories reflect larger systems of power at work. Such networks of differential privilege and oppression are not always apparent in the controlling narratives about reproduction, but they increasingly play an outsized role as reproductive freedoms are eroded in the US and as restrictive policies disproportionately affect multiply marginalized

1. We use the word "people" as well as gendered words such as "woman" and "women" in this introduction. The latter are universalizing terms that are not necessarily gender-affirming and that may be unacceptable in some contexts. We use them to reference any person who chooses to apply such terms to themselves, while acknowledging that they can obscure the uneven and unjust experiences of a variety of people in relation to reproductive concerns.

2. See the Southern Poverty Law Center website for a policy timeline beginning in 2017.

people. Despite whether examples like these draw public attention, are downplayed or ignored, or are experienced quietly, they all demonstrate how instances of reproductive politics reflect complex, compound, and ongoing rhetorical situations—ones that call for, among other things, listening, sharing, analysis, advocacy, and deliberation.

These opening examples of reproductive politics, though stories of exclusion and loss, also illustrate the expansiveness of reproductive justice,[3] the guiding framework for *Inclusive Aims: Rhetoric's Role in Reproductive Justice*. "Reproductive Justice" is a social movement that is rooted across time and place but that began with women of color responding to lived struggles as well as to the exclusion they experienced by primarily white feminist reproductive organizers and activists working under the banner of reproductive rights (see Price). The movement has since broadened and coalesced. It includes three tenets, each of which aligns with the opening stories: the right to have a child, the right to not have a child, and the right to parent children in safe and dignified environments (Ross and Solinger 9). As helpful as these three principles are to imagining the many connecting points of reproductive justice as a method for seeking change, the movement's potential remains greater than the sum of these parts. The principles invite a wide array of people to converge and share their communal, familial, and individual experiences in alliance—a type of coming together that is rare and challenging amid the often-disorienting context of reproductive political concerns. The voices of reproducing people are infrequently those central to such deliberation; instead, decisions about reproductive matters and possibilities too commonly perpetuate the power, privilege, and preferences of a few. This capacity for enduring, strategic, and coalitional justice-seeking emerges from the movement's unwavering allegiance to a generative human-rights framework and corresponding positive freedoms, or freedoms *to* rather than freedoms *from*. As explained by thought leaders Loretta J. Ross and Rickie Solinger, "Reproductive Justice reintegrates human rights and civil rights and looks to the international human rights framework as a sturdy moral, political and legal structure through which reproductive justice goals may eventually be accomplished" (79). Reproductive justice encourages people to replace the goal of securing individual rights

3. Throughout this introduction we capitalize "reproductive justice" when specifically referring to the social movement and use lowercase letters when referring to the theory and framework.

by degree with a generative and holistic process of working toward just reproductive lives for all.

In addition, the movement's call for white allies who heed its wisdom, its practices, and its commitments invites us, Heather and Nancy, as editors, to work at the intersection of, on one hand, this movement's theory and call to action and, on the other, our training as rhetorical scholars (Ross, "Conceptualizing" 223–26). We must take care to grapple with the affordances and limitations of our shared positionalities—as white, cisgender, heterosexual, (mostly and temporarily) able-bodied teacher-scholars of rhetoric in higher education—and our unique perspectives and experiences. Therefore, we engage with this work to rigorously and ethically do our part in support of reproductive justice without speaking over or appropriating the intellectual and material efforts of movement participants. Rather, we seek to align with and extend these efforts through our explicit attention to rhetoric and our desire to bring together various voices and perspectives through this collection. As rhetorical feminists, it is our belief that "public and private language use can be a means to create a different kind of world characterized by a different set of practices and values, ones that establish *eudaemonia,* the greatest good for all human beings" (Glenn 5).

Across *Inclusive Aims: Rhetoric's Role in Reproductive Justice*, we argue that rhetoric, a facilitator and act of movement, enables reproductive justice in three ways: (1) rhetoric is an approach and mindset that makes visible reproductive politics' systemic injustices hidden in normative practices and established policies; (2) rhetoric functions as an instrument for analyzing and advocating, enacting reproductive justice's reliance on individual and collective stories as a productive tool for furthering social change; and (3) rhetoric operates as a crucial quality of coalitional strategy because it enables specific discursive, embodied, and material tactics necessary for democratic action toward intentional systemic change. Thus, rhetoric further expands reproductive justice's aim to "create a culture shift in reproductive politics and bring fresh voices together to build an expansive vision for universal justice" (Ross et al. 12). For us as editors, the term "reproductive justice" signifies movement—from the term's early social movement roots to its enactments as a concept and framework. Rhetoric, as it is employed across this collection, facilitates and acts as "movement" in all three ways, magnifying the potential for additional and yet-to-be imagined forms of agency, advocacy, and action.

Rhetoric as Movement in Promoting Reproductive Justice

To invite a wide readership into this collection, we define the term rhetoric and explain how it aligns with reproductive change. Despite major decisions (e.g., *Roe's* reversal) occupying a primary place in the public reproductive landscape in the US, we take an especially expansive view in considering reproductive justice as "an emergent radical theory that reframes [a] problem" (Ross and Solinger 113) and, thus, a tactic for pursuing *eudaemonia*. Accordingly, rhetoric, as an approach and mindset, assists in making sense of major grievances and also making apparent otherwise hard-to-decipher injustices of reproductive politics. By "mindset" and "approach," we refer to the agency-oriented possibilities of rhetorical movement—the trans-historical and trans-contextual awareness of opportunities and tactics for intervening in situations and contexts even when the means for doing so are limited or available to the few instead of the many. A rhetorical mindset offers specific ways of thinking and perceiving that are responsive to real contexts and are attuned to how discourse practices and epistemologies reflect and shape realities. Assuming a rhetorical mindset refers to the change-seeking intellectual labor of assessing situations to determine how they are rhetorical—determining whose perspectives and voices are present, what assumptions and beliefs are at play, how power is operating, and what insights this type of analysis offers to those wishing to intervene, resist, advocate, raise awareness, or otherwise make change. Rhetoric is a lens of analysis that can be used to critique social, political, and legal situations of injustice and neglect and to question what matters—and to whom and why.

We intentionally resist and reframe the popular usage of the term, which connotes discourse that is especially unproductive or insincere. Instead, we employ a contemporary, scholarly definition of rhetoric across this collection, considering it a lens for exploring the interanimation of discursivity with bodies, spaces, practices, and objects across time. As Thomas Rickert argues, rhetoric "must diffuse outward to include the material environment, things (including the technological), our own embodiment, and a complex understanding of ecological relationality as participating in rhetorical practices and their theorization" (3). Rickert's move is one that other scholars employ as they reconsider traditional Western academic theory alongside non-Western ways of knowing and being.[4] Bringing this broader definition of rhetoric in conversation with reproductive justice allows activist-scholars and scholar-activists to identify reproductive injustices and possibilities for change.[5] Jacqueline Jones Royster and Gesa E. Kirsch argue that such an expansive approach to rhetorical work "asks us to imagine bold futures, futures worth living, fighting, and working for; futures that begin to address grand challenges while training our rhetorical ear and eye toward the consequences and impact of words and actions" (119).

With this scope of possibility in mind, we further differentiate between two ostensible modes of change: motion and movement. Parsing these two terms helps situate why a rhetorical approach is an appropriate response to often disorienting, overwhelming, and even discouraging reproductive contexts—why rhetoric is meaningful given that the state of reproductive affairs is lamentable for those who have "fallen prey to the seductive lure of a dominant US cultural logic, that of evolutionary history progress, or the idea that each generation marches ever onward and upward" (Ratcliffe 35). The controlling narratives of reproductive politics—the stories told *to* and *about*, not the stories told *by* and *with*—often mask the power orientations and partial allegiances that are manifest in systemic policies and practices. Controlling narratives, then, tell us stories of motion—that is, action related to change that *seems* to move people to *eudaemonia* but that reinforces a status quo of facilitating the greatest good for some but not for all. Motion and movement differ to us in that "motion" is passive; it sponsors the *idea* of movement without remaining accountable to, nor reflecting on, those who are excluded from consideration. In recent years, the US government seems to have had motion in its decisions about reproductive issues, whether addressing immigration, the pandemic, the transgender ban in the military, a crisis in Black maternal health, limitations on abortion and transgender support, etc. Such motion, however, is piecemeal, often responsive to a single issue, and overly reliant on notions of US constitutional claims

4. For more on this discussion, see Royster and Kirsch, p. 123–25.

5. In a 2022 *Rhetoric of Health and Medicine* dialogue, Maria Novotny and Lori Beth DeHertogh use the term *scholar-activists* to refer to those working in reproductive justice. We understand activist-scholars and scholar-activists to reflect slightly different positionalities and perspectives. Activist-scholars work in post-secondary education and employ their activism professionally and/or personally. Scholar-activists are more fully engaged in activism, using their writing and research to advocate for change.

to individual freedoms that articulate to privacy rights. Subsequently, these instances have failed to bring about more intentional and expansive movement that can address the structural needs of various communities or the varied, often intersectional, concerns of those of any (and multiple) identity affiliation(s). Movement, in our way of engaging the term, draws upon both theories of reproductive justice and rhetoric in understanding that purposeful reproductive action, although often personal, is never fully private. When we aim for movement, we are encouraged to grapple with the effects of interlocking systems of oppression and the potential for "root transformations" in society (de Onís 506). Movement must be social and communal. Its aims must be inclusive and transformational.

Rhetoric as approach and mindset, then, offers a foundational way of engaging with reproductive politics as a broad and pervasive domain of personal, communal, and public activities. Its breadth and ubiquity mean that its presence, as well as its effects, can be difficult to discern or explain. When Laura Briggs contends that "In the United States . . . there is no outside to reproductive politics, even though that fact is sometimes obscured" (4), we hear the echo of rhetoric as an everywhere and often invisible phenomenon. In addressing the interrelationships between rhetoric and reproductive justice more fully, we call attention here to Briggs's ability to explain how reproduction touches so many wide-reaching and political issues in the US: foreign policy on immigration, school funding tied to digital access for online instruction, and economic issues tied to the availability and affordability of menstrual hygiene, birth control products, and infant care, housing precarity, and more. Despite this ubiquity, reproductive injustices remain invisible, only partially considered, or disconnected from other wide-ranging issues in the imaginary of many people. Relatedly, the people whose lives and bodies are most affected by reproductive politics have been—and still are—infrequently called upon (to share their wisdom), listened to, heard, and heeded.

Reproductive politics in the US especially are framed through rights to privacy and many aspects of reproduction are experienced within non-public contexts and in ways that can invoke feelings of shame due to imbalances of power and/or white, heteronormative notions of purity (i.e., at the doctor's office, when living in poverty, through sex education, and in situations of assault). These framings and contexts intensify the effects of injustice, which become more apparent when considering reproductive politics transnationally and imagining this area as a site of global responsibility and possibility. Even those whose work aligns with adjacent and overlapping reproductive justice aims (i.e., stigma related to "good mothering" directed to people who use drugs, see Nichols et al.) may need to situate their social movement efforts so that they are legible within wider public contexts that tend to recognize discreet, rather than intersecting, calls for justice. In these ways and more, the possibilities of justice in the realm of reproductive politics remain unmet.

Our invocation of reproductive politics specifically functions as an invitation for *rhetorically* responding to needs related to people's reproductive health, wellness, safety, and dignity. At a time when state legislatures—not medical experts—are defining "abortion" to restrict a reproducing person's access to care even when their life is at stake, keen rhetorical awareness and deft rhetorical action are needed. Simultaneously, we focus on reproductive justice as a theory of change that offers the most appropriate and coalitional lens to use in considering how to leverage rhetoric in service of an inclusive and responsive vision. With this focus, we simultaneously respond to Shui-yin Sharon Yam's call for intersectional rhetorical research that "is committed to noticing, clarifying, and critiquing how dominant discourses and ideologies in different sociopolitical areas come to inform reproductive politics and regulate the bodies of marginalized people" (32). We must be clear, however; our efforts here are in no way meant to co-opt, erase, or diminish the unique contributions of various activists who individually and collectively have shaped the reproductive landscape in earlier decades. That is, we are not advocating a politics of unproblematic and global feminist sisterhood. Nevertheless, we purposefully use reproductive politics, an intentionally broad term as we engage it, in the spirit of finding rhetorical proximity and relation, if not always common ground. Activists' and scholars' situations, aims, and needs will necessarily be different, but their strategies can be (more explicitly), if temporarily, coalitional, and their efforts more mutually beneficial. Here we are considering this appeal to coalition based on the definition offered by Karma Chávez, Adela C. Licona, and Nana Osei-Kofi: "Coalition requires proximity, and that proximity can be geographic, emotional, intellectual, or ideological among others. Being in relation to or seeking a relation to someone or some group is fundamental to coalition. Being in or seeking a relation to someone or some group also requires a responsiveness to the lived histories of that someone or that group" (148–9). Without a rhetorical mindset and approach, alliances and activist practices can too easily result in motion rather than movement toward systematic change.

Reproductive Justice Stories as Rhetorical Movement

Across sites of reproductive in/justice, rhetoric also functions as an instrument, an essential means for engaging with reproductive political harms and for pursuing just movement through critique, theory-building, activism, and advocacy. By naming rhetoric an instrument, we emphasize the dynamism and potentiality of rhetoric as movement toward justice and dissuade readings of "instrument" that suggest a more static connotation that separates rhetoric and action. The scope of this work is suggested by Stephanie Tillman and Amber Johnson, who assess the constraints of the divisive political discourses of abortion as just one form of the "decision making processes regarding a body's reproductive potential": "people must dedicate a lifetime to learning what decisions are one's own and how to talk about abortion socially, religiously, politically, secretly, and publicly" (436). Such robust rhetorical challenges, we contend, are usefully explored through story. The Reproductive Justice Movement recognizes story as a key rhetorical instrument to illustrate, support, and build its theory of change. It further relies on storytelling as a strategy for sharing various lived experiences and invites new rhetorical uses of story to imagine more inclusive and just possibilities. In so doing, the movement supports social change by generating "a culture of collaboration" with the goal of "revolutionaliz[ing] our approach to reproductive politics" (Ross and Solinger 116). Willing to use story to identify connections and to center the otherwise marginalized, reproductive justice figures itself as a "sort of open-source code" (Ross et al. 19) that can and should adapt to those who find themselves part of the movement. This openness echoes in the words of activist and cultural critic Mikki Kendall: "Reproductive justice needs to be reframed to include the entire spectrum of choices surrounding every stage of women's health, reproductive and otherwise" (220).

Rhetoric not only invites a focus on what stories apparently convey but also what stories do and can do, often in more tacit, if still provocative ways. Stories are not only a means of disclosure but afford opportunities for perspective-building—an obvious assertion, but one that can be more widely leveraged for coalitional movement. Stories are sites of telling that also enable individual and group reflection and facilitate identifying patterns of shared experience and contrasts across bodies, time, traditions, communities, and physical and social locations. As a dynamic rhetorical instrument, one story compounded by many stories becomes a shared indictment of injustice and a collaborative vision of possibility. Conversely, stories as sites of disclosure can reproduce hierarchies that threaten to undercut the aims of reproductive justice. Tasha N. Dubriwny and Kate Seigfried's analysis of publicly shared "later abortion narratives" are a case in point. These stories, which have gained traction among those advocating for the right to abortion care, engage in a "motivational vocabulary of mercy and good motherhood" (200). Garnering significant attention in a US context, these stories implicitly promote reproductive rights primarily for those (white, heterosexual, and economically secure) people who are imagined as having the potential to be "good mothers." The stories, then, shore up the logic of access for some but fail to make abortion an inclusive and public issue. By engaging a rhetorical mindset, those calling for, sharing, and listening to stories can detect such tacit patterns of exclusion and articulate, as do Dubriwny and Seigfried, the urgent need for alternative and more inclusive rhetorical vocabularies.

Stories, then, in all their forms, provide a textual basis for doing the intellectually and emotionally challenging work of discerning the upstream causes and downstream implications of injustices—those that are too frequently experienced individually and that too often are felt but not fully understood—so as to activate resistance or broader change. In her study on women's suffrage movements, Lee Ann Banaszak argues that to create change, social movements must develop and maintain "values and perceptions that encourage confrontation, reform, or challenge of the political system" (222). Story sharing as a means of change takes time, and it can be emotionally difficult work. Engaging stories means listening for unexpected places of reproductive justice and then laboring (intellectually, affectively, and materially) toward "a unified movement for human rights" (Ross and Solinger 59). The politics of recognition and accountability implicated in story sharing, however, can be a site of struggle. Striving toward greater recognition through story sharing frequently requires care and negotiation, sometimes results in unintelligibility and even failure, and can easily slip into appropriation. Keeping stories of reproductive injustices relevant and accurate requires care in light of neoliberal tendencies, for storytelling potentially introduces harm, enabling stories to be co-opted, especially within market economies (Zavella 109–10) as several contributors in this collection illustrate. Further, as we open ourselves to the democratic potential of engaging more stories, we must ask ourselves "what legitimate interests might we be missing that motivate substantial pluralities of our polity-mates to oppose our rhetorics so vehemently?" (Condit 444). Compelled to take up such critical and recursive work, we can engage story, as an act of rhetorical movement, to support reproductive justice activism and change.

Central to the project of this collection, then, is drawing from the wisdom of those whose efforts have enabled this work, from the social movement history of reproductive justice activists and coalitions. Because the Reproductive Justice Movement often tells its story of development, this history will be familiar to some readers and unfamiliar to others. Recounting it here is a matter of accountability and a commitment to the project of sharing "collective *public* stories" related to "organizing and the histories of women of color and their communities" (Price 44). Further, as we advocate for rhetoric's ability to help people make sense of what garners (public) attention, what perspectives are persuasive, and what sites of silencing and oppression exist, we recognize the significance of amplifying Reproductive Justice Movement histories.[6]

Although there is no singular "story" of the Reproductive Justice Movement, Black feminist organizing that contributed to movement efforts in the US was well underway by the 1970s. The Combahee River Collective, an Afrocentric Black feminist group that began meeting in 1974 to develop an "integrated analysis and practice" in response to "major" and "interlocking" systems of oppression, published a statement in 1977 that articulated a distinct lack of coalition in the mainstream, middle-class, white feminist movement:

> As Black feminists we are made constantly and painfully aware of how little effort white women have made to understand and combat their racism, which requires among other things that they have a more than superficial comprehension of race, color, and Black history and culture. Eliminating racism in the white

6. We take a similar approach here as do Novotny and DeHertogh in calling attention to the value of Temptaous Mckoy's concept of "'amplification rhetorics,' or the process of 'forging a space' for marginalized voices, contributions, and lived experiences within a broader scholarly field'" (378). In attending to amplification as a process of coalition, we explicitly consider how we amplify across various non-academic and academic locations.

> women's movement is by definition work for white women to do, but we will continue to speak to and demand accountability on this issue. (Combahee)

This portion of the Collective's statement captures a vital truth: that despite many successes, first- and second-wave middle-class white heterosexual feminists "failed rhetorically," because they missed "perfect opportunities" to transcend their differences and use their collective activism to "speak to and from the margins, invite dialogue, lift up vernaculars and [the] experiences of all participants, and foreground hope and possibility" (Glenn 31).

Significantly, the Collective draws from the realities of Black women's "day-to-day existence" to explain how the experiences of racism, sexism, and oppression of poor people are frequently interconnected (Combahee). It also makes apparent the prevalence of sexual and other forms of physical and emotional violence that Black women faced. As one of the authors, Beverly Smith, has explained, the perspectives in the statement were shaped in large part by its writers interacting with women they encountered in their working lives—people who they took the time to listen to and in whom they trusted ("The Combahee"). Critically, the Collective wielded great rhetorical power in listening to the stories of others and using that knowledge to directly inform their statement for change. Additionally, as Keeanga-Yamahtta Taylor's scholarship has demonstrated, the Combahee River Collective's analysis of oppression did not just stop at that—analysis—but also synthesizes and articulates a plan for collective action.

Despite it being less inclusive than it could be, as Smith herself now recognizes, the Combahee River statement articulated truths that have been more widely experienced and reiterated by other people of color, including those who have directly supported "traditional" reproductive rights organizations ("The Combahee"). Reproductive Rights Movement leaders (a group that is primarily white) have long failed to meaningfully address human rights violations related to reproducing people of color, including state-directed sterilization abuses and other population- and community-directed oppressions that have disproportionately affected non-white people. Historically, mainstream reproductive rights activism has also fallen short in addressing intersectional issues such as the Hyde Amendment restrictions on access (Price 45–46). Additionally, the pro-choice/pro-life framework that has, at this point, circulated for more than fifty years, centers access to abortion as the exclusive concern of reproductive rights. The binary upholds choice as a matter of privacy and individual responsibility in a way that abandons an earlier movement focus on "equality and abortion laws that discriminated based on class and economic resources" and fails to accommodate intersectional and marginalized identities (de Onís 497; see also Harper 77–82).

Because of these shortcomings, the National Black Women's Health Project (an organization emerging from a conference in Atlanta, Georgia in 1983) and a range of other reproductive health organizing efforts by people of color in the 1980s and 1990s increasingly crystalized their focus on allowing reproducing people to "control their own bodies and destinies" while responding to the needs of their communities (Silliman et al. 2). These groups include, but are not limited to, the Black Women's Health Imperative, the National Latina Health Organization, the Native American Women's Health Education Resource Center, and Asian Pacific Islanders for Choice (Zavella 2). The efforts of many such groups were long "undocumented, unanalyzed, and unacknowledged" (Silliman et al. 1), even though they contributed to what would become the reproductive justice framework.

By 1994, the term *reproductive justice* was coined by twelve Black "founding RJ mothers," thus rhetorically anchoring a set of values and aims (Leonard 39). SisterSong Women of Color Reproductive Justice Collective, a subsequent entity emerging from this early collective activism, was formed in 1997 and introduced a cohesive social movement strategy at its national conference in 2003. One year later came the publication of the first book on the subject, *Undivided Rights: Women of Color Organizing for Reproductive Justice*, which documented activist efforts and supported further awareness and coalition-building. SisterSong remains a central organization in the social movement as reproductive justice is taken up in increasingly disparate sites and among various activists and allies.

As editors of this collection, we are making a mindful choice to engage in a reproductive justice method and analysis, doing so in an effort to listen to these activist thought leaders and respond (as white women) as they so often have asked us to do. Simultaneously, we do so in the spirit of learning from—thinking alongside and with—rather than appropriating the insights of the more inclusive and coalitional Reproductive Justice Movement. Although the history of the social movement suggests that reproductive justice emerged from the needs and perspectives of people of color, and while a necessary aspect of doing reproductive justice work is centering these same people, their ideas, and their concerns, it is time for all people—including white people—to learn about and work mindfully in support of reproductive justice aims. Learning from antecedent labor enables recognition, contribution, and wider coalition. Like Maria Novotny, Lori Beth De Hertogh, and Erin A. Frost, we also agree that "it's time for non-Black folx to acknowledge and contribute to the work [that] Black [and indigenous] Women began" (8).

Listening in allyship also means remaining especially attentive to the Reproductive Justice Movement's ongoing efforts. For instance, in September 2021, twelve legal and reproductive justice scholars filed at the US Supreme Court a brief of *amici curiae* ahead of the 2022 *Dobbs* decision. The brief offered the justices a rigorous interpretation of the Mississippi law that, if passed, would effectively ban abortions after fifteen weeks of pregnancy and set off a ripple effect across conservative states. The brief opens by explaining: "*Amici* are law professors who are scholars in the field of reproductive rights and justice . . . Notably, as reproductive *justice* scholars, *Amici* appreciate that abortion access is a key element of racial justice, and they recognize that the denial of abortion access is a form of racial subordination" ("Brief" 1). We read this brief as both doing legal work and functioning as an alternative form of story—one that recounts critical and contextual details of the lives of those real people affected by constraints on reproductive freedom, corrects inaccuracies and oversights in the dominant narratives of reproductive "choice," and configures these insights for the specific context of a Supreme Court decision. Specifically, the brief delivers sound and compelling arguments as to the "breathtakingly constrained social conditions" of Black women living in Mississippi (20), which include disproportionately high levels of poverty, un-insurance, and intimate partner violence and reproductive coercion (5). *Amici* also explain that many Mississippians "do not receive, or are denied by law from receiving, information about sexual and reproductive health in their schools" and report that this mix of factors contributes to higher rates of unanticipated pregnancy among reproducing people there than in other parts of the US (5). Doing more than merely reporting this factual information, the brief rigorously argues that "an overhaul of *Roe*" is an act denying "the reality of black women in this country" and that the proposed "Ban" would result in state-level efforts to "*coerc[e]*" reproducing people into continuing their pregnancies (12–13). Countering a false, politically wielded, narrative that "abortion is black genocide," the authors affirm that "black women have demanded abortion rights for themselves" and that publics should simply "trust black women to do what is best for themselves, their families, and their communities" (25, 29). With these rhetorical moves, the authors center the reproductive justice framework to illuminate how relevant and useful it is in relation to the *Dobbs* case—all the while reminding that the framework's three pillars—the right to have a child, not have a child, and parent a child with dignity—are to be considered "simultaneously" instead of being considered in piecemeal, and politically convenient, ways (29). Though directed to the Court, the brief provides cogent arguments that rhetorically model how reproductive justice's stories can be leveraged to oppose renewed sites of reproductive oppression.

This cluster of stories about reproductive justice—those starting with the Combahee River Collective Statement, those of the Reproductive Justice Movement taking shape, and the brief of *amici curiae* that illustrates movement leaders' ongoing advocacy—evidence variable forms of alliance that have enabled rigorous analysis and theories of change. In addition to amplifying such stories, we must also contend with the knowledge that they yield for us, people deeply concerned with unjust reproductive politics but not historically part of the Reproductive Justice Movement. As editors, we mindfully heed the call of reproductive justice scholar Caroline R. McFadden who insists that the theory "offers invaluable insight into the fight for social justice that white feminists *must* seek out, listen to, and learn from" (243). We listen further to Ross, who draws on theories of bell hooks and Audre Lorde: "We do not need to share a common oppression to fight equally to end all oppressions," because "it takes all of our differences to make us whole, and differences only become barriers that break us into fragments if we let them" ("Conceptualizing" 226). To be sure, this work of finding points of alliance and models of effecting change through story must attend to critical race theory's interest in counterstory methodology—an explicit way of using story to resist unjust, controlling narratives. As Aja Y. Martinez explains, counterstory "recognizes that experiential knowledge of people of color is legitimate and critical to understanding racism that is often well disguised in the rhetoric of normalized structural values and practices" (3). Even though "we've *all* been telling stories, *all* along" (Martinez 1), it is essential to remain diligent in recognizing whose stories inform our alliances and how those stories are ethically engaged.

Through story, we embrace rhetorical action that draws from the wisdom of others across time and experience while remaining open to new questions. Following Yam, we take seriously that reproductive justice demands that both storyteller and audience "grapple with the structural causes of their lived experiences and narratives" (22). Such interrogation is certainly needed in our contemporary moment, when reproductive futures are actively being (re)written by those in power—people who are too often intent on *not heeding* the wisdom of reproducing people and their allies. To have hope for the future of reproductive justice, both activism and academe must work together "to theorize, strategize, and organize" for the rights and justice of all (Ross and Solinger 111). This collection aims to join in the work of reproductive justice by taking up a capacious reproductive political approach. It includes chapters that document stories of others not included in those controlling narratives and others that retell stories through what Clare Hemmings in *Why Stories Matter* refers to as "recitations," retellings in order to expose "half-submerged native traces from the starting point of political exclusions haunting the present" (165, 195).

Rhetoric as a Crucial Quality of Coalition Building for Change

In a culture of division, finding avenues for alliance is a pressing challenge. As Kimberly Harper explains in recounting historic and ongoing efforts to expand safety, justice, and care to reproducing people not represented by the mainstream feminist movement, coalitions are, fundamentally, groupings that "on the surface might seem dissimilar but [that] are really fighting for the same thing" (81). Coalescing through stories—to share them, listen to them, and learn from them—opens paths for alliance and action that may necessarily be "multifaceted and multiphased, allowing time for all sides to listen, keep silent, consider and weigh" (Glenn 42–43). For people in coalition, rhetoric enables unique discursive, embodied, and material tactics that enable people's collective movement toward purposeful systemic change. We acknowledge that such movement, in the words of Cheryl Glenn, "creates possibilities, not blueprints for an imagined utopian future" (193) and is taken up through coalition-building that is "strategic [and therefore] temporary" (43). Significantly, the explicitly public quality of rhetoric is central to this endeavor. As Chávez reminds, "It is crucial to understand coalitional moments and possibility through public rhetoric because publicity creates not only visibility and accessibility but also accountability" (15).

While coalitional rhetoric encourages awareness of social location and context, it can also reveal the concerns of representation and recognition that come with alliance.[7] Despite such cautions, alliance can be an avenue to power, especially when marshaled in service of inventive and "contingent" forms of inclusion (Winderman and Hallsby 423). Detecting such possibilities and acting upon them is both challenging rhetorical work and a crucial avenue for structural change.

This collection's chapters advocate for and function as coalition. Our valuing of story as a central thread that runs through this collection extends the Reproductive Justice Movement's call "to organize with people who think differently about issues or who focus on different issues but who agree to work together to achieve human rights goals" (Ross and Solinger 116). By gathering together contributors with varied disciplinary, experiential, and epistemological perspectives, we wish to actively disrupt—or, in decolonial terms "delink"—existing matrices of power (Cushman et al.; Mignolo). A tactical approach to coalition building, then, puts rhetoric to work for change through opportunities to speak up, interrupt, and/or speak out within or against discourses of reproductive politics—to communicate and/or use rhetorical awareness to navigate lived experiences. We—Heather and Nancy—recognize that the work of reproductive justice should not be taken up by only some identity groups, and that allyship is a concept that should remain dynamic and responsive to social contexts (see Harris). As coalitional strategy, rhetoric does more than just accumulate stories; to wit, it facilitates insightful and just responses. Leandra Hinojosa Hernández teaches, through an analysis of the violence "accompanying migrant family separation at the US-Mexico border," that such "extreme forms of reproductive injustice" require multiple lenses of theoretical and/or activist analysis; without such diversity of perspective and thought, those committed to movement will fall short of understanding the "constellation of effects and outcomes" that such experiences represent (131–32). Rhetoric, itself a tradition of democracy, affords a unique opportunity to bring different types of thinkers together to work in varied ways toward reproductive justice. As Banaszak notes about the importance of inclusivity, "Without

7. Wendy Hesford, drawing on the work of Arabella Lyon, argues that coalitional efforts can enable "recognitions in between"—sites of awareness of differential privilege that can "serve as an empowering bridge" for instance, "for nonblack allies to show solidarity that respects the black lives and experiences" that are the basis for anti-racist activism (553).

a movement 'community' and intense social interaction among activists, a social movement will remain divided" (223). This collection as an enactment of inclusive allyship highlights the real ways that public discourse, politics, information economies, and so many other aspects of contemporary life function to divide and separate individuals and groups from networks of care, resulting in detachment and isolation.

Rhetorical Action for Reproductive Justice

The collection's title—*Inclusive Aims*— reflects a disposition of radical inclusivity that we have tried to ensure is present in each chapter of this book. This work requires a centering of human rights as the foundational value of reproductive justice—an approach that, for us, simultaneously reflects our moves outward and inward. Specifically, we grapple with the wisdom gained from the Reproductive Justice Movement's national and transnational coalitional efforts, the ethical and practical desires of many to work toward reproductive justice across (and sometimes despite) geo-political borders, and the reality that this collection largely centers work to be done here "at home" in the US, and from our editorial location in the US South, where so much crucial organizing has taken place.

Considering these concerns of scope and scale is no easy matter. In their afterword, Yam and Natalie Fixmer-Oraiz usefully look to transnational feminist scholarship by Ashwini Tambe and Millie Thayer to engage with the concepts of "scaling out" and "scaling up." The afterword writers do so by explaining that these concepts reflect Tambe and Thayer's insistence that it is "insufficient to pay attention to singular domestic issues without attending to their intersections with other systems of oppression in a transnational context." Calling on readers to actively pursue ways to connect the local geographic context of this collection's chapters to global concerns of reproductive justice as a rhetorical pursuit, the writers articulate that "scaling out" affords opportunities for finding how people across various divides are often "interpellated" by similar issues. Additionally, they explain how "scaling up" remains relevant for examining "how seemingly domestic exigences generate activism, collaborations, and solidarities across national boundaries."

Heeding these insights and dialogically engaging with Yam and Fixmer-Oraiz's arguments, we—Heather and Nancy—have labored to further situate this collection alongside these timely calls for action. As an act of rhetorical movement, we ally ourselves with the "scaling out" that

Yam and Fixmer-Oraiz identify and theorize in the afterword and call attention to our own complementary engagement with what we term "scaling in." We understand the collection—as a series of chapters connecting rhetoric and reproductive justice—to be "scaling out" by addressing "the disturbing political developments of our time" (Tambe and Thayer 26). "Scaling out" calls attention to the digital porosity and migratory flows of our contemporary moment (26–31) while still allowing our contributors to scale in on local injustices past and present. One rhetorical instrument that yokes scaling out with scaling in is story sharing. Scaling in names the process of using stories like those in the subsequent chapters, to draw people together, learn, dialogue, and act in ways that work toward reproductive justice through rhetorical alliance and rhetorical practices. Thus, through this allyship of local and global rhetorics for reproductive justice, the chapter contributors, as activist-scholars and scholar-activists, focus on US reproductive politics of the past and present to better understand the permeable borders of time, space, and culture within this geographic location. Rhetoric provides tools that allow people to recognize and analyze sites of injustice; to identify rhetorical tactics for *doing*—be that advocating, working in an activism capacity, or exercising agency in another way; and to use these tools as a larger coalitional strategy. By scaling in, we create additional avenues and possibilities for the crucial work of scaling out as articulated by the afterword writers.

This collection's contributors work together to forward rhetoric's role in reproductive justice and to demonstrate how theory and activism can coalesce and resist what Ross calls "the artificial binary between the activist and scholar communities" ("Conceptualizing" 181). As activist-scholars and scholar-activists, we foreground and address the injustices in reproductive politics to facilitate reproductive justice's goals as a concept, a framework, and a movement. Glenn explains the intricate connection among academe, politics, and activism: "When rhetoric and feminism become allies in contention with the forces troubling us all, our shared goal is to articulate a vision of hope and expectation" (212). As allies working together, we possibly can enable hope, expectations, and accountability in others, and, as rhetoric likes to claim, make them probable realities through our work together. Activist-scholars and scholar-activists can adopt the goals of reproductive justice, pursuing inclusive aims toward rights and dignity for all.

Works Cited

Banaszak, Lee Ann. *Why Movements Succeed or Fail: Opportunity, Culture, and the Struggle for Woman Suffrage*. Princeton UP, 1996.

"Brief of Amici Curiae Reproductive Justice Scholars Supporting Respondents," 20 Sept. 2021. www.supremecourt.gov. Accessed 1 May 2023.

Briggs, Laura. *How All Politics Became Reproductive Politics*. U of California P, 2017.

Chávez, Karma R. *Queer Migration Politics: Activist Rhetoric and Coalitional Possibilities*. U of Illinois P, 2013.

Chávez, Karma R., Adela C. Licona, and Nana Osei-Kofi. "From Afro-Sweden with Defiance: The Clenched Fist as Coalitional Gesture?" *New Political Science,* vol. 40, no. 1, 2018, pp. 137–50.

Combahee River Collective. "Combahee River Collective Statement." *Combahee River Collective.* 1977, combaheerivercollective.weebly.com/the-combahee-river-collective-statement.html. Accessed 3 Feb. 2022.

"The Combahee River Collective Statement." *A People's Anthology*, 23 Feb. 2021, podcasts.apple.com/us/podcast/5-the-combahee-river-collective-statement/id1555138719?i=1000510379378.

Condit, Celeste. "Rhetorical Strategies for Retrieving Abortion Rights." *Quarterly Journal of Speech,* vol. 108, no. 4, 2022, pp. 441–45.

Cushman, Ellen, Rachel Jackson, Annie Laurie Nichols, Courtney Rivard, Amanda Moulder, Chelsea Murdock, David M. Grant, and Heather Brook Adams. "Decolonizing Projects: Creating Pluriversal Possibilities in Rhetoric." *Rhetoric Review,* vol. 38, no. 1, 2019, pp. 1–22.

de Onís, Kathleen M. "Lost in Translation: Challenging (White, Monolingual Feminism's <Choice> with *Justicia Reproductiva.*" *Women's Studies in Communication*, vol. 38, no. 1, 2015, pp. 1–19.

Dubriwny, Tasha N., and Kate Siegfried. "Justifying Abortion: The Limits of Maternal Idealist Rhetoric." *Quarterly Journal of Speech,* vol. 107, no. 2, 2021, pp. 185–208.

Glenn, Cheryl. *Rhetorical Feminism and This Thing Called Hope*. Southern Illinois UP, 2018.

Green, Emma. "A World Without Children." *Atlantic,* 20 Sept. 2021, www.theatlantic.com/politics/archive/2021/09/millennials-babies-climate-change/620032/. Accessed 15 May 2023.

Greenberg, Alissa. "The Pandemic Disrupted Tens of Thousands of IVF Cycles." *NOVA.* 14 May 2021, www.pbs.org/wgbh/nova/article/ivf-covid-pandemic-infertility/. Accessed 18 Feb. 2022.

Harper, Kimberly C. *The Ethos of Black Motherhood in America: Only White Women Get Pregnant*. Lexington, 2021.

Harris, Tina M. "Being Our Sister's Keeper: Rethinking Allyship Amid Multiple Pandemics." *Women's Studies in Communication,* vol. 44, no. 2, 2021, pp. 146–50.

Hemmings, Clare. *Why Stories Matter: The Political Grammar of Feminist Theory.* Duke UP, 2011.

Hernández, Leandra Hinojosa. "Feminist Approaches to Border Studies and Gender Violence: Family Separation as Reproductive Injustice." *Women's Studies in Communication,* vol. 42, no. 2, 2019, pp. 130–34.

Hesford, Wendy S. "Surviving Recognition and Racial In/justice." *Philosophy and Rhetoric,* vol. 48, no. 4, 2015, pp. 536–60.

Kendall, Mikki. *Hood Feminism: Notes from the Women That a Movement Forgot.* Penguin, 2021.

Leonard, Toni M. Bond. "Laying the Foundations for a Reproductive Justice Movement." *Radical Reproductive Justice: Foundations, Theory, Practice, Critique,* edited by Loretta J. Ross, Lynn Roberts, Erika Derkas, Whitney Peoples, and Pamela Bridgewater Toure. Feminist P, 2017, pp. 39–49.

Martinez, Aja Y. *Counterstory: The Rhetoric and Writing of Critical Race Theory,* National Council of Teachers of English, 2020.

McFadden, Caroline R. "Reproductively Privileged: Critical White Feminism and Reproductive Justice Theory." *Radical Reproductive Justice: Foundations, Theory, Practice, Critique,* edited by Loretta J. Ross, Lynn Roberts, Erika Derkas, Whitney Peoples, and Pamela Bridgewater Toure. Feminist P, 2017, pp. 241–50.

Mignolo, Walter. "On Pluriversality." *Walter Mignolo,* 20 Oct. 2013, www.waltermignolo.com. Accessed 2 Nov. 2017.

Nichols, Tracy R., Amber Welborn, Meredith R. Gringle, and Amy Lee. "Social Stigma and Perinatal Substance Use Services: Recognizing the Power of the Good Mother Ideal." *Contemporary Drug Problems,* vol. 48, no. 1, 2021, pp. 19–37.

Novotny, Maria, and Lori Beth De Hertogh. "Amplifying Rhetorics of Reproductive Justice within Rhetorics of Health and Medicine." *Rhetoric of Health and Medicine,* vol. 5, no. 4, 2022, pp. 374–402.

Novotny, Maria, Lori Beth De Hertogh, and Erin A. Frost. "Editors' Introduction: Rhetorics of Reproductive Justice in Public and Civic Contexts." *Reflections,* vol. 20, no. 2, 2020, pp. 7–13.

Osaka, Shannon. "Should You Not Have Kids because of Climate Change? It's Complicated." *Washington Post,* 2 Dec. 2022, www.washingtonpost.com/climate-environment/2022/12/02/climate-kids/. Accessed 15 May 2023.

Price, Kimala. "What Is Reproductive Justice? How Women of Color Are Redefining the Prochoice Paradigm." *Meridians: feminism, race, transnationalism,* vol. 10, no. 2, 2010, pp. 42–65.

Ratcliffe, Krista. "Silence and Listening: The War On/Over Women's Bodies in the 2012 US Election Cycle." *Retellings: Opportunities for Feminist*

Research in Rhetoric and Composition Studies, edited by Jessica Enoch and Jordynn Jack. Parlor P, 2019, pp. 34–53.

Rickert, Thomas. *Ambient Rhetoric: The Attunements of Rhetorical Being.* U of Pittsburgh P, 2013.

Ross, Loretta J. "Conceptualizing Reproductive Justice Theory: A Manifesto for Activism." *Radical Reproductive Justice: Foundations, Theory, Practice, Critique,* edited by Loretta J. Ross, Lynn Roberts, Erika Derkas, Whitney Peoples, and Pamela Bridgewater Toure. Feminist P, 2017, pp. 170–232.

Ross, Loretta J., Lynn Roberts, Erika Derkas, Whitney Peoples, and Pamela Bridgewater Toure. Introduction. *Radical Reproductive Justice: Foundations, Theory, Practice, Critique,* edited by Loretta J. Ross, Lynn Roberts, Erika Derkas, Whitney Peoples, and Pamela Bridgewater Toure. Feminist P, 2017, pp. 11–31.

Ross, Loretta J., and Rickie Solinger. *Reproductive Justice: An Introduction.* U of California P, 2017.

Royster, Jacqueline Jones, and Gesa E. Kirsch. "Ethics and Action: Feminist Perspectives on Facing the Grand Challenges of Our Times." *After Plato: Rhetoric, Ethics, and the Teaching of Writing,* edited by John Duffy and Lois Agnew. Utah State UP, 2020, pp.117–40.

Searcy, Julie Johnson, and Angela N. Castañeda. "On the Outside Looking In: A Global Doula Response to COVID-19." *Frontiers in Sociology,* vol. 6, 613978, 2021, pp. 1–9.

Silliman, Jael, Marlene Gerber Fried, Loretta Ross, and Elena R. Gutierrez, eds. *Undivided Rights: Women of Color Organizing for Reproductive Justice.* Haymarket, 2016.

Southern Poverty Law Center. "Family Separation—A Timeline." *SPLC.* www.splcenter.org/news/2020/06/17/family-separation-under-trump-administration-timeline. Accessed 15 Sept. 2021.

Tambe, Ashwini, and Millie Thayer, eds. *Transnational Feminist Itineraries: Situating Theory and Activist Practice.* Duke UP, 2021.

Taylor, Keeanga-Yamahtta, editor. *How We Get Free: Black Feminism and the Combahee River Collective.* Haymarket, 2017.

Tillman, Stephanie, and Amber Johnson. "Abortion Language, Nesting Dolls Theory, and an Autoethnographic Plea for Radical Transformation." *Quarterly Journal of Speech,* vol. 108, no. 4, 2022, pp. 436–40.

Winderman, Emily, and Atilla Hallsby. "The *Dobbs* Leak and Reproductive Justice." *Quarterly Journal of Speech,* vol. 108, no. 4, 2022, pp. 421–25.

Yam, Shui-yin Sharon. "Visualizing Birth Stories from the Margin: Toward a Reproductive Justice Model of Rhetorical Analysis." *Rhetoric Society Quarterly* vol. 50, no. 1, 2020, pp. 19–34.

Zavella, Patricia. *The Movement for Reproductive Justice: Empowering Women of Color through Social Activism.* New York UP, 2020.

Rhetorics of Alliance

1 Liberation: The Souths' Rhetorical Framework for Reproductive Justice

Fabiola Carrión

My personal and professional background as an Afro-Indigenous woman born and raised in Peru and as an advocate living in the United States South compelled me to write this account on the resonance of reproductive justice in the Souths—the South of the US (the diverse region within the country) and south of the US (the diverse region below the US border). I grew up among feminist activists, including my mother, who integrated into their advocacy the connections between repressive regimes, racism, poverty, and women's struggles. After receiving most of my formal education in the US, I worked for a US-based organization that offered support to Latin American reproductive rights advocates. As someone who developed her feminist consciousness from the US Reproductive Justice Movement, I naively thought I would propagate its theory during my work trips to Latin America. I had full faith, and still do, that the tenets of reproductive justice can resonate with women[1] from the Global South. However,

1. When I use the words "woman" or "women," I do not intend to be exclusionary as cisgender and transgender women and gender non-conforming and non-binary individuals are active participants of the feminist movements, receive reproductive health care, and have a lot at stake in the fight for reproductive liberation. I have tried to limit these terms when necessary to explain a person's identity, when cited in research, or to reflect the fight against the subjugation of a person because of their sex, gender, or appearance thereof.

I was humbled when the consistent response to my preaching was somewhat like, "Duh. . . . We already know this." I realized that reproductive justice is not necessarily a novel framework for Latin American advocates because it mirrors modes of resistance to oppressions that exist among women of color in the US and among women who live south of the US border. Not much has been written about the commonalities between what I am referring to throughout this chapter as the *reproductive liberation* movements in the Souths—known as reproductive justice in the US and reproductive rights in Latin America and the Caribbean (LAC).[2] Why is it that these connections are not part of our common and shared knowledge? Since both movements were influenced by the human rights framework, are they bound to have the same inevitable successes and challenges? I write this chapter as a witness, active participant, and liaison to the Reproductive Justice Movement and the reproductive rights movement of LAC. I am an embodied form of what Anne Freadman describes as "uptake" because my existence and experience crosses borders; I am in the middle as well as part of both realms, and I work to unite their efforts (43). I hope that this piece not only explains the similarities among the activists of the Souths, but also highlights how their advocacy strategies run parallel to each other and form the pathway to achieving full reproductive liberation in the Americas.

This chapter articulates how the embodied experiences of the women of the Souths and the human rights framework that birthed reproductive justice shaped the most important global texts on reproductive liberation. These concepts are largely the products of the United Nations' 1994 International Conference on Population and Development that met in Cairo, Egypt and the UN's 1995 Fourth World Conference on

2. In the US, reproductive justice is defined as the human right to maintain personal bodily autonomy, have children, not have children, and parent children in safe and sustainable communities. Reproductive justice acknowledges the different experiences of reproduction as well as serves as a political and organizing mechanism. In contrast, "reproductive rights" in the US constitute the individual legal rights to reproductive health care services. LAC activists also adopt a more intersectional approach, recognizing that reproductive rights are human rights that should be fully accessible. In this sense, what is understood as "reproductive justice" in the US constitutes "reproductive rights" in Latin America and the Caribbean. As such, I use the term "reproductive liberation," to include intersectional, human-rights frameworks led by women activists of the two Souths: what women of color in the US call "reproductive justice," and LAC women consider "reproductive rights."

Women in Beijing, China. I analyze how these two international conferences of the mid-1990s were pivotal for these movements as activists contributed to and were influenced by a human rights framework that gave voice to their multiple and intersecting demands. The conferences were also instrumental because they convened the international movement's highest number and most diverse set of participants who engaged in rhetorical dialogue and collaboration. As the most inclusive space for reproductive rights up to that point, the conferences engendered official agreements containing language that established a rhetorical framework of what reproductive liberation would look like in the future (including what it looks like now). Accounting for and analyzing these conferences and their effects reinforces "*ethos* as a social act" in reproductive liberation work; as both theory and practice, it is "a mode of inquiry" *and* "a site of struggle" (Hesford 199).

I argue that the trajectories and rhetorical consequences of the two Souths—as facilitated by the conferences—led to the present models of reproductive liberation in three main ways. First, the Cairo and Beijing conferences reframed earlier discursive appeals to limit population growth by instilling a new commitment: to promote reproductive health and rights as universal and moral imperatives. Second, these conferences articulated the importance of an intersectional approach that abandons the separation of the different oppressions experienced by women of the Souths. Third, the Souths' activists returned to their home countries and employed the conferences' rhetorical frameworks to advocate for reproductive rights and justice. For these reasons, Cairo and Beijing marked *kairotic* moments in the push for reproductive liberation. Largely in response to these conferences, these movements have encountered intense opposition in the last twenty-five years, both influencing discourse and leading to some policy losses, particularly in the US. At the same time, some gains have been slowly but steadily achieved in LAC thanks to the transnational organizing and the discourse that was largely developed in these conferences. As so often happens, the past augurs the future. As the Cairo and Beijing conferences showed, now is the time to once again center the experiences of women of the Souths and support intersectional advocacy that rejects a narrow discourse in favor of an inclusive and broader vision for reproductive liberation.

My own experiences serving as an advocate and attorney in the US, including in the US South, as well as my professional and personal trajectory in LAC as a program officer and a child raised by feminists, have shaped the questions I pose and my approach to answering them. In addition to relying on secondary scholarship, my research included interviewing a former colleague, physician Virginia Gómez de la Torre from Ecuador, as well as two Peruvian feminist leaders: feminist theorist Virginia Vargas and sociologist Susana Galdos. I also had a long and insightful conversation with Loretta Ross, who is one of the founders of the US Reproductive Justice Movement, a Southerner, and a Beijing conference participant. Finally, I owe huge thanks to sociologist and communicator Patricia Córdova who facilitated some of these connections and worked with my mother on a feminist magazine called *MUSA* in the early 1990s. In what follows, I recount the findings of this research to tell the story of these conferences, point to their rhetorical legacy, and suggest their potential for helping activists understand reproductive liberation moving forward.

How the Multiple Paths of the Souths Converged for Reproductive Liberation

The Souths have a common history that has resulted in similar frameworks for reproductive liberation. Since European colonization in the Americas, Indigenous peoples and African slaves endured the harshest forms of oppression, with women bearing the brunt of exploitation. In addition to brutal working conditions, their bodies were weaponized through systemic rape, reproductive coercion, and family separation. Having many reasons to avoid pregnancy, preserve their families, and control their fertility, Black and Indigenous women consumed herbs to end their pregnancies throughout generations (Ross and Solinger 20). From their lived experiences, these women knew that their reproductive health was directly connected with their project of life and the survival of their families.

By the mid-twentieth century, Black women, specifically from the US South, pioneered efforts to achieve reproductive liberation along with other rights that were critical to them, their families, and their communities. In the 1960s, the first Black female legislator in Tennessee, Dorothy Lavinia Brown, introduced a bill to legalize abortion when the pregnancy was caused by rape or incest. Other Southern Black women acknowledged the connection between the lack of reproductive freedom with other forms of oppression experienced in their communities. For example, Black women involved with the Arkansas Women's Project in the 1970s and 1980s worked on issues of intimate partner, reproductive health, and sexual violence while delivering anti-racism and anti-homophobia workshops. They understood that they could not separate one topic from the other and that being a feminist required being anti-racist (University of Central Arkansas Archives).

Meanwhile, LAC feminists played a critical role in defying the military and authoritarian regimes that killed, tortured, and disappeared hundreds of thousands of people from the mid to the late twentieth century. Women activists, through the Vaso de Leche (Cup of Milk) program in Peru and the Casas de la Mujer in Nicaragua, engaged in intersectional advocacy in support of poor and oppressed people, including Indigenous and Black women. In contrast to the second wave feminism dominated by white women in the US, LAC feminist advocacy included Indigenous and Black women like my mother. LAC women knew that working across sectors was critical to full liberation. With the transition to democracy in the 1980s and their experience advocating against systemic violence, LAC women in the next decade increased their political participation by demanding equal rights and addressing their concerns as women, such as the rights to bodily autonomy and access to sexual and reproductive health care.

The 1990s were also a turning point for Black women in the US. A group of twelve Black women[3] participating in a conference on healthcare reform in 1994 decided to convene separately in a hotel room because they were frustrated by the ways that health and reproductive rights were siloed from other social justice issues important to Black women like poverty, the environment, and intimate partner violence (Ross and Solinger 64). Further, they maintained that the second wave of the feminist movement, which was primarily represented by middle class and wealthy white women, could not fully defend the needs of women of color and other non-dominant populations because it limited its focus to abortion and failed to understand the multiple oppressions experienced by women of color. The next month, some of these women and other activists of color—many of them from the South—would go to Cairo to attend the International Conference on Population and Development,

3. This group, which called itself "the Women of African Descent for Reproductive Justice and included leaders from the US South," was comprised of Toni M. Bond Leonard, Reverend Alma Crawford, Evelyn S. Field, Terri James, Bisola Marignay, Cassandra McConnell, Cynthia Newbille, Loretta Ross, Elizabeth Terry, 'Able' Mable Thomas, Winnette P. Willis, and Kim Youngblood.

which offered them a unique opportunity to assert their beliefs and comprehend a human rights framework that would eventually help them conceptualize reproductive justice.

The women of the Souths had become incrementally familiar with the human rights framework by attending international conferences a decade before the events in Cairo and Beijing (Ross, Personal Interview). In gatherings like the 1984 Second International Conference on Population in Mexico, LAC women denounced coercive practices in contraceptive research and proposed that reproductive choice be based on the right to bodily integrity and control (Berro Pizarrossa 4). The 1985 World Conference to Review and Appraise the Achievements of the United Nations Decade for Women in Kenya elevated the plight of Afro-descendants from around the world in addressing racial discrimination along with gender oppression (Ross, Personal Interview). These rhetorical spaces provided these activists with crucial lessons about the human rights framework and the importance of building transnational movements for reproductive liberation.

The human rights framework also offered a conceptual model more conducive to intersectional advocacy that better resonated with the Souths' activists. Legal theory characterizes human rights as universal, interrelated, interdependent, and indivisible. They also involve "positive" and "negative" obligations. Positive rights are those rights governments must guarantee by setting up systems and infrastructures, like the right to health. Negative rights are those that governments must refrain from unduly interfering with, like the right to privacy. As human rights are interdependent and interrelated, reproductive rights encompass various basic protections that relate to and build from one another, such as the rights to health, life, autonomy, privacy, information, as well as to be free from tortuous, cruel, and inhumane treatment (Ross and Solinger 78–89). These human rights characteristics formed the theoretical structure of reproductive justice. The human rights framework also articulated how LAC feminists integrated their particular role within a larger social justice movement. While the conferences in Mexico and Kenya helped to build an understanding of human rights and reproductive liberation, the 1994 International Conference on Population and Development in Cairo and the 1995 Fourth World Conference on Women in Beijing became the pinnacle in UN activism on reproductive liberation.

All Coming Together: The Cairo and Beijing Conferences

The International Conference on Population and Development represented a global and multi-sectoral commitment to promote reproductive health and rights in novel ways. More than eleven thousand participants from 179 governments attended this conference while an adjacent forum welcomed 1,500 nongovernmental organizations (NGOs) including more than 4,200 activists (United Nations, *Programme of Action*, iii). Galdos highlights that LAC members of civil society had prepared agendas in their countries in order to present these to their official delegations during the conference (Personal Interview). When NGOs and official delegations arrived in Cairo, they were ready to collaborate and negotiate formally and informally. In contrast to Karma R. Chávez's recounting of troubled and contentious coalition building between immigrant and LGBTQ groups in Arizona (133–34), the Global South activists who went to Cairo were ready to redeploy or readapt to multiple perspectives and political pressures in order to come to a general consensus that would result in the Programme of Action. Galdos also posits that Cairo was the first space in which these stakeholders worked in this cooperative manner. As a result, the conference's agreement integrated the experiences of many activists who had been previously ignored or, more starkly, who had been seen as enemies of the State for opposing tyrannical administrations and harsh austerity measures of the 1970s and 1980s.

The 1994 Cairo Conference also offered US women of color an open space for participation and coordination. Six organizations representing Asian and Pacific Islander, Black, Latine, and Native American women, known as the US Women of Color Coalition for Reproductive Rights, organized to have an impact at the Cairo Conference. Along with other Global South activists, they presented the "Statement on Poverty, Development, and Population Activities," which articulated the connection between their oppressions as US women of color with the status of women in the Global South (Silliman et al. 48–49). This type of statement has benefited the reproductive liberation movement in the short- and long-term because it acknowledges differences while understanding that activists are connected through the common roots of their oppressions (Chávez 114). The end result of this new rhetorical framework marked a significant shift in the conference's paradigm from a narrow, technical, and medical approach focused on population control to a human rights framework based on women's rights.

Through the conversations that transpired before and during the conference, government delegations, UN representatives, and activists negotiated the language of a unanimous and transcendental agreement known as the Programme of Action. The Programme's Preamble expressed the shared aims of advocating for human rights by addressing the relationship between poverty, underdevelopment, and reproduction in a context that rejects a sole concern for population control (6–7). It made clear that the issues of population, poverty, and the environment cannot be considered in isolation. The Programme of Action therefore connected reproductive health with other issues like education, political and economic development, maternal and child mortality, migration, and violence against women. This new understanding, argues Alexandra Garita, would not have been possible without the "active role of a strongly articulated and well-organized transnational feminist movement," which included US women of color and LAC women (271). Ross also credits activists from the Global South with the Programme's recognition of maternal health and morbidity, childbearing, and child-raising as critical components of human rights ("Understanding").

Language that eventually became part of the reproductive justice mantra appeared first in Cairo's Programme of Action (9). Principle #4 explained that "the human rights of women and the girl child are an inalienable, integral and indivisible part of universal human rights" in the way that reproductive justice embraces human rights and their universal application (9). All individuals, established Principle #8, have the "basic right to decide freely and responsibly the number and spacing of their children and to have the information, education and means to do so" (10). This Principle went beyond describing the general right of reproductive health to emphasize the means to actually achieve that right in the same way that the reproductive justice framework demands that reproductive liberation involves full access and not merely choice. In the exercise of this right, the Programme of Action contended, governments should "take into account the needs of the living and future children and their responsibilities towards the community" (46) just as reproductive justice emphasizes the right for everyone to live in "safe and sustainable communities." Thus, the Programme conceptualized a definition of rights beyond individualistic protections akin to reproductive justice's community-centered approach. Similarly, LAC feminist activists, primarily those experiencing poverty and of African and/or Indigenous descent, possessed the experience of creating "soup kitchens" in order to feed their communities through mutual aid, which additionally served as incubators for political education and consciousness. Activism that was cultivated of a collective necessity to care for their families and communities imbued LAC advocates with the innate skills and understanding to make these connections in the Programme of Action. The Cairo conference was a turning point in arriving at a new global consensus based on human rights because it created the first explicit global agenda borne out of the direct experiences of those mostly impacted by them. The Programme of Action offered both US and LAC activists with a unique set of tools to reclaim their rights back home, but more work, greater buy-in, and additional opportunities were also on the horizon.

Only a year after the Cairo convening, 17,000 government delegates and 30,000 activists arrived at the Fourth World Conference on Women in Beijing, making it the largest gathering on reproductive rights to this day. Beijing welcomed more than seven times the number of activists who participated in Cairo. Representatives from 189 governments attended the conference while activists participated in a parallel forum in Huairou, two hours away from the official site.[4] Beijing also gathered the largest international congregation of LAC activists, among them Vargas. The LAC contingency possessed more resources that enabled their participation, Vargas contends, and were better equipped with the skills learned from Cairo a year before (Personal Interview).

The Beijing Conference provided an opportunity for many more activists who had never participated in international spaces. It was a "rich moment of learning," asserts Vargas, who was also the NGO forum coordinator for Latin America (Personal Interview). The founders of the Reproductive Justice Movement, like Southern-based Ross and Newbille, also returned to this global forum and brought many more activists with them. They formed a US Women of Color coalition that offered information, leadership training, and strategic planning skills to women of color (Silliman et al. 49). Because of the diversity of voices and the agreement that ensued, Beijing became an expanded rhetorical gathering.

4. The International Women's Tribune Centre reports that 35,000 individuals registered for the forum: 12,336 from Asia and the Pacific, 3,245 from Africa, 2,020 from Latin America and the Caribbean, just under 1,000 from the Middle East, and almost 15,000 participants from Europe and North America.

The consensus reached in Beijing resulted in the most enduring language on reproductive liberation to this day. It was during this conference that then-US First Lady Hillary Rodham Clinton proclaimed, "Women's rights are human rights," which was incorporated in the conference's Declaration and Platform for Action and became a rallying cry for women's rights activists worldwide. Moving beyond the Cairo consensus, the Beijing conference articulated that poverty, social development, and women's rights were critical to global social justice. The Beijing Platform for Action established that "[t]he advancement of women and the achievement of equality between women and men are a matter of human rights and a condition for social justice and should not be seen in isolation as a women's issue" (United Nations, *Beijing* 16). Furthermore, the Platform for Action established that peace was inextricably linked with the advancement of women in the way that reproductive justice demands living in safe environments (3). It also made clear that development and peace are necessary for women to attain optimal health throughout the life cycle (35). The Platform for Action would therefore articulate the language that became the complete reproductive justice definition: "the human right to maintain personal bodily autonomy, have children, not have children, and parent the children we have in safe and sustainable communities" (SisterSong website).

Beijing's Platform for Action built from and exceeded Cairo's Programme for Action by unequivocally demanding change to structural problems that intersect with one another. It denounced the inequities and obstacles that remain for women around the world, particularly women from the Global South. It also recognized that while oppressions apply to all, they affect individuals differently, especially through the experience of violence, poverty, and racial as well as other forms of discrimination. The Platform acknowledged that some women face additional barriers to full equality and advancement "because of such factors as their race, age, language, ethnicity, culture, religion or disability, because they are indigenous women or because of other status" (United Nations, *Beijing* 18). The Platform became a transnational response and rejection to the notion that "sisterhood is global" and that all women are equally subjugated. In this sense, Beijing exemplifies how the global feminist movement has always accounted for and wrestled with difference, a challenge that has largely become its strength. Reproductive justice similarly recognizes that while every individual has the same human rights, not everyone is oppressed the same way, at the same time, or by the same forces. As explained earlier, reproductive justice was born out of the frustration that white feminists failed to acknowledge that their conditions differed from the struggles experienced by women of color. The Platform for Action was also unique in condemning governments who placed reservations or self-imposed exemptions on fulfilling certain components of global agreements. It stated that unless human rights are "fully recognized and effectively protected, applied, implemented, and enforced," they exist in "name only" (90). The Platform for Action would therefore condemn governments against breaking their own promises in ways that no other international agreement had done before. Lastly, the Platform for Action explicitly summoned governments to review the laws that punish women who undergo abortions and not just simply aim to reduce unsafe abortions, taking one step closer to recognizing the human right to abortion in ways that Cairo stopped short of doing (40).

Beijing's Platform for Action outlined the most progressive blueprint thanks to the multitude of diverse voices who were part of the conference as well as the deepening political education of a growing transnational movement. Beijing was the culmination of a long and ongoing process to mobilize more women to fight for the expansion of their rights with an intersectional approach. While Cairo was important because it fostered collaboration between civil society and governments, the numbers and diversity of activists in Beijing resulted in much greater implications for feminist organizing and rights discourse as evidenced by its influence on reproductive justice principles and LAC feminist advocacy. As the feminist voices of the Latin American Association of Social Sciences proudly declared, "*Nosotras no llegamos a Beijing; nosotras inventamos Beijing.*" (*We didn't arrive to Beijing; we invented Beijing.*) (FLACSO 13).

The Souths' feminists reached a peak during the Cairo and Beijing conferences that they have not been able to surpass in other international gatherings. Vargas postulates that Beijing and the NGO forum represented the highest global point in addressing women's issues ("Los Feminismos"). Alternatively, Ross admits that more could have been done in Beijing, particularly in advocating for sexual freedom, pleasure, and sexual orientation ("Understanding"). Galdos reacts similarly by pointing to Cairo's exclusion of sexual health and rights in its Programme of Action (Personal Interview).

Even with the compromises that were reached, no other conferences are referred to more than Cairo's and Beijing's. Gómez de la Torre contends that the conferences' agreements are considered more effective advocacy instruments than treaties because their texts represent the input of a more diverse set of voices, including NGOs. My experience in LAC advocacy confirms that Cairo and Beijing had an empowering effect among activists, who recognized commonalities among women's conditions globally; thus, their texts more closely aligned with other activists' goals, experiences, and concerns.

The Impact of the Conferences Back in the Souths

It would be difficult to overstate the conferences' impact on feminist organizing and reproductive rights policy throughout Latin America and the Caribbean. As articulated by Vargas, advocates hoped to influence the actual "texts" of government reports and UN documents, and they considered Beijing to be an exceptional opportunity—a "pretext"—for remobilizing and revitalizing movements and fostering debates on women's rights (Álvarez et al. 553). Nonetheless, this form of advocacy did not take place without criticism. Some LAC activists dismissed the notion that rights could truly be advanced at the UN because it was an institution dominated by Western countries. They also criticized the origins of the funding that paid for participants' attendance, as US and European donors favored already privileged NGOs with English-speaking staff (554). Álvarez and others further contend that these global efforts still denied advocacy access to grassroots organizations who were less likely to conduct policy assessment, project execution, and social services delivery (562). Vargas acknowledges these critiques and employs the term "gender technocracy," which she defines as the cooptation of feminist discourse in these types of advocacy spaces ("Los Feminismos").

Gaining more attention and acceptance from LAC policymakers also came at some cost. Then-Peruvian President Alberto Fujimori joined his country's delegation in Beijing where he defended his goal of "carrying out a modern and rational policy of family planning" (United Nations, "Unofficial"). When he returned to Peru, Fujimori founded the Ministry of Women and Vulnerable Populations as well as the Women and Family Commission in Congress (Córdova). It would seem like women's rights were central to his agenda, but an intersectional human rights analysis demonstrates that it was quite the opposite. His "modern and rational policy" was actually a nationwide program to forcibly and unsafely sterilize poor and Indigenous women in order to control their reproduction. One of the darkest periods of recent Peruvian history, this sterilization program has been condemned internationally, including through cases like *María Mamérita Mestanza Chávez v. Peru* at the Inter-American Commission on Human Rights.

After the conferences, LAC activists continued to meet through informal gatherings known as "*encuentros*" (or encounters) in order to build solidarity, strategize, and elaborate new discourses that employed a more intersectional framework (Rosenberg 537). They also formed more affinity groups that represented different identities, such as the Latin American and Caribbean Black Women's Network as well as the Lesbian Feminist Network. Through the creation of these groups, LAC activists have developed improved strategies to address racism, heterosexism, and other issues within their movements. Galdos concurs that Black and Indigenous leadership is far more visible than it was in the past, although leaders were always part of the feminist movement. Furthermore, these networks created, joined, and worked with more specialized issue groups such as the Latin American and Caribbean Women's Health and Reproductive Rights Network (Rosenberg 546). Growth, specialization, and collaboration have been critical to some of the more recent successes of the LAC feminist movement. Meanwhile, in the 1990s and on, Black and other women of color in the US would have their own reckoning and formulate a concept that would transform the discourse of reproductive and sexual rights, broaden the movement, and reshape activism for new generations.

When US activists returned from Cairo and Beijing, they were determined to build a national movement led by women of color that would incorporate the ideological foundation of human rights (Silliman et al. 49). In 1997, two years after the Beijing conference, some of those who participated at the global conferences formed SisterSong, a Southern-based, national membership organization that uses a human rights framework to "create a national, multi-ethnic Reproductive Justice Movement" (SisterSong website). The term "reproductive justice," however, was not defined until SisterSong began to plan its first national conference in Atlanta in 2003, which sponsored plenary and workshop sessions to explore the concept of reproductive justice (Ross, "Understanding"). A year later, a large contingent of women of color marched under the banner "Women of Color for Reproductive Justice" in the March for Women's Lives in Washington, DC. Reproductive justice leaders, particularly Ross, had successfully pushed the march's organizers to change the name of the March from "the March for Freedom of

Choice" to the "March for Women's Lives" in order to embrace a reproductive justice mantra that acknowledged every aspect of women's lives in ways that are critical to achieving reproductive liberation as articulated at the conferences (Ross, Personal Interview). Thanks to the organizing efforts of women of color, the march brought over one million participants to the US Capitol. Such turnout demonstrated that the Reproductive Justice Movement was needed to take on the reproductive and other oppressions experienced by BIPOC[5] women for too long.

In defining reproductive justice, advocates turned to the global human rights framework because the US lacked a sufficient legal foundation to guarantee women of color safe and reliable access to health care and other rights. For example, the US Constitution does not articulate a right to health care in contrast to international legal instruments and other national constitutions. As a result of their participation in international conferences and the cross-learning that emerged with activists from the Global South, the founders of the Reproductive Justice Movement understood that the US legal system could not adequately resolve the "simultaneous vectors of oppression." Human rights, an alternative framework, effectively addresses intersectional concerns (Ross and Solinger 181). The founders believed that only a comprehensive human rights-based approach could address access to health care and grapple with the intersecting issues of class, race, and gender that affect BIPOC women (Silliman et al. 24).

Leaning on the international agreements, reproductive justice founders developed more practical goals that addressed race, gender, and class prejudices in intersectional ways. The human rights characteristics of universality, indivisibility, and inalienability also appealed to the founders, who observed that the reproductive justice framework offered basic protections that all human beings should enjoy (Ross and Solinger 127). Reproductive justice recognizes the common struggles for universal human rights that include everyone but prioritizes those who have been historically oppressed. As both a negative and positive human right, reproductive justice also demands that the government not interfere with reproductive decision-making while insisting on its obligation to create the conditions to freely exercise these decisions (169). As Ross and Solinger articulate, reproductive justice "looks to the international human rights framework as a sturdy moral, political, and legal struc-

5. I use the terms women of color and BIPOC women interchangeably. BIPOC stands for Black, Indigenous, and Other People of Color.

ture through which reproductive justice goals may eventually be accomplished" (79).

In the same way that the reproductive justice founders contributed to and learned from reaching global consensus, reproductive justice also understands that a movement requires the unity of a "polyvocality of experiences" (Ross and Solinger 59). These multiple and varied perspectives resemble what Chávez calls "dissonance" because they "promote a heightened awareness of, and attentiveness to, the need for constant work and reflexivity." In other words, the movement's success comes from its constant grappling with the tensions that stem from these different experiences (136). The human rights framework and the conferences that adopted it also offer reproductive justice advocates new theories of agency and power they never felt in the US (68). By building from an international human rights framework, Ross argues, reproductive justice connects local and national issues to the "global struggle for women's human rights that would call attention to our commitment to the link between women, their families, and their communities" ("Understanding"). Vargas feels the same way about the LAC reproductive rights context since she believes that the world conferences proved the importance of constructing a new global space ("Los Feminismos").

Over the years, based in part from the language and lessons learned from the conferences, reproductive justice leaders and SisterSong have conceptualized the principles of reproductive justice. This new theoretical paradigm centers three interconnected human rights: the right not to have children using safe birth control, abortion, or abstinence; the right to have children under the conditions individuals choose; and the right to parent children in safe and healthy environments (Ross and Solinger 9–57). Reproductive justice is also a political and organizing movement that weaves reproductive rights with social justice, representing the activist pivot that resulted from the Beijing Platform and a rejection of the dichotomy of the pro-choice/pro-life debate (Ross and Solinger 42–43; Ross, Personal Interview). Reproductive justice requires a fight across social movements to build a united demand for human rights (Ross and Solinger 69–70). This framework recognizes the leadership of women of color and their ability to change the discourse, activism, and new knowledge that can transform the US political, cultural, and socio-economic landscape (258–59). Reproductive justice theory is articulated from the lived experience of BIPOC women and therefore its authenticity cannot be denied.

The Movements Merge . . . Again

Since the Beijing and Cairo conferences, more groups have been created to advance the causes of BIPOC and LGBTQ women in the Souths in ways that acknowledge their multiple identities. New theories and submovements have emerged to further conceptualize reproductive rights through racialized and other identities. For instance, novel terminology like *Amefricanidad* rejects the Eurocentric underpinnings of *mestizaje,* which downplays the Indigenous and African identities of Latin America and the Caribbean (Rivera Berruz). Supported by seasoned advocates, LAC feminism now involves a more diverse group that is also involved in the fight for racial equality, the right to the land, and sexual diversity.

Similarly, a more diverse movement of activists in the US adheres to a reproductive justice framework that links political, economic, and social rights. Black women, LGBTQ individuals, and young people are advancing the mantra of reproductive justice and forming coalitions across movements. Just as they did decades before, they are pioneering efforts to achieve reproductive liberation in the US South. For example, a BIPOC-led abortion fund purchased a clinic in Alabama to provide abortions across the Southeast. In addition, Black women from the South continue to speak in international human rights spaces like the UN Human Rights Council. With young people at the helm, the Souths' movements have also increased in capacity and heightened public consciousness on reproductive rights and justice.

When it comes to legal protections, Latin America has enjoyed some notable successes since the Cairo and Beijing conferences. Ecuador and Chile have liberalized laws by permitting abortions on certain grounds. Colombia, Mexico, Argentina, Uruguay, and Guyana have joined Cuba's long-standing law decriminalizing abortion altogether. The same is not true in the US, where in 2022 the Supreme Court reversed almost fifty years of precedent by holding that abortion is no longer a constitutionally protected right. This devastating decision is accompanied by states' failure to expand Medicaid access leading to rising maternal mortality rates, particularly among Black and Indigenous women in the US South.

Reproductive rights in the Souths are also increasingly threatened by fundamentalist groups. In Latin America and the Caribbean, an alliance has been formed between the Catholic Church and Evangelical Churches, who are establishing political parties, electing officials, and inculcating among their congregants their staunch opposition to anything related to sexual and reproductive rights. Fundamentalism has also expanded across the US South as shown by the strong bonds created between fundamentalist Christian groups with elected officials who are advancing a successful anti-abortion agenda in Southern state legislatures and the courts. When reflecting on the impact of the conferences, advocates confess they had no idea how religious conservatism would aggressively respond to the global feminist movement of the 1990s and halt the progress achieved (FLACSO 25).

Women of color in the US may have more in common with LAC activists than white women in their own country. They come from similar trajectories of colonialism and white supremacy, their needs are the same as they lack access to critical rights, and their holistic approach to advocacy is similar. Health-care systems and infrastructures in both regions continue to fail BIPOC women because they are less likely to have access to health care while being more prone to chronic conditions that correlate with intergenerational trauma. The COVID-19 pandemic has clearly exposed these disparities as Black and Indigenous peoples in the Americas have been disproportionately impacted by the coronavirus. As the Souths continue to fight fundamentalism, racism, and economic exploitation, an emphasis on reproductive liberation could bridge the disconnect between existing laws and the lack of economic and social resources to achieve those rights.

When I asked Ross how reproductive justice could be advanced in other countries, like those in Latin America and the Caribbean, she seemed hesitant since the framework came from the human rights principles that advocates around the world had jointly developed particularly in Cairo and Beijing. It would seem obvious to advocates from the Global South that these rights are intersectional, that access is just as important as legal recognition, and that advocates must work together to achieve full liberation. Perhaps rhetorically amplifying reproductive justice as also reproductive liberation—a term that names the Souths' rhetorical coalitional work past, present, and future that I described in this chapter—can serve as a reminder of the Souths' common struggles and aligned agenda. The powerful, intersectional, and nuanced text that was created from the Cairo and Beijing conferences, different from earlier global gatherings, would not have occurred but for the strong presence and preparation of those who brought their own experiences to these global spaces. Women of color activists returned to the US with a human rights framework that they called reproductive justice in order to articulate their demands. In a country that will soon be majority-minority, this intersectional understanding of reproductive justice as a result of BIPOC leadership must continue for reproductive liberation to be fully realized.

Similarly, the continued success of reproductive liberation in LAC depends on the leadership of Afro-descendant, Indigenous, and LGBTQIA individuals. Across these geopolitical sites, this critical rhetorical, activist work of liberation can best move forward with structural support. More government and philanthropic resources should be directed to grassroots organizations that are led by historically underserved communities. A leadership pipeline must be created and sustained so that more activists from the Souths have the ability to participate in any future international fora and hold their governments accountable. By the same token, *encuentros* should be ongoing and well-financed without ideological interference. This support is warranted because reproductive liberation includes an integrated analysis in the same way in which Vargas calls the Latin American feminist movement the "text and the pretext." It is both the goal and the method. Reproductive liberation is the acknowledgment that advocates must work across social justice movements to build a united struggle for human rights. For the goals of Cairo and Beijing to be fulfilled, the movements will have to continue pushing for bolder policies and investing in leaders who can advocate from their embodied experiences.

A lot has happened in the last twenty-five-plus years since the conferences. In addition to a few policy victories in Latin America and the Caribbean, LAC advocates are more connected, LGBTQ visibility and sexual rights are more prominent, and some practices like inter-partner violence have been largely condemned. The challenges are arguably bigger as well. COVID-19 has exacerbated the feminization of poverty, and a religious push against reproductive and sexual health is stronger than it has ever been. Neither South is near fulfilling the goals of the Cairo and Beijing conferences, but advocates do have powerful texts and the possibility for stronger goals whenever more activists from the Souths reengage in these spaces—hopefully in leadership positions and in stronger numbers.

Works Cited

Álvarez, Sonia E. et al. "Encountering Latin American and Caribbean Feminisms." *Journal of Women in Culture and Society*, vol. 28, no. 2, 2002, pp. 537–79.

Berro Pizzarossa, Lucía. "Here to Stay: The Evolution of Sexual and Reproductive Health and Rights in International Human Rights Law." *Laws*, vol. 7, no. 3, 2018, /www.mdpi.com/2075–471X/7/3/29. Accessed 30 Jan. 2021.

Chávez, Karma R. *Queer Migration Politics: Activist Rhetoric and Coalitional Possibilities*. U of Illinois P, 2013.

Córdova, Patricia. E-mail to the author. 28 Apr. 2020.

FLACSO Argentina. "Decisiones en Contextos de Cambios: Interpelaciones e Inspiraciones de la Conferencia de Beijing." *Sinergias: Cuadernos del Área Género, Sociedad y Políticas,* vol. 5, 2005, www.somosiberoamerica.org/wp-content/uploads/2016/10/G%C3%A9nero-y-Desarrollo-inspiraciones-desde-Beijing.pdf. Accessed 30 Jan. 2021.

Freadman, Anne. "Uptake." *The Rhetoric and Ideology of Genre: Strategies for Stability and Change*, edited by R.M. Coe, L. Lingard, and T. Teslenko. Hampton, 2002, pp. 39–53.

Galdos, Susana. Telephone interview with the author. 1 Oct. 2020.

Garita, Alexandra. "Moving toward Sexual and Reproductive Justice: A Transnational and Multigenerational Feminist Remix." *The Oxford Handbook of Transnational Feminist Movements,* edited by Rawwida Baksh and Wendy Harcourt. Oxford UP, 2014, pp. 271–94.

Gómez de la Torre, Virginia. Telephone interview with the author. 28 Apr. 2020.

Hesford, Wendy S. "Ethos Righted: Transnational Feminist Analytics." *Rethinking Ethos: A Feminist Ecological Approach to Rhetoric*, edited by Kathleen J. Ryan, Nancy Myers, and Rebecca Jones. Southern Illinois UP, 2016, pp. 198–214.

Rivera Berruz, Stephanie. "Latin American Feminism." *Stanford Encyclopedia of Philosophy*. 2018, plato.stanford.edu/archives/fall2020/entries/feminism-latin-america/. Accessed 30 Jan. 2021.

Rosenberg, Martha. "A Decade after Cairo in Latin America: An Overview." *Indian Journal of Gender Studies*, vol. 13, no. 2, 2006, pp. 275–91.

Ross, Loretta J. Telephone interview with the author. 3 May 2020.

—. "Understanding Reproductive Justice" *SisterSong*. May 2006, d3n8a8pro7vhmx.cloudfront.net/rrfp/pages/33/attachments/original/1456425809/ Understanding_RJ_Sistersong.pdf?1456425809. Accessed 30 Jan. 2021.

Ross, Loretta J., and Rickie Solinger. *Reproductive Justice: An Introduction*. U of California P, 2017.

Silliman, Jael, Marlene Gerber Fried, Loretta Ross, and Elena R Gutiérrez. *Undivided Rights: Women of Color Organize for Reproductive Justice*. South End P, 2004.

SisterSong Women of Color Reproductive Justice Collective. SisterSong. www.sistersong.net/. Accessed 13 June 2020.

United Nations, *Beijing Declaration and Platform of Action*, Adopted at the Fourth World Conference on Women. 27 Oct. 1995, www.un.org/en/

events/pastevents/pdfs/Beijing_Declaration_and_Platform_for_Action.pdf. Accessed 31 Jan. 2021.

United Nations, *Programme of Action*, Adopted at the International Conference on Population and Development, Cairo, 5–13 September 1994. United Nations Population Fund, 2004, www.unfpa.org/sites/default/files/event-pdf/PoA_en.pdf. Accessed 30 Jan. 2020.

United Nations, *Report of the International Conference on Population and Development, Cairo, 5–13 September 1994*, www.un.org/en/development/desa/population/events/pdf/expert/27/SupportingDocuments/A_CONF.171_13_Rev.1.pdf.

United Nations, Unofficial Translation from Spanish Original Speech Given by the President of the Republic of Peru Alberto Fujimori, Before the IV World Conference on Women, 15 Sept. 1995. Beijing, China, www.un.org/esa/gopher-data/conf/fwcw/conf/gov/950915131946.txt. Accessed 30 Jan. 2020.

University of Central Arkansas Archives. "M95–03 Women's Project, Transformation Newsletters." University of Central Arkansas, uca.edu/archives/m95–03-arkansas-womens-project-collection/m95–03-womens-project-transformation-newsletters/. Accessed 30 Jan. 2021.

Vargas, Virginia. "Los Feminismos Latinoamericanos Construyendo Espacios Transnacionales: Beijing y los Encuentros Feministas Latino Caribeños." 2020. Personal collection.

— Telephone interview with the author. 6 May 2020.

2 Self-Help Clinics, Transphobia, and Reproductive Justice

Hannah Dudley-Shotwell

In a 2019 article, Meera Shah, MD, associate medical director of Planned Parenthood Hudson Peconic (serving multiple counties in New York state), asserted that it was high time we stopped using the phrase "women's health," because this construction "ignores all the other people—with or without a uterus—who have reproductive health needs." Shah's point is about more than semantics; as she notes, most gynecological and obstetric practices reflect cisnormative and even downright transphobic structures that make it nearly impossible for many transgender and gender nonconforming (GNC) people to receive care.

I came across Shah's article as my book, *Revolutionizing Women's Healthcare: The Feminist Self-Help Movement in America* was literally on its way to the printer.[1] My immediate response was, "STOP THE PRESSES. I can't publish a whole book with 'women's healthcare' in the title when I completely agree with Shah's point that this phrasing is exclusionary, transphobic, and even dangerous." Further thinking calmed my knee-jerk response. *Revolutionizing Women's Healthcare* is a historical monograph. It documents the *history* of the self-help movement and its intersections with the feminist and women's health movement from the early 1970s through roughly the early 1990s. Self-help activists did (and often still do) use the term "women's healthcare." They employ(ed) this language strategically—exactly for the purpose of centering "female-bodied" people and of making the point that these people deserved quality healthcare that paid attention to the unique needs of women with female reproductive bodies. Historically, in many (though certainly not all corners) of the self-help, feminist, and women's health movements, there ran strains of both hetero- and cisnormativity. These theoretical, rhetorical, and practical strains continue to impact access to and the quality of reproductive healthcare for people of all genders today.

1. Portions of this chapter first appeared in my book, from Rutgers UP (2020).

The history of feminist self-help efforts and their manifestation in exclusive spaces for political and health activism (and care) is a critical arena for considering contemporary issues of feminist transphobia because of the nature of the roots, branches, and fruits of this movement. Roots: women of all races, classes, and sexualities shaped the self-help movement. Branches: the movement extended to countless geographical locations and impacted both mainstream and alternative healthcare as well as federal and state law. Fruits: the effects of this movement are still seen today in the wide array of birth control options available to consumers, classes and support for nursing parents, "natural" family planning and birth, and innumerable other manifestations of healthcare provision.

The rhetorical practices developed in and used by feminist clinics from the 1970s, with attention to the female body as *the* factor in determining entry into the category of "woman," have had long-lasting effects for how gynecological care is offered today, even in feminist settings. In clinics, self-help activists developed what scholars call "spatial rhetorics" because they delineated, as Jessica Enoch writes, the "purpose of the space; the actions, behaviors, and practices that should happen inside that space; and the people who should occupy it" (6). More directly relevant to this discursive analysis, self-help activists as rhetors developed an entire language around their praxis, laying claim to terms such as "self-help," "self-exam," and "feminist." But they also laid claim to the category of "woman" and in the process expressed a rhetorical othering of those they saw as outside of that category. Many self-help activists insisted that belonging in the category of woman also meant that you were suited to add to knowledge about self-help. Consequently, discursive configurations of "woman" that reified in 1970s self-help circles continue to have real meaning for trans and GNC people seeking healthcare today. A number of scholars have begun to document the myriad ways members of the queer community are marginalized in health and reproductive care.[2] In this essay, I expand upon this work by examining the ways the rhetoric and praxis of the feminist self-help movement contributed to this marginalization. I consider how a reproductive justice framework might guide those providing quality healthcare for people of all gender experiences and expressions (e.g., queer, gender nonbinary,

2. See Briggs; Mamo; Marsh and Ronner; Romesburg; and Stryker.

trans), especially in contemporary feminist clinics with historical ties to this movement.[3]

A Brief History of the Welcoming (and Exclusionary) Self-Help Clinic

Feminist gynecological self-help, which emerged in the early 1970s, was predicated on women's frustration with men's control over their bodies. Women who wanted an abortion were usually at the mercy of men (sympathetic doctors and back-alley abortionists).[4] To get birth control, a woman had to convince her (usually male) doctor that she needed it. Doctors and medical boards forced women to be sterilized against their will. Husbands could rape and abuse their wives with relative impunity. The list goes on. A woman's body was not her own.

In 1970, members of the Los Angeles feminist community supported two male abortion providers when they opened an illegal abortion clinic but soon began to feel uncomfortable about it, fearing that the men were "male chauvinist pigs." The women began contemplating developing a space of their own: opening their own underground, *woman-controlled* abortion clinic. With this radical goal in mind, they began carefully observing abortions and other procedures in the clinic. Here, local activist Carol Downer saw a woman's cervix for the first time: "I was absolutely amazed . . . it was so close!" She swiped a plastic speculum from the clinic, went home, and tried it for herself. Lying in her bed, she used the plastic speculum, a flashlight, and a mirror, and conducted what she would later call a "self-examination." Seeing her own cervix—so close and accessible—made Downer begin to feel confident that she and other

---

3. This essay is largely concerned with gender expression, as opposed to sexual identity (though the two intersect). Occasionally, throughout this text, I use the term "queer" to indicate a wide variety of gender expressions and sexualities, not just those who identify as trans or gender nonconforming. Some Planned Parenthood clinics successfully implement diversity and inclusion initiatives for people of all genders but are beyond the scope of this essay. Also beyond the scope are more local, self-help based types of care that are still happening (outside of clinics), though many of these forms of care center queer health and reproduction.

4. A notable exception was Chicago's Jane Collective, an underground abortion service in which feminist laywomen provided an estimated 11,000 illegal abortions in the four years preceding *Roe v. Wade.*

laywomen could easily learn to perform abortions and get men out of at least *one* women's space (Eberhardt 15).

Later, in a safe, woman-only space, the back room of the Everywoman's Bookstore in Venice, California, the women met to discuss opening their own abortion clinic. Downer showed the other women how easily she could do a "self-exam" and how accessible the cervix was (Downer, Personal Interview). Eager to see their own cervixes, several other women in the group took a turn doing self-exams (Downer, "No Stopping").

Excited by their findings, the group wondered: If the cervix was so accessible, but no woman in the group had ever examined hers before, what else did she not know about her body? Most importantly, how could cervical self-exam allow a woman increased control over her own health? How could she use this knowledge to take control of the most personal space of all—her own body? After this meeting, several of the women began gathering on a regular basis for gynecological "self-help groups," taking turns doing cervical self-examination, performing uterine size checks on each other using a bimanual exam, doing breast exams, and dialoguing about their gynecological health. By regularly examining each other's bodies and discussing them at length, these self-help groups furthered their understanding of how women's bodies varied (Fishel 29–32).

Gynecological self-help spread quickly around the nation, and the rhetorical situation in which the movement emerged was "networked" (Dingo; Edbauer). As Jenny Edbauer argues in her work on rhetorical ecologies, "this rhetoric emerge[d] already infected by the viral intensities that [were] circulating in the social field" (14). That is, preexisting notions of which women *qualified* as women already existed within feminist circles just by the fact that the women in these circles were the products of a cisnormative society. This cisnormativity would pervade their work for decades, circumscribing their revolutionary ideas. Via fax, phone, and in-person conferences, a network of self-help activists emerged, each contributing to the burgeoning discourse of self-help. The movement grew rapidly. Some groups began to monitor their menstrual cycles and keep careful calendars charting their basal body temperature. Others kept journals describing the quality of their vaginal secretions. A few donned white lab coats, bought urine pregnancy tests at a medical supply store, and then practiced using them.[5] Some groups acquired microscopes to closely examine secretions, discharges, and menstru-

5. At the time, even these simple tests were administered only in a doctor's office.

al blood (Murphy). Many set out "to just rap" about their experiences (West Coast Sisters). While the meaning of self-help varied from rhetor to rhetor, audience to audience, location to location, what most of these rhetorical situations had in common was an assumption that "woman" only included a certain group of people.

In self-help groups, the female body itself took on both visual and metaphorical rhetorical importance. Possession of a cervix, vagina, uterus, clitoris, etc. was the metaphorical password into a club centered on a burgeoning brand of feminism, which celebrated and revered the "biologically" female form. Gynecological self-help activists lifted the female form up on a pedestal and reminded the world through visual and performative rhetoric (print media, films, conferences, etc.) that it was something to be admired, cherished—something to pen songs, forge statues, and render paintings about. By placing the female body, especially the cervix, at the center of their analysis, self-help activists necessarily contributed to rhetoric that represented the female reproductive anatomy as the primary constituent of a woman's lived experience. Their role in developing and using such discourse implicates these activists in the (intentional and unintentional) historic marginalization of trans and gender-nonconforming people. Self-help activists were not unique in this glorification of the female form, women's reproductive capabilities, or the power and strength of conceiving, carrying, birthing, and feeding a child; yet, these activists' influence as rhetors was particularly powerful and widespread, especially amongst other 1970s and 1980s feminist circles. Their writings appear in the records of dozens of other contemporary feminist groups and individuals.

Transphobia in the contemporary feminist movement is a result of discourse, assumptions, and ciswoman-only rhetorical spaces—in particular, places that celebrated and investigated the female body, especially its capacity for reproduction (and its related potential for abuse). One such space was the feminist self-help-based clinic—the material locations that emerged from self-help activist group activity. Throughout the 1970s, in an effort to create safe spaces, self-help activists built and ran feminist clinics and overhauled gynecological care.[6] Most clinic founders were white women from middle-class families. A fair number were lesbians, and while many did not conform to "gender norms," I have

6. For the most part, feminist clinics were "women only" spaces. The most significant exception was physicians. Women rarely held medical degrees in the early 1970s, so many had to hire male doctors to perform abortions.

never come across a 1970s self-help activist who publicly identified as trans.[7] Before these clinics existed, people needing reproductive healthcare usually encountered their (typically male) gynecologist when they were reclined on an exam table with their feet in stirrups. Their pelvic exam might be painful, their doctor brusque, demanding, and patronizing. He might scold them for asking about birth control, particularly if they were unmarried. If he believed they needed a medical procedure, he would likely perform it without explaining it to them or giving them much choice in the matter. Conversely, in new feminist clinics all around the country, laywomen health workers (staff with no previous medical training) and clients intentionally learned from each other in physical spaces that were conducive to this sharing. Clients could access and edit their own medical records during visits (Feminist Women's Health Center, "A Visit"). Women met in groups with other women for their visit instead of going one-by-one into exam rooms (Spain 123). Health workers decentered physicians and recognized women (read: ciswomen) as the experts on their own biologically female bodies. Both the health workers and the clients contributed to the emerging conversation about self-help, adding layers to the discourse by sharing their own experiences. Because trans women (at least "out" trans women) did not apparently contribute to this knowledge creation, their voices are absent from 1970s rhetoric about self-help. Possession of a cervix meant the possession of a voice in this movement. Trans voices were rhetorically foreclosed.[8]

In spite of (or because of) activists' revolutionary aspirations, conflicts over "inclusivity" arose early in the history of feminist clinics. Many self-help activists argued that women of all races, classes, and sexualities could benefit from a self-help group. (Note: gender expression

7. Twenty-first century self-help activists *do* often run the gamut of gender. It is also likely that some 1970s clinic founders and users (who may have identified as masculine lesbians, for example) have more recently begun to identify as GNC or trans masculine, but I have not come across them.

8. This activism took place in the context of many other feminist experiments in acting "separately." Most famously, groups like the Washington, DC–based Furies tried to organize their entire lives separate from mainstream institutions, eschewing patriarchal and heteronormative systems of both work and family. Feminists established their own bookstores, credit unions, and dozens of other institutions where they promoted feminist ideology while simultaneously offering jobs and services to women. Separatism was also in keeping with Black Power activism, which encouraged the creation of businesses and institutions that furthered Black values and valued racial pride.

and gender identity are not on that list.) In many cases, lesbian women were well-integrated into the staff but then had to work to create spaces within clinics where they could dialogue about their specific reproductive healthcare needs, such as coming out to a doctor, infection transmission between same-sex partners, insurance discrimination, and donor insemination. In other cases, clinics discovered that lesbian clients were reluctant to use their services because of clinics' emphasis on contraception and reproductive health (Berkeley Women's Health Collective; Feminist Women's Health Center, "Lesbian"; Gay Women's Liberation Collective; Klein; O'Donnell).

Black women, Indigenous women, Asian women, and Latinas have participated in gynecological self-help from its inception; some joined predominantly white self-help groups, and others created gynecological self-help groups specifically for non-white women. A few women of color were clinic founders, dozens worked in feminist clinics as health workers, and scores of others used clinic services. Yet many women of color and Indigenous women believed the movement did not fully consider their needs in its services, strategies, politics, policies, goals, and outreach. These grievances led to rhetorical responses that continue to be an instructive part of feminist self-help care.

Beyond gynecological self-help, in the hands of women of color and Indigenous women, the self-help movement came to encompass a whole range of both praxis and discourse that included a more intersectional and holistic look at the raced female body and the health implications of just *existing* as a woman of color or Indigenous woman. In the 1980s and 1990s, women of color and Indigenous women began forming self-help-based organizations to address issues of racial and economic inequality in the women's health and reproductive rights movements. When these national organizations came on the scene as rhetors contributing to self-help discourse, they developed new uses for and understandings of self-help, and in doing so, completely redefined the parameters of the movement. These groups insisted that race and sex were *inextricable* aspects of lived experience and were determined that dealing with physical health necessitated addressing mental health, particularly the effects of internalized and institutionalized racism and colonialist structures. In essence, women of color and Indigenous women did for the self-help movement what they did for many other mainstream feminist undertakings in the late twentieth-century: they insisted that the movement grapple with and articulate notions of intersectionality and assemblage and enact those theories into their everyday practice and language.

Women of color in the National Black Women's Health Project developed "psychological self-help," a process for examining the way institutional and internalized oppression affected peoples' lives. Each time a psychological self-help group met, they picked an issue like domestic and sexual violence, teenage pregnancy, infant deaths, chronic illness, stress, or self-esteem, and shared their lived experience and discussed their feelings about it. The idea was that after using self-help to work through their emotions on an issue that affected their health, the women in the group would feel empowered to take action and make changes for themselves and others. "The whole process of self-help was supposed to lead to social justice work," health activist Loretta Ross explains. "You get rid of this baggage, this remembered pain, so that you can free up your body, your soul, your spirit to do more work and service to your community." In this way, the act of conversation was meant to lead to transformation (Ross, "Voices" 203–05). Psychological self-help groups embodied a notion that rhetorical scholar Cheryl Glenn expresses: Feminism and rhetoric can change each other.

Activists using psychological self-help contributed to a wider movement that became known in the 1990s as "reproductive justice." In 1997, women from sixteen women-of-color organizations representing Latinas and Native American, African American, and Asian American women formed the SisterSong Women of Color Reproductive Justice Collective. SisterSong has since become the major voice of the Reproductive Justice Movement; they argue that bodily autonomy must include the right to have children, not to have children, and to parent those children in safe and healthy environments (SisterSong.net). The organization used psychological self-help as a way to dialogue while working in coalitions. Observing the success and importance of the reproductive justice framework, some feminist clinics began trying to incorporate reproductive justice into their provision of care, with varying degrees of success. While this intervention has expanded feminist self-help care, exclusionary logics and practices among practitioners—in medicalized and self-help contexts—prevent fully inclusive care.

The Need for More Inclusive Feminist Healthcare Spaces

Trans and GNC people may need many of the same forms of reproductive and gynecological healthcare that cisgender people need, including routine gynecological healthcare, contraception, abortion, fertility treatments, prenatal care, and child birthing; they also sometimes require additional medical interventions—including hormone therapy, gender affirming surgeries, and fertility interventions—in order to live comfortably in their bodies or bear children. A close examination of the rhetorical choices of contemporary feminist clinics shows that much is at stake for these spaces and those potentially or actually using them. Folks in need of healthcare increasingly turn to the internet to locate providers. If a clinic's website or social media presence does not *at the very least* make it clear that they are aware and affirming of and responsive to variations in gender identity, trans and GNC people will not know that a clinic is "friendly" and may never walk in the door. Attention to such inclusive language is of heightened importance in light of the 2022 *Dobbs vs. Jackson Women's Health Organization* decision, the resulting state laws that limit (or ban) access to reproductive healthcare, and the care provided in so-called "sanctuary" states where care remains accessible, including to those traveling from more restrictive areas. Even a name of a clinic that includes the word "woman" (e.g., Atlanta Feminist Women's Health Center, Women's Health Specialists) could potentially be off-putting or unintentionally exclusionary. Fear of discrimination from providers means that queer people are less likely to attend regular screenings (for cervical and breast cancer, for example), which then increases their risk for late diagnosis (Ussher et al.). Clinic websites, social media, and other literature must include rhetorical choices that demonstrate explicitly that their intended audience includes trans and GNC folks.

When queer people do attempt to access healthcare, especially obstetric and gynecological care, boundaries may include blatant homophobia and transphobia, exclusion of any same-sex partners, inappropriate questioning, and even complete refusal of services (Hayman). Trans women who are over fifty need screening if they have been on estrogen for more than five years. Trans masculine people may practice chest binding, which can cause extra pain during a breast exam; if they have had a chest reconstruction, they still need annual chest exams over the age of fifty (for the remaining tissue). Gynecological care can be especially challenging for trans men with a cervix; an exam can be more painful because testosterone can lead to vaginal dryness. Of course, these challenges are further compounded by the fact that trans and GNC people are more likely to be disadvantaged in both education and employment and therefore more likely to live in poverty and homelessness. Body dysphoria, emotional distress, shame, and even physical pain may be heightened when trans and GNC people encounter healthcare providers who are either ignorant or disrespectful of their healthcare needs and fail to use inclusive language (Faculty of Sexual and Reproductive Healthcare; Ussher et al. 602–03).

Having biological children is yet another complex situation. Reproduction can be uniquely medicalized for queer people, who often fit the medical definition of "infertile" just by virtue of their sexuality or gender identity, even if that is not biologically the case. For example, a queer person might not have access to sperm simply because neither they nor a sexual partner produces it (Mamo; Stacey). When trying to conceive or when pregnant, the language of "husband and wife" or "mother and father" on forms, informational pamphlets, and official records can be off-putting and offensive. Pictures of happily married (white, likely middle-class) heterosexual couples wearing wedding rings abound. Queer and/or nonwhite people may be visually excluded from the representations of families. Trans and GNC people also face the constant imperative of having to explain their situation, identity, and even potential fertility solutions to providers (Thompsen and Morrison 59).

An abortion for a trans or GNC person can mean trauma at the hands of incompetent or non-inclusive caregivers. Jack Qu'emi Gutiérrez, an Afro-Latinx Floridian, recalled such an experience to *Out* magazine. When seeking to terminate a pregnancy, Jack felt they had to hide their non-binary gender identity to avoid tough conversations with providers. The required ultrasound "heightened their discomfort with their body," and the actual abortion plus its aftermath proved to be an "awful" tribulation that enhanced their dysphoria (Berg).

Queering Feminist Spaces Using Reproductive Justice

Adopting a reproductive justice framework to maintain inclusive and welcoming self-help spaces, though a method for addressing these problems, is not so simple. A major constraint to making healthcare more inclusive is transphobia—a site of oppression that exists even among feminists. For instance, many fans and followers of the Harry Potter series and (once) beloved author, J. K. Rowling, now may consider her a "TERF," short for "trans-exclusionary radical feminist." Once seen as a stalwart gay rights and feminist activist, Rowling drew fire in 2019 when she tweeted her support of a cisgender woman who was fired for anti-trans tweets (Rowling). Though Rowling's critics were largely responsible for bringing the term TERF into the zeitgeist, both the term and the ideas espoused by those it describes have a longer history. This history illustrates the multidimensional rhetorical levels—spatial, linguistic, embodied, and procedural—operating as self-help clinics further incorporate inclusive reproductive justice practices.

In 1979, feminist scholar Janice Raymond published *The Transsexual Empire*, in which she described "transsexuals"[9] as simply a creation of modern medicine, an institution that works to both reinforce gender stereotypes and patriarchy. Raymond saw trans women as victims of this "empire," and Trojan horses, designed by the empire to invade women's spaces "disguised" as women (Raymond). In the 1990s, despite being increasingly denounced, transphobia continued to exist within some feminist circles. But when the large Michigan Womyn's Music Festival refused to allow a trans woman to attend, claiming "MichFest" was only for "womyn-born-womyn," a huge protest ensued, and battle lines were drawn. The term "womyn" was one of several alternative spellings used by radical feminists to avoid the word "men." It was a move away from patriarchal linguistic conventions that assumed the masculine as default. In this context, it specifically *excluded* transgender women (Kerr).[10] In relation to the self-help movement, in 2016, Downer contributed to *Female Erasure: What You Need to Know About Gender Politics' War on Women, the Female Sex, and Human Rights*, summarizing her fear that trans people were threatening women-only spaces. Since her introduction of cervical self-exam to the feminist community in 1971, Downer has undoubtedly been the most well-known gynecological self-help activist. Her depictions of trans invasion of women's spaces, which she ar-

---

9. The term "transsexual" is largely considered outdated, and some members of the queer community find it offensive, both because the term has often been used pejoratively and because it has distinct clinical connotations, implying that this category only includes those people who are using medical interventions to change their physical body to align with their gender identity.

10. The term "womxn" is a more recent, twenty-first century invention and specifically includes trans and GNC people.

ticulated partially in response to the "bathroom bill" controversy during Barack Obama's presidency, are worth a close examination both because of her influence over the self-help movement and late twentieth century feminism and because of how these movements influenced her.[11]

On one level, Downer's concerns are about physical space. Historian Daphne Spain writes, "Women's rights were tied inextricably to the places created by Second Wave feminists. They were made by and for women, and autonomy from men was central to their identity" (xi). Feminist clinics were a prime example of such spaces. Downer argues, "Denying women their own spaces will have a devastating effect on women's individual self-image and group solidarity." She goes on to argue that if women did not have their own spaces, it would be impossible for them to develop a "mass feminist consciousness" (Downer, "Queer Theory's" 335). A review of *Female Erasure* that appears on its dust jacket summed up the concerns of Downer and her co-authors this way, "If you believe that women, including those who have been sexually assaulted by males, should not be forced against their will to share their most vulnerable spaces with males, this book is for you." The key word here is "vulnerable." As Downer and other feminists have argued since the 1970s, in order to develop a feminist consciousness, women need space—physical and rhetorical—to be vulnerable together, to safely socialize with other women, dialogue, and develop their politics.

On another level, Downer's concerns are about language. She writes, "I am shocked and upset at the transgender movement leadership's aggressiveness toward women. It upsets them when females refer to our own sexual or reproductive organs or claim menstruation, pregnancy and birth as female concerns, so they insist that we change language to be 'inclusive'" ("Queer Theory's" 335). Downer sees much of this conflict over language as a watering-down of the meaning of "woman." She also vehemently opposes the prefix "cis-," arguing that "a group of males who prefer to identify as women are attempting to create a hierarchy within the term 'woman' and to push females lower in it." To Downer, who sees transgender women unalterably as *men*, opening up language in this fashion is yet another example of the kind of language oppression that has plagued women under the patriarchy for centuries (350).

On a third level, this fear is about bodies. Downer expresses the kind of essentialism that undergirded much of 1970s gynecological self-help

11. Though, as I have argued elsewhere, the movement quickly spread out of her control and far beyond what Downer imagined.

activism, delineating who is a "woman" by using their physical characteristics. She is clear about the rhetorical exclusions of "woman" and insists, "Women have vulvas, vaginas, uteruses, ovaries, and female-sexed cells through their bodies. The category doesn't exclude females whose uteruses never developed or which have been surgically removed. The category excludes those with a male body" ("Queer Theory's" 341). One aspect of TERF philosophy that confounds some onlookers is their acceptance of trans men, people born with biologically female bodies but who identify as men. In fact, it is this acceptance that strikes at the heart of TERF philosophy and is most connected to the lessons of gynecological self-help and radical 1970s feminism. Downer and others believe that trans *men*, by virtue of being born into the world with uteruses, ovaries, vaginas, and so forth, can have a feminist consciousness, whereas those who were not born with these body parts cannot. She sees womanhood as written on and in the female body. Womanhood is not only immutable; it is worthy of protection from those who would seek to steal it for themselves. Her insistence that there is a "female experience" means that biologically female persons should be able to lay claim to language that describes their bodies. Of course, this idea that males and females are fundamentally different because of their biology pervades much of Western culture, including many strains of twentieth century feminism.

The feminist clinics with roots in self-help that I have explored do not *explicitly* claim transphobic notions of womanhood. Yet, their deep roots in gynecological self-help mean that they must be particularly careful to foster inclusivity if they wish to be accessible for all who might need their services. I argue that a more thorough embrace of the principles of reproductive justice and attention to the psychological self-help branch of their lineage can help them do just that; to be truly inclusive, self-help based clinics need to adopt a more holistic view of health, just as psychological self-help activists called for.

While early iterations of the reproductive justice framework (in the 1990s) did not explicitly spell out its usefulness for trans and GNC people, their logics are inclusive (SisterSong "Principles of Unity"). In more recent years, SisterSong and other reproductive justice organizations have been more explicit, using phrases like "marginalized women and trans* people" in their literature.[12] Alliances between queer-centered and reproductive justice organizations have also emerged (SisterSong.

12. Some organizations add the asterisk here to encompass a broad range of gender identities and expressions.

net; Thomsen and Morrison). Ross, one of the original architects of the framework, sums up how reproductive justice can be effective for trans and GNC liberation: "Not only biologically defined women experience reproductive oppression. By highlighting the distinction between biological sex and socially constructed gender, our analysis includes transmen, transwomen, and gender-nonconforming individuals" ("Reproductive Justice" 290). Ross argues further that the "open-endedness" of the reproductive justice framework means that it can evolve (300). In 2010, the current director of SisterSong, Monica Simpson, came to the organization from work in a gay and lesbian community center and in criminal justice reform. For her, this role was a "revelation" because "In doing LGBTQ+ work, it couldn't hold my Blackness. In doing work around the prison industrial complex, you couldn't talk about queerness . . . The Reproductive Justice Movement felt like my political homecoming" (Berg). Further, Simpson claimed that "She sees the ability for queer and trans people to self-determine at the core of the movement, from rejecting violence against transgender women to addressing the 'very unique challenges' queer people face when they want to become parents" (Berg).

Listening to reproductive justice activists means appreciating how this framework is a natural companion for queer liberation movements. Both center on "the ability of all people to have freedom and self-determination over their own body, health, and life" (Wong). These movements historically are met with resistance by some common foes, especially those who characterize them as "anti-family" (Stacey). "The animus against those who support LGBT rights and against those who believe we should have bodily autonomy and reproductive choice flows from the same poisonous tree . . . It's a sense that individuals are not entitled to their own autonomy, to their own authentic lives, if it runs afoul of a certain code of how we should behave," argues Kate Kendall, executive director of the National Center for Lesbian Rights. Further, legal victories for reproductive justice are often legal victories for queer health, and vice versa (Luna; National LGBTQ TaskForce). Those interested in reproductive justice who use the term, perhaps even without knowing its history, need to critically examine how it might be used by and for people of all genders. Political scientist Cathy Cohen argues that queer politics can and should include anyone who has not benefited from heteronormativity (Cohen). The same might be said for reproductive justice applying to anyone who has experienced reproductive injustice, broadly defined.

This inclusive impulse, though, presents additional rhetorical challenges. Consider, for instance, Carly Thomsen and Grace Tacherra Morrison's analysis of "End Fake Clinics" (EFC), a student club from the University of California, Santa Barbara that brought queer theory and reproductive justice together in unique ways in the early twenty-first century. EFC believed that crisis pregnancy centers were a "threat to reproductive justice," but also, significantly, that these institutions relied on "the very gendered and sexual ideologies that feminist and queer studies scholars and activists have long worked to disrupt" (727). In trying to articulate the importance of a "queer" reproductive justice framework, the group found itself confounded. Thomsen and Morrison write,

> Connecting the movements by claiming that reproductive issues impact LGBTQ people seemed insufficient politically and epistemologically . . . It seemed obvious that trans men might want to give birth, LGBTQ parents may struggle to retain custody of their children, and LGBTQ people may experience difficulty adopting or accessing reproductive technologies—but all of these examples are built upon . . . "pronatalism." Could we craft a queer reproductive justice politic that . . . was relevant beyond individuals' immediate reproductive needs, and that understood 'queering' beyond examining an issue in relation to LGBTQ-identified people? (718)

The group further posited questions that feminist clinics should consider when starting to reflect on any inclusive/exclusive ideology undergirding their missions, their practices, and their rhetorics. Most importantly, they acknowledge the complexities of language that clinics might attend to:

> Do we talk about women, or is that essentialist and even trans-antagonistic? How might we acknowledge that sexism drives the materiality of reproduction and thus that (people who experience the world as) women experience reproductive issues in ways that most men do not—without reproducing a gender binary? At the same time, how can using ostensibly gender-neutral phrases such as "pregnant people" and "parent" operate in the service of sexism? (Thomsen and Morrison 719)

Grappling with such questions at an organizational level may help feminist clinics on a quest for inclusivity. Another organization doing the work to "queer" reproductive justice is the Atlanta-based SPARK Reproductive Justice Now. "Without Queer and Trans liberation, there is no Black liberation," they argue. "There can be no Reproductive Justice when Black womxn are criminalized, Black trans and non-binary people are marginalized, and Black parents cannot see their children grow in peace. It is imperative that we continue to challenge the erasure of Black womxn, and Queer and Trans folx in the conversations and actions around police violence, brutality, and killing of ALL BLACK LIVES" (SPARK). Clinics with roots in the self-help movement must also consider such criminalization, marginalization, erasure, and violence as they consider how to provide inclusive care to all people who need it.

Clinics should integrate *both* components of self-help—gynecological and psychological—and integrate reproductive justice principles if they truly want to serve trans and GNC people. I conclude by examining three clinics with deep roots in the self-help movement: Women's Health Specialists (WHS) in Chico, Redding, and Grass Valley, California; the Emma Goldman Clinic (Emma) in Iowa City, Iowa; and the Feminist Women's Health Center (FWHC) in Atlanta, Georgia. All three opened in the 1970s and offered self-help based gynecological care and abortions. Today, these clinics proudly proclaim *both* their roots in self-help *and* their eagerness to serve clients of diverse gender expressions—and attending to their language choices (as reflected on their websites in 2020) suggests how they might be perceived or experienced as rhetorical spaces that are created for certain people.

The WHS website specifically notes that it provides services for "women, men, trans* folks, and youth." Yet, in an informative section on birth control, the website also reads, "Most women are concerned about how a method works and how to use it." A section on the FemCap (a type of barrier birth control that works by blocking sperm from entering the cervix) lists an advantage of the FemCap as "controlled by the woman." Because the FemCap is a non-hormonal form of birth control (and therefore would not conflict with testosterone therapy, for example), this device might be an excellent choice for trans men who have uteruses, ovaries, and so forth and who have sex with partners who have sperm. Here, activists might return to the basic pillars of reproductive justice framework: the right to bodily autonomy, including the right to have a child, not have a child, and to parent one's child in safe and sustainable environments (SisterSong.net). Given the possibility of using the reproductive justice framework, how might WHS strive toward even more inclusive languages? For example, could adapting language to be more inclusive engage a wide audience while also indicating to potential trans and GNC clients that the clinic had considered their needs as people who may or may not want to have children and included them in their provision of healthcare (WomensHealthSpecialists.org)?

Similarly, the Emma clinic proclaims that it "exist[s] to empower women and men in all life stages through the provision of quality reproductive health care." Yet a close examination of the section of their website devoted to emergency contraception (EC) might send a different message to trans and GNC clients: "Women should not take EC if they have any of the following [conditions] . . . " and "EC may make some women feel sick . . . Some women may have sore breasts." Testosterone therapy is not a replacement for contraception, and trans men and GNC folks with a uterus may be at increased likelihood for needing EC (Faculty of Sexual and Reproductive Healthcare). Folks using testosterone must stop their hormone treatment if they get pregnant yet may be unaware of these facts or simply unwilling or unable to use contraception due to gender dysphoria, discrimination from healthcare providers, or financial instability. Again, by returning to the tenets of reproductive justice, which affirm all human beings' right to retain true bodily autonomy and choose the timing of their pregnancies, Emma might choose to make explicit on its website the usefulness and availability of EC for trans men (EmmaGoldman.com).

Of the three, the Atlanta FWHC is the only clinic whose website explicitly states that their work is "influenced by the work of reproductive justice leaders like Loretta Ross and SisterSong Reproductive Justice Collective," perhaps because of the clinic's proximity to the Atlanta-based organization. The organization writes that this work encouraged them to "adopt an intersectional framework approach and move away from a pro-choice centered framework," which has led to the development of a host of programs that tackle systemic inequalities in healthcare and society (key concerns of the psychological self-help groups that are part of FWHC's ancestry). It is worth noting that the Atlanta FWHC commonly uses the words "people" and "patients" instead of "women." I have not found a place on their website where they say "women" with reference to a service that should actually be available to people across the gender spectrum, including on the pages where they describe their abortion services. Importantly, however, this clinic has retained its original name, which includes the word "women" in the title (FeministCenter.Org).

Ross writes that Black women "offered [the reproductive justice framework] to the intellectual commons of inquiry" ("Reproductive Justice as Intersectional Activism" 290), yet uptake of the framework remains uneven at best. Several questions for future consideration arise. What are other potential impacts of more broadly applying a reproductive justice framework to trans and GNC healthcare? Does this application only expand the impact of the movement? Does it in any way diffuse the meaning and usefulness of the framework? How can feminist clinics continue to imagine rhetorical (discursive and spatial) ways of overcoming legacies of essentialism and exclusion, especially in a post-*Roe* America? As Glenn argues, "rhetoric and feminism are slowly transforming each other," an observation that suggests hopefulness in terms of the types of care I have discussed in this chapter (2). The revolutionary nature the feminist clinics born from the self-help movement make them the ideal space—figuratively and materially—to continue transforming reproductive healthcare, and the rhetorical choices they make can help create this change. As such revolutionary spaces, they are ideally situated to take lessons from the Reproductive Justice Movement and adapt them to make their clinics less cisnormative. Scholar-activists and activist-scholars should extend discursive analysis (as I have presented in this chapter) and would be well-suited to engage more explicitly spatial analyses of clinics as they change over time and across locations. It is only through attention to both aspects of the self-help movement (gynecological and psychological) that the self-help movement's offspring (feminist clinics) can fulfill their revolutionary ideals and offer quality care for people with a wide array of gender and sexual expressions. The revolution continues.

Works Cited

Berg, Alex. "Why Reproductive Justice is an LGBTQ+ Rights Issue." *Out Magazine*. 19 Feb. 2019, www.out.com/out-exclusives/2019/2/19/why-reproductive-justice-lgbtq-rights-issue. Accessed 17 Dec. 2020.

Berkeley Women's Health Collective, "Lesbian Clinic" flyer in Lesbian Health Activism The First Wave: Feminist Writings from the Early Lesbian Health Movement, December 1973, Feminist Health Press, box 9, folder 28: "Brochures/factsheets/publications: publication: Lesbian Health Activism: the

First Wave, 2001," Records of the Mautner Project, Schlesinger Library, Harvard University, Cambridge, MA.

Briggs, Laura. *How All Politics Became Reproductive Politics: From Welfare Reform to Foreclosure to Trump.* U of California P, 2017.

Cohen, Cathy. "Punks, Bulldaggers, and Welfare Queens: The Radical Potential of Queer Politics." *GLQ*, vol. 1, no. 4, 1997, pp. 437–65.

Dingo, Rebecca. "Linking Transnational Logics: A Feminist Rhetorical Analysis of Public Policy Networks." *College English*, vol. 70, no. 5, 2008, pp. 490–503.

Downer, Carol. "No Stopping: From Pom-Poms to Saving Women's Bodies." *On the Issues Magazine*, www.ontheissuesmagazine.com/2011fall/2011fall_downer.php. Accessed 3 Dec. 2020.

—. Personal Interview. 26 Mar. 2014.

—. "Queer Theory's Suppression of Feminist Consciousness." *Female Erasure: What You Need To Know About Gender Politics' War On Women, the Female Sex and Human Rights*, edited by Ruth Barrett. Tidal Time, 2016, pp. 335–56.

Dudley-Shotwell, Hannah. *Revolutionizing Women's Healthcare: The Feminist Self-help Movement in America.* Rutgers UP, 2020.

Eberhardt Press. "Free to Choose: A Women's Guide to Reproductive Freedom." 2006, www.eberhardtpress.org/pdf/freetochoose.pdf. Accessed 19 Nov. 2015.

Edbauer, Jenny. "Unframing Models of Public Distribution: From Rhetorical Situation to Rhetorical Ecologies." *Rhetoric Society Quarterly*, vol. 34, no. 4, 2005, pp. 5–24.

Emma Goldman Clinic. Emma Goldman Clinic, www.emmagoldman.com. Accessed 7 Dec. 2020.

Enoch, Jessica. *Domestic Occupations: Spatial Rhetorics and Women's Work.* Southern Illinois UP, 2019.

Faculty of Sexual and Reproductive Healthcare of the Royal College of Obstetricians & Gynaecologists. "CEU Statement: Contraceptive Choices and Sexual Health for Transgender and Non-binary People." 16 Oct. 2017, www.fsrh.org/documents/fsrh-ceu-statement-contraceptive-choices-and-sexual-health-for/. Accessed 8 Dec. 2020.

Feminist Women's Health Center, "A Visit to a Clinic or Physician," August 15, 1978, box 6, folder: Women's Health in Women's Hands (8 of 9), Feminist Women's Health Center Records, Sallie Bingham Center for Women's History and Culture, Duke University, Durham, NC.

Feminist Women's Health Center, "Lesbian Well-woman Clinic," flyer in Lesbian Health Activism The First Wave: Feminist Writings from the Early Lesbian Health Movement, December 1973, Feminist Health Press, box 9, folder 28: "Brochures/factsheets/publications: publication: Lesbian Health

Activism: the First Wave, 2001," Records of the Mautner Project, Schlesinger Library, Harvard University, Cambridge, MA.

Feminist Women's Health Center. www.feministcenter.org. Accessed 7 Dec. 2020.

Fishel, Elizabeth. "Women's Self-Help Movement: Or, Is Happiness Knowing Your Own Cervix?" *Ramparts*, Nov. 1973.

Gay Women's Liberation Collective, "In Amerika They Call Us Dykes," quoted in "Lesbian Health Care: Issues and Literature," in Lesbian Health Activism The First Wave: Feminist Writings from the Early Lesbian Health Movement, December 1973, Feminist Health Press, box 9, folder 28: "Brochures/factsheets/publications: publication: Lesbian Health Activism: the First Wave, 2001" Records of the Mautner Project, Schlesinger Library, Harvard University, Cambridge, MA.

Glenn, Cheryl. *Rhetorical Feminism and This Thing Called Hope*. Southern Illinois UP, 2018.

Hayman, Brenda et al. "De Novo Families: Lesbian Motherhood." *Journal of Homosexuality,* vol. 64, no. 5, 2017, pp. 577–91.

Kerr, Breena. "What Do Womxn Want"? *New York Times*, 14 March 2019.

Klein, Paula. "Health Needs Assessment in a Lesbian Community," September 10, 1980, box 44, folder: "Lesbian Health Issues," Emma Goldman Clinic Records, University of Iowa Special Collections, Iowa City, Iowa.

Luna, Zakiya. "Black Celebrities, Reproductive Justice and Queering Family: An Exploration." *Reproductive Biomedicine and Society Online,* vol. 7, 2018, pp. 91–100.

Mamo, Laura. *Queering Reproduction: Achieving Pregnancy in the Age of Technoscience,* Duke UP, 2007.

Marsh, Margaret and Wanda Ronner. *The Pursuit of Parenthood: Reproductive Technology from Test-Tube Babies to Uterus Transplants*. Johns Hopkins UP, 2019.

Murphy, Michelle. "Immodest Witnessing: The Epistemology of Vaginal Self-Examination in the US Feminist Self-Help Movement." *Feminist Studies,* vol. 30, no.1, 2004, pp. 115–47.

National LGBTQ TaskForce. "Queering Reproductive Justice: A Toolkit." March 2017, www.thetaskforce.org/wp-content/uploads/2017/03/Queering-Reproductive-Justice-A-Toolkit-FINAL.pdf. Accessed 8 Dec. 2020.

O'Donnell, Mary. "Lesbian Health Care: Issues and Literature," in Lesbian Health Activism The First Wave: Feminist Writings from the Early Lesbian Health Movement, December 1973, Feminist Health Press, box 9, folder 28: "Brochures/factsheets/publications: publication: Lesbian Health Activism: the First Wave, 2001" Records of the Mautner Project, Schlesinger Library, Harvard University, Cambridge, MA.

Raymond, Janice. *The Transsexual Empire: The Making of the She-Male*. Beacon Press, 1979.

Romesburg, Don, editor. *The Routledge History of Queer America*. Routledge, 2018.

Ross, Loretta. "Reproductive Justice as Intersectional Feminist Activism." *Souls,* vol. 19, no. 3, July-September 2017, pp. 286–314.

—. "Loretta Ross." By Joyce Follett. Voices of Feminism Oral History Project, Southampton, MA: Smith College, 2004–2005.

Rowling, J.K. "J.K. Rowling Writes about Her Reasons for Speaking out on Sex and Gender Issues." 10 June 2020, www.jkrowling.com/opinions/j-k-rowling-writes-about-her-reasons-for-speaking-out-on-sex-and-gender-issues/. Accessed 21 Apr. 2023.

Shah, Meera. "Why We Should Stop Using the Phrase 'Women's Health.'" *Vice*, 5 March 2019, www.vice.com/en_us/article/kzdxgn/why-we-should-stop-using-the-phrase-womens-health. Accessed 3 Dec. 2020.

SisterSong. "Principles of Unity." *Collective Voices*, 2004, in folder: "Collective Voices Winter 2004," SisterSong WOC Reproductive Justice Collective Records, Sophia Smith Collection, Smith College, Northampton, MA.

SisterSong: Women of Color Reproductive Justice Collective. www.sistersong.net. Accessed 8 Dec. 2020.

Spain, Daphne. *Constructive Feminism: Women's Spaces and Women's Rights in the American City*. Cornell UP, 2016.

SPARK. "There Is No Black Liberation without Queer and Trans Liberation." 4 June 2020, www.sparkrj.org/uncategorized/there-is-no-black-liberation-without-queer-trans-liberation/. Accessed 21 Apr. 2023.

Stacey, Judith. "Queer Reproductive Justice?" *Reproductive Biomedicine & Society Online*, vol. 7, 2018, pp. 4–7, www.sciencedirect.com/science/article/pii/S2405661818300157. Accessed 8 Dec. 2020.

Stryker, Susan. *Transgender History: The Roots of Today's Revolution*. Seal, 2017.

Thomsen, Carly and Grace Tacherra Morrison, "Abortion as Gender Transgression: Reproductive Justice, Queer Theory, and Anti-Crisis Pregnancy Center Activism," *Signs*, vol. 45, no. 3, pp. 703–30.

Ussher, Jane M, Joan Chrisler, and Janette Perz, eds. *Routledge International Handbook of Women's Sexual and Reproductive Health. The Routledge International Handbooks Series*. Abingdon, Oxon: Routledge, 2020.

West Coast Sisters. "Self-Help Clinic." 1971, box 4, folder: "Self-Help Clinic," Feminist Women's Health Center Records, Sallie Bingham Center for Women's History and Culture, Duke University, Durham, NC.

Women's Health Specialists of California. womenshealthspecialists.org. Accessed 7 Dec. 2020.

Wong, Jon. "Repro Justice Isn't Just for Cis, Straight Women. It's for Queer Folks Like Me, Too." *If When How*. 27 June 2018, www.ifwhenhow.org/pride-2018-queer-repro-justice/. Accessed 21 Apr. 2023.

3 Inclusive Models of Reproductive Justice: Creating Space for Masculine-of-Center Pregnant and Birthing People

James D. Warwood

Ryan had a rough pregnancy; his life postpartum was not much better. Physically, his body managed the labor of pregnancy and childbirth admirably—he describes his body as doing "everything it was supposed to do without giving [him] much trouble" (Wehman-Brown, "People" 00:24:26). It was the dissonance of being a transmasculine pregnant person that traumatized Ryan. The culture of reproduction in the United States is centered around women, meaning that pregnancy and birth are inextricably linked with motherhood; from greeting cards to the names of health clinics, these embodied experiences are unwaveringly understood to be feminine. Additionally, conversations and actions following the 2022 *Dobbs v. Jackson Women's Health Organization* decision have been colored by trans-exclusionary language that refuses masculine-of-center people solidarity in post-*Roe* reproductive justice. This means that for masculine-of-center people like Ryan, pregnancy, birth, and life postpartum can be intensely isolating. Ryan recalls how, during the challenging first weeks of new parenthood, "people didn't know what to do with [him]." He explains that for cisheteronormative women there seems to be "sort of a cultural expectation that you get to have community," one that he could not access with his trans-masculine body (00:32:17–00:32:39).

Ryan is not alone in his experience. Masculine-of-center people, from queer women to transgender men, have always carried and given birth to children, but their stories often go unheard. Some of these stories, however, are impossible to ignore; the last two decades have seen the introduction of "the pregnant man" into the public consciousness, most notably through Thomas Beatie, who announced his first pregnancy in early 2008. Beatie's pregnant body—with his beard and a flat, masculine chest—became a visual spectacle that circulated in the media throughout 2008, culminating in the publication of his memoir in November of that year (Beatie). The national interest in Beatie's pregnancy arose from the visual dissonance of his very masculine pregnant body; when he appeared on *20/20* in November 2008, Barbara Walters emphatically told Beatie that the images of his pregnant body were "disturbing" ("Journey" 00:03:48). Walters' reaction echoed that of people across the country—after all, pregnancy is a female experience and Beatie's pregnant body did not look like it belonged to a woman. His story ran counter to the dominant narrative of reproduction, making his pregnant body illegible to onlookers.

Most masculine-of-center people do not publicize their pregnancies to this extent, of course; the pregnancies of feminine cisheteronormative women, on the other hand, are frequently made visible, whether through recurrent posts on social media or high-profile photo spreads from women like Demi Moore and Beyoncé. Why are stories from people like Ryan so rarely heard? Shui-yin Sharon Yam explains that "the birth stories of marginalized people . . . are 'untellable'" because they challenge audiences to rethink the traditional narrative of reproduction in which a woman becomes a mother, usually with the support of a community of family, friends, and healthcare providers. She argues that this neglect of non-normative people not only "invalidates the reproductive experiences of those who do not fit into the dominant imaginary of birthing people," but also "obscures the reproductive injustice . . . commonly experienced by non-normative birthing people" (22). In other words, because pregnant and birthing masculine-of-center people are not recognizable as women who become mothers, their stories are not typically heard as reproduction narratives. Telling the untellable stories of masculine-of-center pregnant and birthing people is an act of reproductive justice, opening a "safe and dignified context for these most fundamental human experiences" (Ross and Solinger 9).

The task of filling the void of masculine-of-center birth stories has been taken up by individuals who publicly chronicle their family-building journeys as a roadmap for others to follow. For example, these narratives have found a home in the sixteen episodes of *Masculine Birth Ritual*, a podcast about masculine-of-center experiences of pregnancy and birth. The podcast, created by Grover Wehman-Brown, serves as a "conduit" for these untellable stories, creating space for them to be heard and recognized ("Introduction" 00:00:18). Each episode is a conversation between Wehman-Brown and masculine-of-center parents, birth workers who care for them, community leaders, and scholars of US reproduction culture. The stories elicited on *Masculine Birth Ritual* reveal a dominant discourse of reproduction that does not hold space for masculine-of-center people, resulting in experiences of pregnancy, birth, and parenthood that are isolating at best and psychically traumatic at worst.

Ryan was a guest on the fourth episode of *Masculine Birth Ritual*; he spoke about the isolation he experienced during pregnancy and after the birth of his daughter, often struggling to find the words to share stories he had not told before. Near the beginning of the episode, Ryan stops, unsure of how much detail to provide; Wehman-Brown tells him, "I think [candor] is helpful just in terms of normalizing this experience"—an experience, Wehman-Brown adds, in which prospective masculine-of-center parents typically have to "dig into the internet" to learn about ("People" 00:04:27–00:04:44). In the introductory episode, Wehman-Brown explains that the podcast is a space to "ask questions in this public sphere that tend to circulate only in the private or semi-private spheres of closed social media networks and one-on-one conversations" ("Introduction" 00:02:58–00:03:06). These stories remain insulated and precarious because they are culturally untellable—when told in the context of a feminine model of reproduction, masculine-of-center birth stories unsettle. This dissonance is the reason Yam and Wehman-Brown both want such stories told: not only do they reveal the reality of non-normative pregnant and birthing people, but the discomfort they cause prompts us to question the model that figures some bodies as non-reproductive.

This chapter engages with the untellable stories of masculine-of-center pregnant people to address what I call *queer dissonance*. This dissonance is emblematic of the inability to reconcile a perceived body with the norms and ideals of a dominant discourse. For masculine-of-center parents, queer dissonance functionally bars them from accessing the community and resources—e.g., prenatal yoga, birth education classes, chestfeeding support—that are open to cisheteronormative pregnant women due to their masculine bodies.[1] However, alternative access

1. In addition to these more social resources, various legal and policy structures (e.g., mother/father birth certificates and second- or stepparent adoption [necessary to gain parental rights of a child one is not biologically related to]) underscore the precarity of trans parenthood and gender-nonconforming parenthood.

points are being made in shared public spaces like podcasts and social media, as I demonstrate here. My analysis centers around two assemblages of rhetorical strategies for addressing the queer dissonance masculine pregnant bodies cause: first, an assemblage of pregnancy and birth counterstories; and second, an assemblage of further countertactics—which seek to challenge dominant practices and ideologies—for making masculine-of-center pregnant and birthing bodies visible. I argue that these assemblages communicate needed changes in the discourse of reproduction in the US and offer models and practices for a more inclusive reproductive justice to support all non-normative pregnant and birthing people.

Origins of Queer Dissonance

The stock story of reproduction in the US—spanning conception, pregnancy, birth, and parenting—is predicated on the existence of a body that is not only recognizably female but also recognizable as a woman. In other words, reproduction is so powerfully gendered that only a female body is capable of pregnancy, and any body read as pregnant is seen as belonging to a woman; bodies that trouble this paradigm are sources of queer dissonance. In this context, womanhood is contingent on femininity—that is, the characteristics and behaviors stereotypical of Western, white women. In her study of masculine-of-center gestational parents, anthropologist Michelle Walks characterizes feminine pregnancy as a Western cultural fetish, "something that is valued not necessarily for its original use . . . but something with added sexual, spiritual, aesthetic, or commodity . . . value" (12). Feminine pregnant bodies signal a culturally appropriate womanhood. The cultural fetish of feminine pregnancy figures "women who are pregnant [as] *pregnant bodies*," publicly held objects that are constantly "under the surveillance of both strangers and people they know" (12). This surveillance of bodies constitutes a division of the feminine from the masculine and the pregnant from the non-reproductive.

The surveillance of pregnant bodies hinges not only on visual cues of Western, white femininity, but also on the performance of a recognizable feminine pregnancy. As KJ Surkan explains, "there is an enormous amount of effort in shoring up the cultural signification of the pregnant body as female and feminine"; this effort is evident in the regulatory "discourse produced by and about pregnant women" ("That" 59).

This expectation means that in order to remain recognizably feminine, women have to perform their pregnancy in a way that complies with the stock story of feminine reproduction. In their examination of the performance of feminine pregnancy on *Instagram*, Katrin Tiidenberg and Nancy K. Baym recognize that pregnancy is "simultaneously one of the most embodied . . . and one of the most discursively regulated" human experiences (2). For the authors, pregnant women "do" pregnancy, a project that requires them to "a.) learn to be pregnant by seeking information and taking advice; b.) master routines of self-care to guarantee the health of the fetus; and c.) constantly perform pregnancy to ensure that others acknowledge it" (2). This acknowledgement is key: adhering to the regulatory discourses that promote the cultural fetish of feminine pregnancy allows pregnant women to "inhabit a socially viable subjectivity" and access support and resources throughout pregnancy and after birth (10).

Marika Seigel, in her analysis of pregnancy manuals, considers the disciplinary effects of texts such as *What to Expect When You're Expecting,* resources intended to teach women the correct way to "do" pregnancy. She figures these manuals as a form of technical communication that "encourages [pregnant women] to discipline their own bodies and practices" for the good of the fetus (9). Pregnancy manuals—both the texts Seigel examines as well as less formal sources of information that circulate person-to-person and in online spaces—comprise a regulatory discourse that shores up the femininity of the ideal pregnant body. Tiidenberg and Baym point to three strands of this discourse that advance "specific, narrow, overlapping visions" of what this ideal pregnant body looks and acts like:

> The "learn it" discourse operates with an internalized sense of responsibility, intense self-education, and reliance on a lifestyle-specific set of expert knowledge (e.g., medical or new age). The "buy it" discourse is comprised of demonstrations of consumerist expertise; consumerist rituals, which construct new consumers in-utero; and legitimizes the above through the rhetoric of love. The "work it" discourse relies on women showcasing the ability to retain a sexualized female body even while pregnant, and, like the "buy it" discourse, increases its moral power by infusing what could, otherwise, be considered vanity, with maternal love. (11)

To maintain a socially viable subjectivity while pregnant, women are expected to read pregnancy manuals and trust their medical providers (whether obstetricians or midwives); buy new maternity clothes, multivitamins, and the "right" items for their new baby; and be fashionably dressed, made up, and regain their "pre-baby" body quickly. Importantly, the work required to attain this viability is not expected only of white women nor is it reflected only in white culture—though it certainly originates in white ideals of feminine beauty.[2]

In these ways, pregnancy intensifies the gender binary. Pregnancy is the pinnacle of womanhood at the same time that it requires the pregnant body to over-perform femininity. A body that was not recognizably feminine before pregnancy is not recoded as female by virtue of being pregnant (Surkan, "FTM" 3). Surkan argues that under the stock story of reproduction, masculinity and pregnancy are so incompatible that onlookers are either unable or unwilling to recognize masculine bodies as pregnant (58). Many of Wehman-Brown's guests recall how whether they were recognized as pregnant or not depended on how others read their gender: Jacoby remembers how he rarely received unsolicited pregnancy advice from strangers because his pregnant body was often read as belonging to a "chubbier guy" ("Welcoming" 00:16:06–00:16:34). These masculine-of-center pregnant bodies, then, are bodies that struggle to be recognized as such under a discourse that promotes a cultural fetish of feminine pregnancy. In moments when they are recognized as pregnant, such bodies become sites of queer dissonance that disturb onlookers.

The strategies Tiidenberg and Baym name presume a recognizably female body: bodies that are *not* unable to "do" pregnancy in a way that promises a socially viable subjectivity. Consequently, masculine-of-center pregnant and birthing people have difficulty accessing or are barred from the resources, services, and community that are available to feminine, cisheteronormative pregnant women. While telling his story in the fourth episode of *Masculine Birth Ritual*, Ryan notes that he does not

2. In some ways, prominent women of color undertake the work to perform a feminine pregnancy even more visibly than their white peers in order to maintain a socially viable subjectivity. For example, *Vanity Fair* ran a feature on Serena Williams in 2017, detailing the love story that led to her pregnancy (Bissinger). Williams—who is no stranger to being masculinized by the media—posed nude for the cover, visually accentuating her Black femininity alongside her Black maternity. Although the article's striking cisheteronormative imagery did not silence critics, the piece went some way to demonstrate that Williams was "doing" pregnancy correctly.

have a clear picture of what pregnancy and birth are like for cisheteronormative women, but "envision[s] a type of community that [he] had no idea how to access" (Wehman-Brown, "People" 00:34:06–00:34:15). When he searched for resources and services—local and online support structures—he "never found anything that reflected who [he is] in this story" (00:40:58). Some of these support structures include competent and compassionate healthcare; birth classes; pre- and postnatal "mom groups"; and the easy camaraderie parents share with other parents in public spaces like playgrounds. Everywhere he looked, Ryan met exclusive language, imagery, and women who did not know what to do with a pregnant person who would not become a mother. Because masculine-of-center people are not recognized as capable of pregnancy and birth, space is not readily held for their bodies within these support structures. Though the guests on Wehman-Brown's podcast recount varying levels of isolation throughout their pregnancies, all describe ways they have been excluded from these elements of reproductive culture by virtue of their masculine bodies.

Frameworks for Analysis

A central goal of *Masculine Birth Ritual* is to give voice to the experiences that are untellable under the discourse of reproduction in the US. These stories shift the focus of family-building narratives to include masculine-of-center people, highlighting the exclusionary systems that figure pregnancy and birth as necessarily feminine. My analysis of the stories told on this podcast proceeds from an understanding of storytelling that arises from three theoretical frameworks: reproductive justice, critical race theory, and queer assemblage. Each of these frameworks calls for the inclusion of marginalized lived experiences as a means of challenging dominant discourse, a core principle that shapes the assemblages I explore in the rest of this chapter. I argue that these frameworks highlight the necessity of storytelling for inclusive models of reproductive justice.

My use of reproductive justice comes from Loretta Ross and Rickie Solinger. In *Reproductive Justice: An Introduction*, Ross and Solinger identify telling stories as "an act of subversion and resistance"; they go on to say: "Storytelling is a core aspect of reproductive justice practice because attending to someone else's story invites us to shift the lens—that is, to imagine the life of another person and to reexamine our own realities and reimagine our own possibilities" (59). The stories told on

Masculine Birth Ritual are a reclamation of marginal experiences and a "[reaffirmation of] social bonds" between others whose pregnancy and birth stories are silenced and made invisible under the dominant US discourse of reproduction (Yam 22). *Masculine Birth Ritual* shifts the lens away from the familiar story of feminine women becoming mothers to highlight feelings of dissonance and isolation that, for non-normative bodies, exist in tandem with the pursuit of the human right to bear, birth, and parent children (Ross and Solinger 10).

Ross and Solinger note that some stories are kept quiet as a "survival strategy" when the teller cannot "trust others with [their] truths" (59–60). Ryan, for example, withholds parts of his story and acknowledges doing so: "I feel like . . . I'm talking around stuff . . . I know exactly what I could be saying to you that I still have . . . I'm not in a place to say" (Wehman-Brown, "People" 00:49:15–00:49:35). He shields himself both from the scrutiny of Wehman-Brown and their listeners as well as the psychic labor of publicly processing his experiences. Ryan's discomfort sharing his experience of pregnancy and birth as a trans-masculine person emerges in part because of the dearth of similar stories. This emphasizes the value of *Masculine Birth Ritual*: as a publicly available resource, the podcast allows masculine-of-center pregnant people to "work together for strength and safety," building a coalition that recognizes that their "collective power is based on and derived from [their] power to tell [their] own stories" (Ross and Solinger 60).

The second framework informing my understanding of storytelling is critical race theory. Daniel G. Solórzano and Tara J. Yosso define critical race theory as an effort to:

> develop a theoretical, conceptual, methodological, and pedagogical strategy that accounts for the role of race and racism [in US institutions] and works toward the elimination of racism as part of a larger goal of eliminating other forms of subordination, such as gender, class, and sexual orientation. ("LatCrit" 472)

Critical race theory confronts the whiteness—especially the cisheteronormative male whiteness—of institutions that not only discount but also silence the stories of marginalized rhetors. For Solórzano and Yosso as well as for Aja Y. Martinez—a rhetorical scholar also engaging with critical race theory—marginalized rhetors include university students of color; for Yam, they are "gender non-normative people" who are pregnant or giving birth (22). In each instance, stories do the work of addressing mechanisms of subordination. Emerging from this foundation is the practice of counterstorytelling. Counterstories are those untellable stories that come from the margins, running counter to the stock or "majoritarian" stories that "generate from a legacy of [white, cisheteronormative, male, and class] privilege" (Solórzano and Yosso, "Methodology" 28). Martinez explains that a stock story "distorts and silences the experiences of people of color and others distanced from the norms such stories reproduce." In their telling, counterstories "validate, resonate, and awaken" marginalized people to the potential for collective power, strength, and safety (51).

It is important at this point to recognize that the majority of the parents who tell their stories on *Masculine Birth Ritual* self-select as white, meaning that conversations about race and the disparity of reproductive healthcare between people of color and white people do not happen (see Petersen et al.). However, counterstorytelling as conceptualized by critical race theorists remains a useful framework for examining masculine-of-center pregnancy and birth stories; using this framework also proactively opens space for the neglected stories of parents of color. Solórzano and Yosso name several key principles of critical race theory, three of which contribute to my use of counterstorytelling in this chapter: the challenge to dominant ideologies; the commitment to social justice; and the centrality of experiential knowledge ("Methodology" 26). The counterstories of pregnancy and birth told on *Masculine Birth Ritual* contest the stock story of feminine reproduction, demonstrating through lived experiences new possibilities for family-building narrative arcs. As a storytelling space, the podcast invests itself in the pursuit of reproductive justice for gender non-normative pregnant and birthing people.

Finally, I take a cue from Maria Novotny, who filters the counterstory through Jasbir Puar's framework of queer assemblage. As a methodology for addressing the war on terror, queer assemblage favors "spatial, temporal, and corporeal convergences, implosions, and rearrangements" (121). Puar further argues that "queerness as assemblage enables attention to ontology in tandem with epistemology, affect in conjunction with representational economies, within which bodies . . . interpenetrate, swirl together, and transmit affects to each other" (122). In other words, queer assemblage attends to the mess inherent in subjective embodied experiences, challenging linear, coherent, and recognizable paradigms of identity. Queering storytelling in this way allows Novotny to disrupt the stock/counterstory binary of in/fertility; "[capture] non-normative identities, positionalities, and moments of being and becoming"; and "[render] narrative even more slippery than usual . . . embracing multiple, and at times contradictory, moments of becoming" (116–117). For Novotny, a queer assemblage of stories complicates the traditional infertility counterstory—in which a woman learns she is infertile and pursues medical assistance at any cost to become pregnant—illustrating the myriad ways individuals relate to and experience the fertility clinic. The counterstories Novotny assembles feature a trans teen preserving his eggs, a gay couple working with a surrogate, and a cisheteronormative woman deciding against IVF and adoption. Through this particular assemblage, Novotny "advance[s] the ways in which [rhetoricians and healthcare providers] care for those whose stories we are simply not trained to hear" (125).

The stories told on *Masculine Birth Ritual* too represent a queer assemblage. Not all of the guests on the podcast experienced pregnancy, birth, and postpartum as solely traumatic experiences. Some of these stories depict masculine-of-center parents who navigated the exclusionary discourse of reproduction in a way that honored their gender identities; for example, Jacoby and his partner composed a "Germination Proclamation," which laid out language for how they wanted their families to talk about his pregnancy and birth (Wehman-Brown, "Welcoming" 00:17:44–00:18:00). This document honors Jacoby's lived experience as a genderqueer pregnant person at the same time that its composition signals a "limited representation of what an ideal birthing parent should look like" (Wehman-Brown, "Introduction" 00:02:23–00:02:50). The assembled stories that I examine illustrate the myriad ways masculine-of-center pregnant people relate to and experience reproduction in the US. These counterstories are not neatly juxtaposed with the ideal arc of cisheteronormative pregnancy and birth, allowing, as Novotny argues, "for the gaps, the reorientations, the spaces between systems of power that influence identity making and knowledge making" (117).

In short, the stories I retell below come from the margins of US reproduction culture and in their telling confront stock stories of feminine pregnancy and birth. These representations offer ways to reconsider reproductive justice beyond the centrality of anatomy; indeed, Ross and Solinger argue that "[r]eproductive oppressions stem from a determination to exercise power over vulnerable persons" regardless of gender identity or genital configuration (6). Additionally, hearing these stories according to the above frameworks reveals gaps in rhetorical scholarship around reproduction, which has largely focused on cishetero norms of pregnancy and birth. Yam suggests that a reproductive justice model (and, I propose, models informed by critical race theory and queer assemblage as well) "urges rhetoricians to be more mindful and intentional in their language use and to expand their scope of study to encompass the pregnancy and birthing experience of queer, trans, and gender nonconforming individuals to account for the intersections between reproductive and gender politics" (22). These moves not only care for the lived experiences of gender non-normative pregnant and birthing people but also broaden conceptualizations of reproductive justice. Ross and Solinger claim that a central goal of reproductive justice is to "build a united struggle for universal human rights in a way that includes everyone" (70). I contend that the following assemblages offer a guide for expanding that inclusivity.

In addition to these frames, rhetorical listening is a valuable tool for engaging with these assemblages. Krista Ratcliffe defines rhetorical listening as "a trope for interpretive invention," one that can be "employed to hear discursive intersections of any cultural categories . . . and any cultural positions . . . so as to help us to facilitate cross-cultural dialogues about any topic" (196). This practice requires that one listen *with* intent rather than *for* it (220). In other words, the storytellers featured on *Masculine Birth Ritual* should be considered not the agents of cross-cultural dialogue, but the impetus. Rhetorical listening asks an audience to listen beyond the familiar, to "*choose* to listen also for the exiled excess and contemplate its relation to our culture and our selves" (203; emphasis added); in doing so, it becomes possible to "*hear* things we cannot *see*"—things such as the reproductive injustices experienced by masculine-of-center pregnant and birthing people (203). For Ratcliffe, such deep engagement with a text inspires "an ethical responsibility" to advocate for those persecuted by certain cultural paradigms while also questioning the ways those same paradigms enable feelings of safety for others. This responsibility opens up the "potential for personal and social justice" (203). Thus, rhetorically listening to the experiences shared on *Masculine Birth Ritual* makes the gaps in reproductive justice apparent.

Counterstories of Pregnancy and Birth as Assemblage

Similar to Novotny's queer assemblage of in/fertility stories, the counterstories shared on *Masculine Birth Ritual* capture experiences that challenge linear, coherent, and recognizable paradigms of identity. Although all of the guests on the podcast identify as masculine-of-center, not all relate negative or traumatic pregnancy and birth experiences. The queer assemblage of stories offered below demonstrates as much. As Novotny suggests, these assembled counterstories provide "a layered and more complex narrative" of masculine-of-center pregnancy and birth than they would on their own, "inventing new spaces for and pointing to the slippages of narratives that make space for agency in an always-changing identity construction" like masculine pregnancy (117). In other words, the counterstories of pregnancy and birth retold below represent a rhetorical strategy developed by masculine-of-center people to extend reproductive justice to include their own experiences.

As I have already shown, Ryan did not have a fraught relationship with his body during pregnancy; in fact, he explains that he "kind of thought it was cool" to see the changes in his body and feel the baby move. Nor did it affect "how gender works for [him] in the world" (Wehman-Brown, "People" 00:12:00–00:12:29). He continued on as he had been, teaching, finishing coursework for his PhD, and just "try[ing] to stay pregnant" (00:09:10–00:10:50). As he recounts his experience, however, it becomes clear that his trans-masculine body did in fact trouble the way he related to pregnancy and birth. He tells Wehman-Brown that his friends do not see nor treat him as a woman, and they did not have "a script for how to treat someone who was pregnant who wasn't a woman." As a result, Ryan "mostly spent the time by [himself]" (00:15:49–00:15:59). Because his pregnant body did not belong to a woman, Ryan went through pregnancy without support of friends—he does not seem to be aware, though, that this isolation was tied to the canonized stock story of feminine reproduction.

In the stories of his postpartum life, Ryan clearly recognizes the effects of this stock story. He identifies birth as the moment that "messed [his experience of gender] all up" (Wehman-Brown, "People" 00:12:28). While he acknowledges that friends did visit to hold the baby and bring Ryan and his wife food, it seemed like "the entire fact that [he] gave birth got erased about a week after [he] did it" (00:35:39). In other words, as soon as the visible fact of his pregnancy was gone, Ryan's body reverted to its non-reproductive masculinity. Being unrecognizable as a gestational parent meant that Ryan had no way to talk about his experience—perhaps explaining his halting, reserved storytelling on *Masculine Birth Ritual.* About halfway through the episode, Ryan recalls one memory that most clearly illustrates the way the exclusive discourse of reproduction affected his life postpartum. Sometime during the early days of his daughter's life, Ryan's in-laws came to see the new baby. As they stood to go, they kissed Ryan's wife and said—in front of Ryan—"thanks so much for making us grandparents" (00:31:37–00:31:56). This seemingly unthinking erasure of the role of his body in that becoming represents a culmination of the injustices Ryan experienced under a discourse of reproduction predicated on a recognizably feminine body. He explains that he "simultaneously [doesn't] want to be made invisible as a birth parent but [he likes] the idea of someone thinking of [him] as someone who has given birth"; the counterstorytelling space of *Masculine Birth Ritual* allows Ryan to imagine such an experience (00:43:25–00:43:43).

While Ryan's story underscores the harm caused by the gap in reproductive justice, other episodes highlight the complexity of non-normative family-building narratives. The eighth episode of *Masculine Birth Ritual* features J Carroll, a trans-nonbinary single parent by choice. As J tells Wehman-Brown, they had always had a desire to be a parent, regardless of their gender identity (Wehman-Brown, "He" 00:01:15–00:02:00). They see pregnancy as just something their body is able to do—"I'm not feminine," they say, "so it can't be only a feminine thing" (00:32:16–00:32:30). This perspective made their pregnancy and birth less traumatic than it was for Ryan. However, that does not mean that J experienced their family-building journey with the structural support that a feminine cisheteronormative woman might.

As J sought out resources and services to prepare them for birth and parenthood, nothing felt "at home" (Wehman-Brown, "He" 00:14:48)—everything seemed to highlight the fact that reproduction culture in the US excludes gender identities and experiences like J's. From the books they read—such as *What to Expect When You're Expecting*—to apps used to track the growth of their baby, nothing available resonated with J's life. J remembers going to pre-natal yoga classes, which, while generally not contributing to the feminization of pregnancy, occasionally excluded J through language use—calling participants "ladies" or "mommas" for example. Such an atmosphere made J feel slightly awkward, but they found the classes useful and so resolved to "just do the yoga and try not to listen to anything" (00:08:01–00:08:38). J had to make do, revealing a tactic of selective engagement that many pregnant and birthing masculine-of-center people have to use. Not everything is going to be perfect, J tells Wehman-Brown—"you have to take the good things and leave the rest" (00:08:45–00:08:51).

The final piece of this queer assemblage relates yet another experience that does not conform to a single reproduction counterstory arc. As a high school biology teacher, Vanya—who describes herself as a genderqueer butch—is fascinated by the reproductive process and, like J, has always wanted to be pregnant (Wehman-Brown, "Grow" 00:01:02–00:04:00). She recognizes, though, that pregnancy is characterized in our culture as the "ultimate thing you can do as a woman"—this means that, for Vanya, getting pregnant as someone who is not a woman was "a mind trip" (00:07:15–00:07:32). Although she has never tried to pass as such, Vanya is often read as a cisgender male owing to her preference for masculine clothing and the beard she grew during puberty. As her body became more visibly pregnant, onlookers struggled to place her, and she was subjected to the sir-ma'am-sir address typical among cisheteronormative people confronted with a body that defies gender norms. In general, though, Vanya did not dwell on how pregnancy related to her gender—she was just Vanya, "growing a human" (00:08:45–00:09:00). Vanya maintained her preference for masculine clothing, though as her body grew she struggled to find things to wear that were not feminine. She recalls standing in a fitting room and "crying because . . . things fit but they just didn't look right, they looked too feminine. Everything had little frills and it was just terrible for someone who doesn't identify in a feminine way." Instead, Vanya made do with leggings, unbuttoned jeans, and too-big t-shirts (00:11:00–00:11:58). Although the experience of moving in the world with a masculine pregnant body did not leave her feeling traumatized by moments of queer dissonance, the fact that Vanya could not just be a pregnant *person* highlights the exclusive mechanisms of reproduction culture in the US.

As a queer assemblage, the counterstories told on *Masculine Birth Ritual* highlight the impossibility of a single masculine-of-center reproduction narrative. Exclusion from the stock story on its own does not guarantee a negative family-building experience. Indeed, as this assemblage of stories shows—and as Wehman-Brown tells Ryan—"being pregnant and being trans doesn't mean that . . . pregnancy is going to be terrible" ("People" 00:49:01). Trans-masculine pregnancy and birth are figured as unnatural and disruptive according to the exclusionary discourse of feminine reproduction; Ryan's isolation, J's need to make do, and Vanya's struggle to maintain her gender presentation all point to the harm inflicted by such exclusion. However, there are rhetorical countertactics for confronting such harm, "skills" that are familiar to queer and trans people (00:49:05). Producing a podcast to communally hold the experiential knowledge of masculine-of-center pregnant and birthing people is one such countertactic. Sharing and listening to these stories is an act of reproductive justice: this queer assemblage shifts the paradigm of reproduction to create space for masculine-of-center pregnancy and birth experiences.

Inclusive Countertactics as Assemblage

This second assemblage of countertactics developed by masculine-of-center parents represents a skill integral to queer and trans people's survival: the ability to collectively build spaces of power, strength, and safety within the confines of an exclusionary discourse. Masculine-of-center pregnant and birthing people have enacted rhetorical practices of inclusion that take advantage of shared online spaces, language and framing, and material practices and epistemologies to hold space for their non-normative experiential knowledge. Because the podcast makes this knowledge publicly accessible, these countertactics not only provide masculine-of-center people with the tools to navigate pregnancy and birth within a discursive context that privileges femininity, but also offer rhetoricians, activists, and healthcare providers suggestions for implementing more inclusive reproductive justice practices.

At the end of each episode of *Masculine Birth Ritual*, Wehman-Brown invites guests to imagine that they are thirty years in the future, seated beside a masculine-of-center pregnant person: what changes or support would they like to see for this person? Some guests share dreams of better-trained medical professionals or more research on masculine reproduction; tellingly, most guests wish for a world in which knowledge and stories of masculine-of-center pregnancy and birth are collectively held. The power of storytelling, after all, is in the collaborative building of knowledges "with full awareness that while ours may not be the dominant narrative, we may nonetheless highlight the importance of our respective backgrounds, experiences, and material realities" (Cedillo and Bratta 235).

Masculine-of-center people are doing this work on their own, making do with the space available to them. For example, several guests mention a popular *Facebook* group dedicated to trans*, nonbinary, and masculine-of-center parents; this is a space to ask questions, share advice, and recommend resources to others. J explains that they used the group to gather "anecdotal evidence" to answer questions that their midwife could not (Wehman-Brown, "He" 00:14:56–00:15:45). This group assembles experiential knowledge to offer models for navigating pregnancy and birth as masculine-of-center people. Without guides and manuals that reflect their lived experiences or healthcare providers competent in gender neutral reproductive care, masculine-of-center people have to "dig into the internet" to find what they can.

Masculine-of-center parents are also creating linguistic space to help friends and family engage with the reality of their pregnancy and birth. Jacoby's "Germination Proclamation," for example, establishes language preferences with family and friends, disrupting the dominant reproduction discourse; sharing the "Germination Proclamation" on the podcast and online allows other masculine-of-center pregnant people to take up that subversion. Ross and Solinger and Yam all advocate for a shift toward inclusive language and more expansive conceptualizations of reproduction, in scholarship as much as healthcare. Limiting conversations around reproduction to women, motherhood, and the female body overlooks the lived experiences of gender non-normative pregnant and birthing people. This omission reifies the cisheteronormativity that is "prevalent in existing pregnancy and birth discourse" (Yam 22). Reproductive justice and critical race theory frameworks urge us to honor the voices from the margins and listen for the gaps between the stories and dominant ideologies—these gaps signal places for rhetorical inquiry that "encompass[es] intersecting identities, positionalities, and experiences that spill over binary categories" (32).

In addition to confronting the limitations of language, some masculine-of-center people have made the decision to enter birth work to effect change through healthcare. Mac is a queer trans man who became a doula in part to meet the needs of LGBTQ people. His goal is to provide competent and compassionate care through education and empowerment; gender neutral childbirth classes; providing competency workshops to healthcare professionals; and, most importantly, listening to and holding space for his clients (Wehman-Brown, "Possibility" 00:00:49–10:00:00). In addition to providing resources and care that feel comfortable to masculine-of-center pregnant people, Mac's work as a doula and educator begins to revise the stock story of feminine reproduction; not only does this revision expand networks of compassionate and competent care, but it also creates material spaces in which masculine-of-center parents feel safe to birth their babies. These knowledges and practices become collectively held through their telling on the podcast, an offering to a community that is typically excluded from the narrative of reproduction.

The above countertactics are examples of a kind of self-directed advocacy, creating tools for survival outside of institutional spaces. Like generations of queer and trans people before them, masculine-of-center parents have learned to make their own spaces of power, strength, and safety through collective action. I suggest that this work can help rhetoricians, activists, and healthcare providers reconceptualize pregnancy and birth in more just ways. The assemblages explored in this chapter point to serious gaps in care and support for masculine-of-center pregnancy and birth; listening to and learning from these rhetorical strategies provides a useful model for working toward more inclusive reproductive justice practices.

I present these parallel assemblages to demonstrate the harms of an exclusionary discourse of reproduction. The centrality of the feminine restricts access to community and resources for people who do not fit the ideal image of a pregnant person. Such exclusion has led masculine-of-center pregnant and birthing people to find new ways to access support networks, drawing from an assemblage of countertactics to do so. The queer assemblage of the counterstories of Ryan, J, and Vanya highlight the need for these tactics, as each experienced pregnancy and birth as periods of dissonance and isolation. Counterstories and other countertactics do the work that critical race theory calls for, centering experiential knowledge to challenge the dominant ideology of feminine reproduction. These rhetorical strategies represent an act of reproductive justice, working toward the goal of a united, inclusive struggle against reproductive oppressions while also imaginatively constructing more just futures. Rhetoricians, activists, and healthcare providers have much to learn from these queer models of reproductive justice, expanding study and care to include masculine-of-center voices.

The assembled experiences of Ryan and the other guests on *Masculine Birth Ritual* highlight the ways healthcare and medicine fall short of caring for masculine-of-center pregnant and birthing people. Wehman-Brown explains to Mac that a significant impetus for the podcast was an actively transphobic nurse they encountered while in the ICU after their birth. Mac comments that in creating the podcast, Wehman-Brown is saving "a heck of a lot of other people" from having the same experience ("Possibility" 00:55:01–00:56:38). Though *Masculine Birth Ritual* does not necessarily exist for healthcare providers, it still has something valuable to offer. Novotny orients her own model of storytelling toward the fields of health and medicine, arguing that queering counterstory through assemblage "make[s] space to question biomedical practices and discourses that construct bodies of health within paradigms of 'normalcy.'" For Novotny, this means disrupting infertility narratives, "which perpetuate cultural ideals of normalcy in the contexts of both ableism and sexuality" (121). Similarly, masculine-of-center pregnant and birthing people have the right to expect pre- and postnatal care that is not predicated on their genital anatomy. Counterstories and other countertactics like those highlighted on *Masculine Birth Ritual* complicate "understandings of the spaces of becoming" (122). There is no one way to be a masculine-of-center pregnant person, meaning there is no one experience that runs counter to the stock story of reproduction in the US—as evidenced by the stories I have retold here.

As Ratcliffe suggests, rhetorical listening demands a responsibility to the other in meaning-making. This logic of responsibility, she says, "asks us, first, to judge not simply the person's intent but the historically situated discourses that are (un)consciously swirling around and through the person and, second, to evaluate politically and ethically how these discourses function and how we want to act upon them" (210). Rhetorically listening to the counterstories told on *Masculine Birth Ritual* reveals the reproduction discourses that shape a bleak experience of pregnancy and birth for many masculine-of-center people; the evidence of these "(un) consciously swirling" discourses signals a troubling gap in practices of reproductive justice.

The responsibility to bridge that gap, however, does not lie with the storytellers. Rhetoricians; activists; healthcare providers; and friends, family, and caregivers of masculine-of-center pregnant and birthing people have an ethical responsibility to take these queer assemblages and listen for the gaps, the silences that signal injustice. In doing so, they can work together with masculine-of-center parents to imagine inclusive models of reproductive justice that hold space for gender non-normative pregnant and birthing people.

Works Cited

Beatie, Thomas. *Labor of Love: The Story of One Man's Extraordinary Pregnancy.* Seal P, 2008.

Bissinger, Buzz. "Serena Williams's Love Match." *Vanity Fair*, Aug. 2017, www.vanityfair.com/style/2017/06/serena-williams-cover-story. Accessed 27 Jan. 2021.

Cedillo, Christina V., and Phil Bratta. "Relating Our Experiences: The Practice of Positionality Stories in Student-Centered Pedagogy." *College Composition and Communication*, vol. 71, no. 2, 2019, pp. 215–40.

Martinez, Aja Y. "A Plea for Critical Race Theory Counterstory: Stock Story versus Counterstory Dialogues Concerning Alejandra's 'Fit' in the Academy." *Composition Studies*, vol. 42, no. 2, 2014, pp. 33–55.

Novotny, Maria. "In/Fertility: Assembling a Queer Counterstory Methodology for Bodies of Health and Sexuality." *Re/orienting Writing Studies: Queer Methods, Queer Projects*, edited by William P. Banks, Matthew B. Cox, and Caroline Dadas, Utah State UP, pp. 112–26.

Petersen Emily E., Nicole L., David Goodman, et al. "Racial/Ethnic Disparities in Pregnancy-Related Deaths — United States, 2007–2016." *Morbidity and Mortality Weekly Report*, vol. 68, no. 35, Sept. 2019, pp. 762–65.

Puar, Jasbir K. "Queer Times, Queer Assemblages." *Social Text*, vol. 23, no. 3–4, 2005, pp. 121–39.

Ratcliffe, Krista. "Rhetorical Listening: A Trope for Interpretive Invention and a 'Code of Cross-Cultural Conduct.'" *College Composition and Communication*, vol. 51, no. 2, 1999, pp. 195–224.

Ross, Loretta J., and Rickie Solinger. *Reproductive Justice: An Introduction.* U of California P, 2017.

Seigel, Marika. *The Rhetoric of Pregnancy*. U of Chicago P, 2014.

Solórzano, Daniel G. and Tara J. Yosso. "Critical Race and LatCrit Theory and Method: Counterstorytelling." *International Journal of Qualitative Studies in Education*, vol. 14, no. 4, 2001, pp. 471–95.

—. "Critical Race Methodology: Counterstorytelling as an Analytical Framework for Education Research." *Qualitative Inquiry,* vol. 8, no. 1, 2002, pp. 23–44.

Surkan, KJ. "FTM in the Fertility Clinic: Troubling the Gendered Boundaries of Reproduction." 2015, *Academia.edu,* www.academia.edu/11416240/FTM_in_the_Fertility_Clinic_Troubling_the_Gendered_Boundaries_of_Reproduction. Accessed 14 May 2019.

—. "That Fat Man is Giving Birth: Gender Identity, Reproduction, and the Pregnant Body." *Natal Signs: Cultural Representations of Pregnancy, Birth, and Parenting*, edited by Nadya Burton, Demeter Press, 2015, pp. 58–72.

Tiidenberg, Katrin and Nancy K. Baym. "Learn It, Buy It, Work It: Intensive Pregnancy on *Instagram*." *Social Media + Society*, vol. 3, no. 1, 2017, pp. 1–13.

Walks, Michelle. "Feminine Pregnancy as Cultural Fetish." *Anthropology News*, 2013, www.academia.edu/2385525/Feminine_Pregnancy_as_Cultural_Fetish. Accessed 27 Jan. 2021.

Walters, Barbara. "Journey of a Pregnant Man." *20/20 Exclusive*. ABC, 18 Nov. 2008.

Wehman-Brown, Grover, host. "Grow Your Own Parasite! Get Pregnant!" *Masculine Birth Ritual*, episode 2, Spotify, 15 Sept. 2018, www.open.spotify.com/episode/02boTlELBDh2dCiMU5WtSH.

—. "He Was with These Wonderful Queers: An Interview with J Carroll on Nonbinary Single Parenting." *Masculine Birth Ritual*, episode 8, Spotify, 14 Jan. 2019, www.open.spotify.com/episode/7swztMTTnGC2wTMH1Y0pEZ.

—. "Introduction to Masculine Birth Ritual." *Masculine Birth Ritual*, episode 1, Spotify, 1 Sept. 2018, www.open.spotify.com/episode/69H1p3t3OK1yKxZSWfo8ad?si=YT7naq_rS6uh5ka1LvEYQw.

—. "People Didn't Know What to Do With Me." *Masculine Birth Ritual*, episode 4, Spotify, 15 Oct. 2018, www.open.spotify.com/episode/51Q3LXhWMmsDgguB6wbXAl?si=ZDNjeN4URLasrlf5NSa_Pg.

—. "Possibility Models of Parenthood." *Masculine Birth Ritual*, episode 3, Spotify, 1 Oct. 2018, www.open.spotify.com/episode/1KF379Wu05vWlSAlbIzdBn.

—. "Welcoming Whatever Being Came: An Interview with Jacoby Ballard." *Masculine Birth Ritual*, episode 16, Spotify, 19 Aug. 2019, www.open.spotify.com/episode/75LuqoyGdRc6gJqn8dSjTa.

Yam, Shui-yin Sharon. "Visualizing Birth Stories from the Margin: Toward a Reproductive Justice Model of Rhetorical Analysis." *Rhetoric Society Quarterly*, vol. 50, no. 1, 2020, pp. 19–34.

4 #NoTeenShame: A Case Study in Rhetorical Activism, Hope, and Limitations

Meta Henty

In 2013, seven young mothers founded #NoTeenShame, "a movement illuminating the need for shame-free LGBTQ-inclusive comprehensive sexuality education & equitable access to resources and support for young families" (No Teen Shame, *Tumblr*). As many scholars have noted, the dominant discourse surrounding teen pregnancy is steeped in gendered and racialized stigma (Arai; Books; Daniel; Luker; Vinson). #NoTeenShame was founded as a response to the stigmatizing #NoTeenPreg campaign from the Candie's Foundation, a nonprofit teen pregnancy prevention organization launched in 2001 by Candie's CEO Neil Cole. Through rhetorically savvy use of technology, the #NoTeenShame founders—Natasha Vianna, Gloria Malone, Marylouise Kuti, Lisette Engel, Consuela Greene, Christina Martinez, and Jasmin Colon—push back against this stigma. In doing so, #NoTeenShame highlights and promotes two reproductive justice principles that can easily be overshadowed by mainstream feminism's focus on "the right *not to have children*." Namely, these two other principles are "the right *to have children* under the conditions we choose and the right *to parent the children we have* in safe and healthy environments" (Ross et al. 14). In the aftermath of the *Dobbs v. Jackson Women's Health Organization* decision, it may be even more tempting to focus on access to abortion over other reproductive rights, but that would be a mistake and counter to the Reproductive Justice Movement and its theoretical framework. Instead, it is more important than ever that we embrace a complete and nuanced interpretation of reproductive justice. #NoTeenShame is an important site of analysis for reproductive justice scholars and activists not only because of its focus on these overlooked principles, but also because it is a rare multiethnic coalition employing an intersectional, reproductive justice-informed rhetoric to effect change. For reproductive justice advocates organizing post-Dobbs, the story of #NoTeenShame's rhetorical activism serves as both a promising framework for effecting change and also a cautionary tale about how such activism can be erased within dominant narratives.

This chapter serves as a coda to Jenna Vinson's analysis of #NoTeenShame in *Embodying the Problem: The Persuasive Power of the Teen Mother*, where she argues that the #NoTeenShame founders use their position of embodied exigence to "seize opportunities to interrupt the discourses that pathologize them" (104). While Vinson analyzes the exchanges between #NoTeenShame and the Candie's Foundation from April 2013 to May 2014, I focus on #NoTeenShame's subsequent rhetorical activism via social and traditional media, the lasting effects of that activism on the national discourse, and the continued attempts to silence young parents' voices.[1] Vinson ends her examination of the exchange between Candie's and #NoTeenShame by writing that the Candie's Foundation continues to position women as the cause of the inequalities and injustices they face (134). However, since the publication of Vinson's analysis, the conversation surrounding teen pregnancy has shifted significantly. In the years following the exchange with Candie's, which has since ceased operations, #NoTeenShame continued to speak out against teen pregnancy prevention campaigns, including the National Campaign to Prevent Teen and Unplanned Pregnancy (hereafter National Campaign). #NoTeenShame also continued to combat the designation of May as Teen Pregnancy Prevention Month. Essentially, #NoTeenShame continued its work to change the hegemonic rhetoric surrounding teen pregnancy—a non-inclusive, stigmatizing rhetoric that both pathologizes and silences young parents. According to the #NoTeenShame website, "the former dominant narrative of young parenthood is no longer welcome—and we've replaced old messaging with an inclusive, positive, and justice-based language" (No Teen Shame, "About"). The website touts the rebranding of May as "Sex Ed for All" month in 2019 as a major achievement and sign of the movement's success (No Teen Shame, "About").

While #NoTeenShame is not solely responsible for these changes, I argue that the movement has been integral in shifting the hegemonic rhetoric of stigma surrounding teen pregnancy. In this chapter, I analyze

1. This chapter extends Sowards and Renegar's understanding of contemporary rhetorical activism in its focus on the multiple rhetorical strategies of #NoTeenShame and demonstrates Jones's call to use our academic teaching, service, and scholarship to promote rhetorical activism.

#NoTeenShame's rhetorical activism between 2014 and 2019 to illustrate how the movement interrupted and effected change in this hegemonic rhetoric of stigma, specifically in relation to the National Campaign and Teen Pregnancy Prevention Month. Reproductive justice provides the primary theoretical framework for my analysis. At its core, reproductive justice "posits that intersecting forces produce differing reproductive experiences . . . [and] our intersectional identities require different considerations to achieve reproductive justice" (Ross et al. 8). Born in part as a response to white feminists' limited focus on abortion, a recognition of and commitment to intersectionality undergirds reproductive justice. This chapter responds to Shui-yin Sharon Yam's call for a model of rhetorical analysis informed by the intersectional framework of reproductive justice that might "allow researchers to identify and amplify rhetorical practices of survivance and coalition-building from the margin" (21).

Considering its origin as an alternative to mainstream white feminists' focus on abortion, perhaps it is unsurprising that most reproductive justice coalitions have formed along racial lines (Silliman et al.). One thing that makes #NoTeenShame a particularly interesting case study in coalition is that the founders' identities are varied: Black, mixed race, Latina, and white and spanning an age range of twenties to fifties. Thus, #NoTeenShame is a relatively rare multiracial and multigenerational coalition in reproductive justice activism. The diversity of the founders lends itself to another tenet of the reproductive justice framework: an embrace of "polyvocality—many voices telling their stories that together may be woven into a unified movement for human rights" (Ross and Solinger 59).

Along with reproductive justice theory, Cheryl Glenn's "rhetorical feminism" provides a helpful lens through which to view and analyze #NoTeenShame's rhetorical activism, successes, and limitations. Glenn defines rhetorical feminism as "a set of tactics that multiplies rhetorical opportunities in terms of who counts as a rhetor, who can inhabit an audience, and what those audiences can do" (335). Glenn acknowledges that the voices of "Others" are often "disrespected, dismissed, if not ignored altogether by those more powerful." "Yet," she maintains, "without these voices . . . there is no hope" (334). #NoTeenShame's rhetorical feminism offers hope to teen parents and reproductive justice activists. However, although the founders of #NoTeenShame employ what I identify as rhetorical feminism to effect change, they are not always recognized for doing so. Thus, this chapter also offers a case study of how difficult it can be for marginalized rhetors of reproductive justice issues to be heard and seen and become part of the larger story of reproductive change.

Like Vinson and the founders of #NoTeenShame, I, too, am a teen mother. Like Vinson, I wrote a dissertation about the rhetorical power of teen mothers. I am also white. This sets Vinson and me apart from most of the founders of #NoTeenShame and the women of color responsible for the Reproductive Justice Movement. Keeping in mind that contributions by women of color to feminist theory and activism have been "consistently underreported by the media and many historians," this chapter serves as a reminder of the debt owed to women of color in the fight for reproductive justice and as a study in how multiracial coalitions can succeed.

The Rhetorical Landscape

Before analyzing #NoTeenShame's rhetorical activism, I turn to the cultural landscape surrounding teen pregnancy prior to the movement's arrival on the national stage, including the National Campaign's role. There is a long history of aligning teen pregnancy, race, and welfare in the United States. Since the 1980s, teen pregnancy has been blamed for a host of racialized social problems, such as dropout rates, poor maternal and infant health outcomes, and juvenile delinquency; in the 1990s, "teen mother" and "welfare mother," already coded as non-white, became virtually synonymous (Geronimus; Kaplan). In 1996, the passage of the Personal Responsibility and Work Opportunity Reconciliation Act (PRWORA) resulted in "the neoliberal agenda of withdrawing state support from the poor while enforcing the norms of the white, middle-class, heterosexual, consumeristic, nuclear family" (Daniel 4). Formed in the wake of this reform, the National Campaign's original mission included the heteronormative goal of "ensur[ing] that children are born into stable, two-parent families" (National Campaign). Like Candie's, as a neoliberal[2] response to welfare reform, the National Campaign focuses

2. Harvey describes neoliberalism as "a theory of political economic practices that proposes that human well-being can best be advanced by liberating individual entrepreneurial freedoms and skills within an institutional framework characterized by strong private property rights, free markets, and free trade" (2). Neoliberalism, then, values self-sufficiency, autonomy, and capitalistic trade via deregulation and privatization. Within recent scholarly work, neoliberalism is

on personal responsibility and obscures structural forces like race and class. Although teen pregnancy discourse has long been racialized, there is a clear shift in the discourse, particularly in terms of race, in the early 2000s. In late 2007 and early 2008, a series of events and media coverage culminated in a pivotal moment for teen pregnancy in American popular culture—a moment that is important to fully understand #NoTeenShame's exigence and ability to effect change in the National Campaign.

In December 2007, the Centers for Disease Control declared a rise in rates of teen pregnancy (National Center for Health Statistics). Within weeks, the film *Juno* opened in theaters, and Nickelodeon star Jamie Lynn Spears announced her own pregnancy at fifteen. Less than a year later, in 2008, the Gloucester pregnancy pact (eighteen pregnancies in Maryland that were the result of an alleged pact between high schoolers) and Bristol Palin's pregnancy prompted headlines like "The Juno Effect Strikes Again" (Friedman). One very important detail united these teen moms and set them apart from how teen moms had been visually depicted in the 1980s and 1990s: they were white. Media coverage at this time suggested teenage pregnancy was becoming normalized, specifically for white, middle-class girls, creating a moral panic and prompting a revamped prevention strategy from the National Campaign. During the summer of 2008, ABC Family released *The Secret Life of the American Teenager* in partnership with the National Campaign, and the next spring, the National Campaign premiered *16 and Pregnant* in partnership with MTV. Sequels *Teen Mom* and *Teen Mom 2* quickly followed. In the franchise, "shame and gossip are normalized" and even "used as an opportunity to reinforce the 'consequences' of teen pregnancy" (Guglielmo and Wallace Stewart 28–29). Again, with few exceptions, the girls featured are white, and the franchise's neoliberal focus on personal responsibility obscures structural forces like racism and poverty.

Despite the franchise's shame-based rhetoric, *Teen Mom* was soon accused of the same "glamorization of teen pregnancy" it was designed to combat, as evidenced by headlines like "MTV's *Teen Mom* Glamorizes Getting Pregnant" (Henson) and "Does *16 and Pregnant* Prevent or Promote Teen Pregnancy?" (Dockterman). By 2014, two academic studies had attempted to determine the effects of the franchise on teen pregnancy—and had come to quite different conclusions (Aubrey et al.; Kearney and Levine). Of course, tabloid coverage fueled the debate as headlines

---

increasingly understood as constructing individuals as rational, self-regulating actors capable of choice and possessing autonomy.

highlighted scandals in the lives of the young stars. 2013 brought arrests, sex tapes, and rumors of additional pregnancies for the stars (Eby; Majeski). This was the cultural landscape surrounding teen pregnancy in the US when #NoTeenShame entered the conversation in 2013: the National Campaign's *Teen Mom* (and its white cast) was everywhere, but the press was increasingly negative.

This watershed moment caused the stigmatizing rhetoric surrounding teen pregnancy to receive renewed attention in the realm of pop culture. A number of feminist and queer scholars have taken up the issue of shame with some arguing that shame can act as a rhetorical exigence for revisionary work (Burke and Brown; Probyn; Stenberg). Such revisionary work can serve as "an invitational [. . .], critical, and generative rhetorical act" that works "to restore the subject and resist the social structure" (Stenberg 124). #NoTeenShame is doing this revisionary work, combatting this dominant narrative by weaving their individual stories into a coalition for change and by showing that teen moms of all colors can be successful. In addition to serving as exigence, the focus on teen pregnancy in pop culture during this time contributed to the rhetorical landscape for #NoTeenShame's messaging.

#NoTeenShame's Rhetorical Feminism

In 2013, two teen pregnancy prevention campaigns garnered national attention for their use of stigma and shame, including the Candie's Foundation's #NoTeenPreg campaign headed by Neil Cole, which featured the tagline "You are supposed to be changing the world, not changing diapers," effectively arguing that one cannot do both and reinforcing stigmatizing rhetoric that teen pregnancy is life-ending (Candie's Foundation). In response to #NoTeenShame's Change.org petition, "Candie's Foundation: Stop Shaming Young Parents," Cole wrote a *HuffPost* blog denying that Candie's shamed teen moms and suggesting that "we can all agree, children should not be having children." This early exchange demonstrates a recurring theme in #NoTeenShame's story: the activists employ alternative rhetorical tactics, such as social media use, to intervene in the dominant discourse, and those in power turn to traditional mainstream media to erase and silence the activists' voices. Understanding this rhetorical power struggle is central to understanding #NoTeenShame's rhetorical activism.

By claiming the authority to speak, the founders of #NoTeenShame establish themselves and other teen parents as rhetors employing what I identify to be an instance of Glenn's rhetorical feminism to interrupt dominant discourse and effect change. Glenn outlines seven features of rhetorical feminism, writing,

> Anchored in (1) hope, rhetorical feminism offers ways to (2) disidentify with hegemonic rhetoric; (3) be responsible to marginalized people even if we ourselves are marginalized; (4) establish dialogue and collaboration; (5) emphasize understanding; (6) accept vernaculars, emotions, and personal experiences; and (7) use and respect alternative rhetorical practices (336).

#NoTeenShame utilizes the alternative rhetorical practice of engaging online spaces in order to create dialogue and invite collaboration in their quest to disidentify with the hegemonic rhetoric surrounding teen pregnancy. The founders work to replace that hegemonic rhetoric with rhetoric that, instead, emphasizes understanding, honors personal experiences and emotions, and works to be inclusive of marginalized groups. By interrupting that hegemonic rhetoric, they illustrate how such rhetoric has impeded young parents' rights to have children and to parent those children in safe environments, and they argue for a more inclusive rhetoric that affirms these rights. By sharing their lived experiences, the young mothers of #NoTeenShame embrace "polyvocality" and the storytelling central to reproductive justice. #NoTeenShame offers one example of how "many voices" might be "woven into a unified movement" using technology and rhetorical strategies informed by reproductive justice (Ross and Solinger 59).

Although the movement began as a direct response to Candie's, by 2014, the #NoTeenShame activists had shifted their focus to a proactive approach of partnering with organizations interested in working with them. While the original audience for #NoTeenShame's petition was Candie's Foundation CEO Neil Cole, the subsequent movement's social media sites had a larger audience and expanded rhetorical approaches. The #NoTeenShame activists employed a variety of platforms for specific rhetorical purposes, working to effect change through three main rhetorical avenues: social media, traditional print media, and more behind-the-scenes communications, activism, and policy building.

#NoTeenShame employed three social media sites—*Tumblr*, *Twitter*, and *Instagram*—and eventually a traditional website to engage audiences and spread their message online. The use of social media and hashtags is the first and most obvious use of what Glenn terms "alternative rhetorical practices" by #NoTeenShame. Much of the movement's rhetoric is reproduced and shared across media, so while the purpose and audience may change, content on the social media sites does not vary much. Generally, the movement's *Tumblr* targets teen parents and creates a safe online space for sharing, while *Twitter* is used to engage a larger audience and interrupt the dominant discourse.[3] The founders not only employed a variety of social media sites, but also consistently worked to have their voices heard by traditional print media, too. Although guilty of reproducing the stigmatizing teen pregnancy narrative, mainstream media also helped amplify the voices of #NoTeenShame. This proved to be a critical step in #NoTeenShame's ability to move from social media to effecting structural change. While #NoTeenShame was working to change the rhetorical landscape via social and traditional media, the founders were also working behind the scenes and on the ground to build coalitions and change actual policies affecting pregnant and parenting teens.

#NoTeenShame's various rhetorical strategies—social media, mainstream media interviews, and coalition-building and policy initiatives—all work in tandem, fulfilling different rhetorical aims, targeting different audiences, and reproducing the #NoTeenShame message. This network of strategies is easy to overlook. My narrative of this rhetorical activism draws together its various forms to illustrate the complex interplay of messages, rhetors, and power dynamics and to demonstrate its potential and limitations.

Following their initial attempt at dialogue with the Candie's Foundation, the #NoTeenShame founders again attempted to establish "dialogue and collaboration," a feature of Glenn's rhetorical feminism, this time by reaching out to the National Campaign. #NoTeenShame first reached out to Sarah Brown, director of the National Campaign, in 2013 after she and #NoTeenShame co-founder Natasha Vianna were both interviewed by NPR about shame-based teen pregnancy campaigns (Vianna, Personal Interview). This marked the first direct interaction between #NoTeenShame and the National Campaign. According to Vianna, #NoTeenShame offered anti-stigma training and community discussions, but the National Campaign was unwilling to engage (Personal Interview). This direct engagement (or attempts at engagement) with

3. The *Instagram* account has been utilized minimally, and I do not analyze it for that reason.

these powerholders is something that sets #NoTeenShame apart from many online movements and is a key component to their strategic activism. From the beginning, #NoTeenShame was aware of the importance of dialogue and coalition.

Although the National Campaign was not interested in collaborating with #NoTeenShame, others were, and tweets from 2013 illustrate the movement's early rhetorical use of hashtags and *Twitter* to invite other voices, generate dialogue, and build coalition. Aware of the intersectional nature of teen pregnancy, stigma, and their own lived experiences, the founders could see coalitional possibilities and tap into them. As a platform, *Twitter*'s drawback was also its strength: anyone could employ a hashtag on *Twitter*. The founders had no control over how #NoTeenShame was used on the platform[4], but this was the same feature that enabled the movement to successfully target #NoTeenPreg in 2013—by employing both hashtags, #NoTeenShame directly combatted Candie's messaging and targeted its audience. *Twitter* proved an effective tool for entering the conversation and reaching new audiences. During its first year of movement activity, #NoTeenShame was lauded in tweets by the Eastern Massachusetts Abortion Fund, Colorado Organization for Latina Opportunity and Reproductive Rights, California Latinas for Reproductive Justice, Planned Parenthood Advocacy Fund of Massachusetts, Forward Together, and others (California Latinas for Reproductive Justice; COLOR; EMA Fund; Forward Together; Planned Parenthood Advocacy Fund of MA). While these organizations, all sites of reproductive justice advocacy, amplified #NoTeenShame's message against stigma, they also gave credit to #NoTeenShame for leading the charge. By utilizing *Twitter* and the hashtag, #NoTeenShame was able to disseminate their message widely and begin to build a coalition of allies.

Since the initial petition to Candie's, #NoTeenShame has actively worked to directly intervene in the rhetoric of teen pregnancy prevention, and they received another opportunity to do so in January of 2014 when the *New York Times* reported that MTV's *Teen Mom* had reduced teen pregnancy rates (Lowrey). Just as the founders seized the moment in 2013, they again pushed back against the narrative perpetuated by dominant media outlets. Within a week, co-founders Vianna and Malone were interviewed about the study for the women's entertainment and

4. At this point, there was no official *Twitter* account for No Teen Shame. Instead, the co-founders used their own accounts and the hashtag to spread awareness and engage with others.

lifestyle website *The Frisky*, and they used the opportunity to explain how the rhetorics of shame undermine young parents' right to parent their children in a safe and healthy environment (Nathman). In the interview, Vianna argues that stigma in the media encourages viewers to despise and pity young parents, resulting in real and dangerous effects on young parents' lives (qtd. in Nathman). While the *Frisky* interview illustrates the role of more traditional media outlets in the movement's success, it is also important to note that the original article from the more established *New York Times* does not include the voices of teen mothers, bolstering Malone's assertion that "[f]or too long organizations, shows, and older people in society have talked about, over, and for us" (qtd. in Nathman). Although the #NoTeenShame petition received national media attention just months prior, the *New York Times* did not approach the founders for comment. With mainstream media not providing the needed platform, #NoTeenShame again worked to expand their "alternative rhetorical practices" of rhetorical feminism through social media.

In April of 2014, #NoTeenShame launched its *Tumblr* site, which showcases the movement's rhetorical feminism through its commitment to "be responsible to marginalized people" and "accept vernaculars, emotions, and personal experiences" (Glenn 336). The #NoTeenShame *Tumblr's* audience was, first and foremost, young parents; serving as an invitation for their voices, the site was meant to be a safe space, created, moderated, and written by and for young parents. With no official *Twitter* account during these first few years, the movement's *Tumblr* was the most official and comprehensive space for engagement and advocacy.

#NoTeenShame's tagline has changed over time, but the original iteration can still be found at the top of the movement's *Tumblr*: "a movement illuminating the need for shame-free LGBTQ-inclusive comprehensive sexuality education & equitable access to resources and support for young families" (No Teen Shame, *Tumblr*). This statement of purpose, with its inclusion of the LGBTQ community, clearly demonstrates how #NoTeenShame's commitments align with reproductive justice's principles and Glenn's rhetorical feminism through their privileging of storytelling, authentic voices, and marginalized people, as well as their awareness of intersectional experiences. The launch of the *Tumblr* site also marks the creation of the movement's first shareable graphic, which serves to combat the stigmatizing rhetoric of teen pregnancy prevention campaigns. It is through these brightly colored graphics that the movement's argument for reproductive justice, particularly the right to parent in safe and healthy environments, is communicated most succinctly. The first graphic, "5 Ways to Be an Ally to Young Parents," illustrates #NoTeenShame's commitment to dialogue and personal experience through statements like, "invite young parents to the table and give them meaningful and genuine roles" (No Teen Shame, "5 Ways to Be an Ally"). By positioning themselves as authority figures, the #NoTeenShame founders establish an inclusive *ethos* and enact rhetorical feminism—arguing for not only their own voices, but for marginalized voices and experiences more generally.

Another important example of #NoTeenShame's rhetorical feminism and acceptance of "vernaculars, emotions, and personal experiences" is the individually authored posts by teen parents featured on the *Tumblr* site and shared via *Twitter*. Through personal stories of shaming by teachers, friends, and strangers, contributors argue for their right to parent "in safe and healthy environments" by illustrating how shame undermines this right. For example, contributor Amy Lopez captures the pervasive and harmful sentiment that a teen pregnancy is life-ending in "Drowning from the Inside Out: The Stigma Surrounding Early Pregnancy." Lopez shares that when she became pregnant at nineteen, people no longer saw her as the valedictorian with a bright future. Instead, she writes, "it was almost as if they were giving out eulogies rather than congratulations or morale boosters. 'She's so young,' they'd say. 'She had such a bright future. She worked so hard in high school. It's a shame'" (Lopez). Lopez's and other contributors' posts illustrate the rhetorical feminism and reproductive justice tenets of respecting personal experience, emotion, and polyvocality. Furthermore, the co-founders and contributors often include images of themselves and their children, literally and affirmatively giving a face to the faceless "problem" of teen pregnancy and thus combatting the negative stereotypes of teen moms. This powerful, visual act is all the more important because #NoTeenShame is not only countering the dominant narrative discursively, but also showing imagistically that parents of color are the rhetors responsible for this reframing. This rhetoric serves to unite the audience of young parents and reject the hegemonic discourse of stigma that oppresses them.

During Teen Pregnancy Prevention Month in 2014, the Candie's Foundation and *Teen Mom* stars flooded social media with #NoTeenPreg, but through the alternative rhetorical strategy of hashtags, #NoTeenShame directly combatted the hegemonic rhetoric while inviting dialogue and collaboration. In addition to directly pushing back against the #NoTeenPreg posts, the founders held a Q&A session on *Twitter*, inviting dialogue, encouraging understanding, and positioning their experiences as valuable (No Teen Shame, "#NoTeenShame *Twitter* Chat"). Allies like the Illinois Caucus for Adolescent Health and Echoing Ida (an alliance of Black women and non-binary writers) also took to *Twitter* to call out #NoTeenPreg and promote #NoTeenShame (Echoing Ida; Illinois Caucus for Adolescent Health). A tweet from Almost Home, an organization that provides housing and support services for homeless teenage mothers, speaks to the *Twitter* war between the hashtags: "#NoTeenShame #NoTeenPreg don't need to be competing camps. Let's support teen parents while providing comprehensive #SexEducation in schools" (Almost Home). Almost Home's tweet illustrates #NoTeenShame's success in entering the conversation. By sparking this dialogue, #NoTeenShame demonstrably spreads its message.

Several articles in more traditional media outlets also featured #NoTeenShame's war against stigma and #NoTeenPreg in May of 2014. An interview with Malone in *Hello Beautiful* included the "5 Ways to Be an Ally" graphic and highlighted the group's goal of ending Teen Pregnancy Prevention Month. Malone showcased #NoTeenShame's focus on systemic problems, arguing that "teenage pregnancy is also caused by no comprehensive sexual education. It's caused by poverty, it's caused by a lack of access to affordable birth control options . . . Even people who work within the social justice system tend to default to teenage pregnancy as bad" (qtd. in Earl). While scholars have long argued that this neoliberal framing reverses the reality that poverty puts one at a greater risk of becoming pregnant as a teen rather than that teen pregnancy causes poverty (Arai; Books; Daniel; Luker), here Malone, aware of the intersectional forces acting upon young women who become pregnant, and with the help of traditional media, brings this argument into the larger public discourse.

In 2015, #NoTeenShame continued to engage with audiences via social media, creating additional shareable graphics to fight against stigma, but the movement also garnered more mainstream media attention, leading to another attempt at dialogue with the National Campaign. Just ahead of Teen Pregnancy Prevention Month, Malone wrote "What Pregnant and Parenting Teens Really Need" for the *HuffPost* blog where she shared her own pregnancy story, writing her shame and again emphasizing the importance of personal experience. In May, Alex Ronan interviewed Vianna and Malone for a *New York Magazine* Q&A piece outlining the women's experiences as teen moms and activists, as well as the goals of the #NoTeenShame movement. In the interview, Vianna highlights the problem with the focus on teen pregnancy prevention, arguing

> the reality is that preventing a pregnancy does not increase opportunities for young people. It does not improve their equitable access to quality education. It does not make their communities safer . . . we're so focused on making sure teens don't get pregnant before their twentieth birthday that we miss out on conversations about consent, healthy relationships, and agency. (qtd. in Ronan)

This claim from Vianna is significant because it succinctly rebuts the argument for teen pregnancy prevention by illustrating how that focus falls short and fails to educate teens on important reproductive health issues. While teen pregnancy prevention undermines reproductive justice rights, Vianna advocates for reproductive justice through equitable education, opportunities, and discussions about consent and agency. Vianna not only explains why a focus on prevention is problematic, but also provides a potential solution to her national audience, an important rhetorical step in effecting change.

According to Vianna, in 2015, amid growing media coverage of #NoTeenShame, the group was contacted by Bill Albert, the National Campaign's Chief Innovation Officer. Undoubtedly, it was the mainstream media coverage, which was a result of the movement's less traditional and more alternative media efforts, that prompted the communication. However, it is also notable that 2015 is the same year the National Campaign's Sarah Brown announced she was stepping down from her longtime role as chief executive, so the organization was undergoing a change in leadership (Reimer). Vianna says she spoke to Albert over the phone about the stigmatizing Teen Pregnancy Prevention Month and the organization's harmful messaging. Unfortunately, Vianna reported that Albert "seemed open and willing to continue discussions but didn't seem to get the internal support to move forward," and communication ceased (Personal Interview). However, buoyed by the kind of hope that defines rhetorical feminism, the founders pressed on.

While the National Campaign was unwilling to work with #NoTeenShame, others were, and the founders focused on building partnerships and shaping policy. Many founders had existing relationships with organizations fighting for reproductive justice, and these prior relationships enabled future #NoTeenShame collaborations.[5] However, the group also worked to forge new alliances, again illustrating their commitment to dialogue and collaboration. On their website, #NoTeenShame lists numerous "supporters," including Advocates for Youth, National Women's Law Center, American Civil Liberties Union, United Nations of the United States, Healthy Teen Network, California Latinas for Reproductive Justice, National Latina Institute for Reproductive Health, Forward Together, Young Women United, and SIECUS (No Teen Shame, "About").

One example of such partnerships effecting concrete change came in 2015 when #NoTeenShame worked with Boston Public Schools to expand their expectant and parenting student policy, developing and providing anti-stigma training for liaisons of all the district's schools. Reproductive justice activists hoping to employ technology for coalition-building and activism should look to #NoTeenShame's ability to build a bridge from their online work to opportunities in the physical world, which relied on cultivating alliances. #NoTeenShame's website also notes that the movement was involved in shaping legislation for the Day of Recognition for Young Parents, New Mexico Legislature (SM 25) and California Young Parents Day, California Legislature (ACR 201) (No Teen Shame, "About"). When I spoke to Vianna, she was careful to note that although #NoTeenShame supported the bills, "the efforts were led by local partners and amazing local young parents," who "deserve the credit" (Personal Interview), an insistence that further highlights the movement's commitment to supporting marginalized communities and collaboration.

That same year, #NoTeenShame also presented at several conferences and workshops, providing concrete advice for organizations looking to support young parents. #NoTeenShame presented at the Civil Liberties and Public Policy Conference and Annual Conference on Youth + Tech + Health, which were backed by organizations focused on reproductive rights and justice and advancing the health of young adults through technology, respectively (Civil Liberties and Public Policy; Youth, Tech, Health). These collaborations illustrate #NoTeenShame's work building coalitions not only with reproductive justice organizations, but also other activist organizations, thus expanding their reach and potential impact.

5. See Vinson's work for a detailed analysis of these relationships.

A Bittersweet Victory

Finally, in 2017, the National Campaign announced that it would be rebranded as Power to Decide (Ehrlich, "We Are Power to Decide"). Bill Albert, who had reached out to #NoTeenShame two years prior, was listed at the time as Chief Program Officer (National Campaign, "Leadership"), and in 2023, is credited as the Senior Director, Digital Content (Power to Decide, "Leadership"). Although Albert was undoubtedly involved in the changes due to his role, the National Campaign moved forward with the redesign without reaching out to or consulting with #NoTeenShame. It is hard to deny the influence of #NoTeenShame's campaign to end stigma on the revamped Power to Decide (previously National Campaign), yet despite private communications between the two, the organization has never acknowledged the hashtag or the co-founders, illustrating that the voices of "Others" are often "disrespected, dismissed, if not ignored altogether by those more powerful" (Glenn 334) and rendering any apparent victory bittersweet.

The first and most obvious change to the National Campaign is its new name. As #NoTeenShame co-founder Malone stated in 2015, "Honestly, I would like to see the phrase *teen mom* disappear off the face of the earth. Why are we the only demographic of moms that are singled out by our age? Why are we teen moms? Why can't we just be moms?" (qtd. in Ronan). The National Campaign finally got the message, becoming Power to Decide: The National Campaign to Prevent Unplanned Pregnancy. Beyond cutting "teen" from the organization's name, the addition of "Power to Decide" illustrates attention to agency. While the focus was previously preventing teens from becoming pregnant, the new focus is providing teens with knowledge and tools so that they can decide for themselves when to become pregnant, which is more consistent with #NoTeenShame's stance and reproductive justice as a framework. At the same time, the concept of "choice" undergirding the name "Power to Decide" echoes white feminist-dominant discourse that served as the impetus for the Reproductive Justice Movement.

The shift in focus is apparent throughout the revamped website. A direct comparison of the National Campaign's previous and current "Why It Matters" pages emphasizes the significance of the shift in discourse. Prior to the 2018 redesign, the "Why It Matters" page reproduced the misleading "research" indicative of a hegemonic rhetoric of stigma and blame, arguing that preventing teen pregnancy will "significantly improve other serious social problems including poverty (especially child poverty), child abuse and neglect, father-absence, low birth weight, school failure, and poor preparation for the workforce" (National Campaign, "Why It Matters"). The page also featured graphics targeting and pathologizing young mothers, including "Just 38 percent of teen girls who have a child before eighteen get a high school diploma" and "Taxpayers spend about twelve billion dollars annually on . . . women who experience unintended pregnancies" (National Campaign, "Why It Matters").

However, after the organization's name change and website revamp, the "Why It Matters" page looks quite different. The page contains paragraphs of text about the importance of young people having "the power to decide if, when, and under what circumstances to get pregnant" (Power to Decide, "Why It Matters"). Several key phrases illustrate the organization's newfound recognition of differences in class and access, as well as respect for young people—suggesting a recognition of the intersectional forces that result in unwanted pregnancy and aligning with the #NoTeenShame movement's goals. First, Power to Decide notably recognizes that "too many young people—especially those who are economically disadvantaged or marginalized—lack [the] power" to make choices about their reproductive health (Power to Decide, "Why It Matters"). This is a huge step forward for the organization. The page goes on to address contraceptive deserts, a well-known problem in reproductive justice activism, but one that was completely ignored by the National Campaign's "Thanks, Birth Control" campaign a few years earlier. This new attention to socio-economic barriers is a clear move away from the organization's previous neoliberal framework towards a more intersectional and inclusive approach. The main method for empowering young people, the website now suggests, is information; the power to decide is "the power of information" (Power to Decide, "Why It Matters"). While I recognize that there is no one-to-one correlation, Power to Decide, with its emphasis on information and education, seems to be answering #NoTeenShame's call for "shame-free LGBTQ-inclusive comprehensive sexuality education" (No Teen Shame, *Tumblr*).

Additionally, Power to Decide now argues for "[t]he power of respect for young people—in every community and reflected in the news, the entertainment media, and the policies that shape our country" (Power to Decide). This sentence, in particular, bears the mark of #NoTeenShame's argument that all parents, no matter their age, should be able to parent with "respect" and "dignity" (No Teen Shame, *Tumblr*). In fact, the new

Power to Decide website even recognizes that some unintended pregnancies do not end in disaster, acknowledging that young women "have stepped up to become great parents no matter the circumstance. Resilient and determined, they create nurturing homes for their families, even if early parenthood is not exactly what they envisioned" (Power to Decide). While the paragraph goes on to note that parenthood would have been easier if they had waited, the organization's recognition that young parents are stepping up and parenting well, calling them "resilient," "determined," and "nurturing," is nothing short of transformative (Power to Decide). It is also clearly a response to #NoTeenShame's movement, even as it fails to acknowledge the movement itself.

On May 6, 2019, Power to Decide announced the rebranding of May's "Teen Pregnancy Prevention Month" as "Sex Ed for All Month" in a blog post on the website titled "A New Direction for May: Sex Ed for All Month." Ginny Ehrlich opens the article by writing, "We stand alongside our sister organizations, Advocates for Youth, Healthy Teen Network, Planned Parenthood Federation of America, and the Sexuality Information and Education Council of the United States, to announce May as Sex Ed For All Month: Accessing Power, Information, and Rights." While the rebranding is clearly a success born of #NoTeenShame's determination and rhetorical prowess, the movement and its founders are notably absent from the list of sister organizations. If Power to Decide is so committed to the effort to help young people and improve reproductive health, rights, and justice for all, then why not reach out to #NoTeenShame's founders and invite them to the table? Instead of consulting with the movement, Power to Decide has attempted to erase its role in this change, demonstrating that for othered voices, the struggle to be heard continues, and that although activists may enact rhetorical feminism and "use and respect alternative rhetorical practices" to effect change, they are not always recognized for doing so.

However, #NoTeenShame did not accept this silencing. #NoTeenShame co-founder Vianna teamed up with Christine Soyong Harley, President & CEO of SIECUS: Sex Ed for Social Change, to combat this erasure, writing an article that sets the record straight regarding the pressures that led to Sex Ed for All Month. Vianna and Soyong Harley explain, "several leading national organizations, including SIECUS: Sex Ed for Social Change, Advocates for Youth, Answer, Healthy Teen Network, Power to Decide, and Planned Parenthood, finally heeded the call from #NoTeenShame and other on-the-ground advocates from across the country," rebranding May's "Teen Pregnancy Prevention Month" as "Sex Ed For All Month." This framing is important: these organizations heeded the call, but they did not lead the charge. The young parents, whose voices have long been ignored, worked for years to effect this change. There is an irony in Power to Decide's adoption of more inclusive branding alongside its simultaneous failure to recognize key voices that advocated for this change. Historical clarification not only tells a more complete story but also demonstrates how social and cultural change is often the result of both local and national as well as traditional and alternative advocates and coalitions.

Although Power to Decide may not acknowledge #NoTeenShame's role, others have. The article "Youth Power, Information, and Rights Month," published May 2019 by Planned Parenthood of the Pacific Southwest states,

> A coalition made up of Power to Decide, Advocates for Youth, SIECUS, Healthy Teen Network, the Guttmacher Institute, #NoTeenShame, and Planned Parenthood Federation of America was behind this name change . . . young people's sexual health needs go beyond pregnancy prevention and . . . a focus on "teen pregnancy prevention" contributes to stigma around pregnant and parenting youth.

Here, Planned Parenthood acknowledges #NoTeenShame, but in contrast to Vianna and Soyong Harley's article, the movement is categorized as one part of a coalition of marginalized *and* mainstream organizations as opposed to being a catalyst for change among organizations with greater infrastructure and public recognition. Suggesting that Power to Decide and #NoTeenShame were part of the same coalition that effected this change is misleading at best; #NoTeenShame worked to change the discourse, and as arbiter of that discourse, the National Campaign/Power to Decide was one of the targets. However, at least Planned Parenthood is acknowledging the existence of #NoTeenShame and the fact that prevention campaigns reproduce stigma. While the Power to Decide article announcing Sex Ed for All Month makes no mention of stigma, other organizations, like SIECUS and Planned Parenthood, are recognizing not only the problematic dominant discourse, but also the role of #NoTeenShame in changing that discourse.

As we move into the post-*Dobbs* era with renewed attention on reproductive justice advocacy, this chapter serves as an important reminder that emergent stories of change can be co-opted or incomplete as important rhetorical players behind the scenes may be erased. As feminist scholars, it is imperative that we continue to question and examine these stories in order to have a thorough understanding of the rhetorical forces at work and also recognize marginalized rhetors effecting change. While the movement's success may be tempered by the attempted erasure of its role in effecting change, that should not hamper hope for the future. #NoTeenShame has shown that rhetorical action can effect real change in the realm of reproductive justice, and numerous organizations *are* taking notice and crediting the movement. The founders of #NoTeenShame did not simply create a social media campaign for parents—they created a movement that directly engages the people in power. Because of their successful rhetorical moves on social media, the founders of #NoTeenShame were able to garner enough support and attention to be seen and listened to as activist-rhetors, even as they continually struggled to maintain that position. #NoTeenShame's accomplishments illustrate how activist-rhetors can tap into a specific cultural moment and employ available and emerging technologies to successfully target multiple audiences, build coalitions, and interrupt dominant discourses. As a multiracial and multigenerational coalition, #NoTeenShame's success highlights the possibilities of rhetorical activism, the importance of listening to and working with women of color, and the ethical need to acknowledge their intellectual contributions. It also suggests that this work is ongoing, ever shifting, changing, and growing. Finally, #NoTeenShame illustrates how rhetorical feminism can be put into practice to intervene in dominant discourses in concrete ways—and that should give us all hope, which, as Glenn writes, "is more important than ever at this historical moment" (341).

Works Cited

Almost Home [@AlmostHomeSTL]. "#NoTeenShame #NoTeenPreg don't need . . ." *Twitter*, 21 June 2014, twitter.com/AlmostHomeSTL/status/480403554629595137. Accessed 10 Oct. 2020.

Arai, Lisa. *Teenage Pregnancy: The Making and Unmaking of a Problem*, Policy P, 2009.

Aubrey, Jennifer Stevens, et al. "Understanding the Effects of MTV's 16 and Pregnant on Adolescent Girls' Beliefs, Attitudes, and Behavioral Intentions toward Teen Pregnancy." *Journal of Health and Communication*, vol. 19, no. 10, 2014, pp. 1145–60. *EBSCO*, doi:10.1080/10810730.2013.872721.

Books, Sue. "Fear and Loathing: The Moral Dimensions of the Politicization of Teen Pregnancy." *Journal of Thought*, vol. 31, no. 1, 1996, pp. 9–24.

Burke, Tarana, and Brené Brown. "Introduction: A Conversation." *You Are Your Best Thing: Vulnerability, Shame Resilience, and the Black Experience*, edited by Tarana Burke and Brené Brown, Random, 2021, pp. xi-xxiii.

California Latinas for Reproductive Justice [@Latinas4RJ]. "'Age doesn't define a good parent'…" *Twitter*, 28 Aug. 2013, twitter.com/Latinas4RJ/status/372777998761873408. Accessed 10 Oct. 2020.

Candie's Foundation. #NoTeenPreg Carly Rae Jepsen PSA. *Candies' Foundation*, 2013, www.thecandiesfoundation.org. Accessed 10 Oct. 2020.

Civil Liberties and Public Policy. "Who We Are." *Civil Liberties and Public Policy*, www.clpp.hampshire.edu/about-us/who-we-are. Accessed 1 Dec. 2020.

Cole, Neil. "Shame on Who?" *HuffPost*, 11 June 2013, www.huffingtonpost.com/neil-cole/shame-on-who_b_3421988.html. Accessed 30 Jan. 2020.

COLOR [@colorlatina]. "Standing w/former #teenmom . . ." *Twitter*, 26 June 2013, twitter.com/colorlatina/status/350028925973430273. Accessed 10 Oct. 2020.

Daniel, Clare. *Mediating Morality: The Politics of Teen Pregnancy in the Post-Welfare Era.* U Massachusetts P, 2017.

Dockterman, Eliana. "Does *16 and Pregnant* Prevent or Promote Teen Pregnancy?" *Time*, 13 Jan. 2014, www.time.com/825/does-16-and-pregnant-prevent-or-promote-teen-pregnancy/. Accessed 15 June 2020.

Earl, Jade. "#NoTeenShame: A Social Media Movement Pushes Us to Respect Young Mothers & We're All For It." *Hello Beautiful*, 10 May 2014, www.hellobeautiful.com/2721704/no-teen-shame-campaign/. Accessed 15 June 2020.

Eby, Margaret. "*Teen Mom* Farrah Abraham Defends Selling Sex Tape, Asks: 'What Would You Do?'" *New York Daily News*, 3 May 2013, www.nydailynews.com/entertainment/gossip/watch-teen-mom-farrah-abraham-defends-sex-tape-article-1.1334527. Accessed 15 June 2020.

Echoing Ida [@EchoingIda]. "We stand with #NoTeenShame . . ." *Twitter*, 22 May 2014, twitter.com/EchoingIda/status/469473531693395969. Accessed 15 Dec. 2020.

Ehrlich, Ginny. "A New Direction for May: Sex Ed for All Month." Power to Decide, 6 May 2019, https://powertodecide.org/news/new-direction-for-may-sex-ed-for-all-month. Accessed 10 Dec. 2020.

—. "We Are Power to Decide." *Power to Decide*, 4 Dec. 2017, www.powertodecide.org/news/we-are-power-decide. Accessed 10 Dec. 2020.

EMA Fund [@EMA_Fund]. "'And I see young mothers not just participating in our #reprojustice . . .' http://ow.ly/ms47S #NoTeenShame." *Twitter*, 27 June 2013, twitter.com/EMA_Fund/status/350336002218409984. Accessed 10 Oct. 2020.

Friedman, Roger. "The *Juno* Effect Strikes Again." *Fox News*, 2 Sept. 2008, www.foxnews.com/story/the-juno-effect-strikes-again. Accessed 15 June 2020.

Forward Together [@FwdTogether]. "RT @icah: Love all the #noteenshame imgs & info on *Tumblr* . . ." *Twitter*, 27 Aug. 2013, twitter.com/FwdTogether/status/372429184616120320. Accessed 15 Oct. 2020.

Geronimus, A.T. "Damned If You Do: Culture, Identity, Privilege, and Teenage Childbearing in the United States." *Social Science and Medicine*, vol. 57, no. 5, 2003, pp. 881–93.

Glenn, Cheryl. "The Language of Rhetorical Feminism, Anchored in Hope." *Open Linguistics*, vol. 6, no. 1, 2020, pp. 334–343, doi.org/10.1515/opli-2020–0023.

Guglielmo, Letizia, and Kimberly Wallace Stewart. "*16 and Pregnant* and the 'Unvarnished' Truth about Teen Pregnancy." *MTV and Teen Pregnancy: Critical Essays on 16 and Pregnant and Teen Mom*, edited by Letizia Guglielmo, Scarecrow P, 2013, pp. 19–34.

Harvey, David. *A Brief History of Neoliberalism*. Oxford UP, 2005.

Henson, Melissa. "MTV's *Teen Mom* Glamorizes Getting Pregnant." *CNN*, 4 May 2011, www.cnn.com/2011/OPINION/05/04/henson.teen.mom.show/index.html. Accessed 15 June 2020.

Illinois Caucus for Adolescent Health [@ICAH]. "For some, it's #teenpregnancyprevention #noteenpreg day..." *Twitter*, 7 May 2014, twitter.com/ICAH/status/464075572251873280. Accessed 10 Oct. 2020.

Jones, Rebecca. "Rhetorical Activism: Responsibility in the Ivory Tower." *Activism and Rhetoric: Theories and Contexts for Political Engagement.* 2nd ed., edited by JongHwa Lee and Seth Kahn. Routledge, 2019, pp. 26–37.

Kaplan, Elaine Bell. *Not Our Kind of Girl: Unraveling the Myths of Black Teenage Motherhood*, U of California P, 1997.

Kearney, Melissa S., and Phillip B. Levine. "Media Influences on Social Outcomes: The Impact of MTV's 16 and Pregnant on Teen Childbearing." *American Economic Review*, vol. 105, no. 12, 2015, pp. 3597–632. *EBSCO*, doi:www.aeaweb.org/aer/.

Lopez, Amy. "Drowning from the Inside Out: The Stigma Surrounding Early Pregnancy." *#NoTeenShame*, *Tumblr*, 12 Apr. 2016, NoTeenShame.tumblr.com/. Accessed 15 June 2020.

Lowrey, Annie. "MTV's *16 and Pregnant*, Derided by Some, May Resonate as a Cautionary Tale." *New York Times*, 13 Jan. 2014, www.nytimes.com/2014/01/13/business/media/mtvs-16-and-pregnant-derided-by-some-may-resonate-as-a-cautionary-tale.html. Accessed 15 Aug. 2020.

Luker, Kristin. *Dubious Conceptions: The Politics of Teen Pregnancy*, Harvard UP, 1996.

Majeski, Ashley. "Has *Teen Mom* Lost Its Original Message?" *Today*, 14 Mar. 2013.

Malone, Gloria. "What Pregnant and Parenting Teens Really Need." *Huffpost blog*, 28 Apr. 2015. www.huffpost.com/entry/what-pregnant-and-parenting-teens-really-need_b_7157074. Accessed 15 Sept. 2020.

Nathman, Avital Norman. "Real Talk: Real-Life Teen Moms Sound Off on Study Claiming "Teen Mom" Reduced Teen Pregnancies." *The Frisky*, 16 Jan. 2014. *Internet Archive*, web.archive.org/web/20140126075957/http://www.thefrisky.com/2014–01–16/real-talk-real-life-teen-moms-sound-off-on-study-claiming-teen-mom-reduced-teen-pregnancies/. Accessed 20 Nov. 2020.

National Campaign to Prevent Teen and Unplanned Pregnancy. "Leadership." *The National Campaign to Prevent Teen and Unplanned Pregnancy*, 2017, web.archive.org/web/20171020205029/http://thenationalcampaign.org/about/leadership. Accessed 20 April 2023.

National Campaign to Prevent Teen and Unplanned Pregnancy. "Why It Matters." *The National Campaign to Prevent Teen and Unplanned Pregnancy*, 2016. *Internet Archive*, web.archive.org/web/20160306110623/http://thenationalcampaign.org/why-it-matters. Accessed 20 Jan. 2018.

National Center for Health Statistics. "Teen Birth Rate Rises for First Time in 15 Years." *Centers for Disease Control and Prevention*, 5 Dec. 2007, www.cdc.gov/nchs/pressroom/07newsreleases/teenbirth.htm. Accessed 20 Jan. 2019.

No Teen Shame. "About." *#NoTeenShame*, www.NoTeenShame.com/about. Accessed 20 Apr. 2020.

—. *#NoTeenShame*, *Tumblr*, 2014–2020, NoTeenShame.tumblr.com/. Accessed 15 June 2020.

—. "#NoTeenShame *Twitter* Chat on 4/17/2014." *#NoTeenShame, Tumblr*, 19 Apr. 2014, noteenshame.tumblr.com/post/83203236789/noteenshame-teen-pregnancy-young-parenthood-repro. Accessed 15 June 2020.

—. "5 Ways to Be an Ally to Young Parents." *#NoTeenShame*, *Tumblr*, 30 Apr. 2014, https://noteenshame.tumblr.com/image/84330345141. Accessed 15 June 2020.

— [@NoTeenShameOrg]. *NoTeenShame*, *Twitter*, twitter.com/NoTeenShameorg. Accessed 15 June 2020.

Planned Parenthood Advocacy Fund of MA [@PPAdvocacyMA]. "Teen mothers..." *Twitter*, 4 Oct. 2013, twitter.com/PPAdvocacyMA/status/386242245240045568. Accessed 10 Oct. 2020.

Power to Decide. "Leadership." *Power to Decide*, 2023, https://powertodecide.org/about-us/leadership. Accessed 20 Apr. 2023.

Power to Decide. "Why It Matters." *Power to Decide*, 2020, powertodecide.org/what-we-do/information/why-it-matters. Accessed 5 July 2020.

Probyn, Elspeth. *Blush: Faces of Shame*. U of Minnesota P, 2005.

Reimer, Susan. "Teen Pregnancy Visionary Steps Down." *Baltimore Sun*, 13 May 2015, www.baltimoresun.com/opinion/op-ed/bs-ed-reimer-national-campaign-20150513-column.html. Accessed 15 June 2020.

Ronan, Alex. "Teen Moms Need Support, Not Shame." *The Cut*, 8 May 2015, www.thecut.com/2015/05/teen-moms-need-support-not-shame.html. Accessed 15 June 2020.

Ross, Loretta J., et al. Introduction. *Radical Reproductive Justice: Foundation, Theory, Practice, Critique*. Feminist P, 2017, pp. 7–14.

— and Rickie Solinger. *Reproductive Justice: An Introduction*, U of California P, 2017.

Silliman, Jael, Marlene Gerber Fried, Loretta Ross, and Elena R. Gutierrez, eds. *Undivided Rights: Women of Color Organizing for Reproductive Justice*. Haymarket, 2016.

Sowards, Stacey K., and Valerie R. Renegar. "Reconceptualizing Rhetorical Activism in Contemporary Feminist Contexts." *Howard Journal of Communications*, vol. 17, no. 1, 2006, pp. 57–74.

Stenberg, Shari J. "'Tweet Me Your First Assaults': Writing Shame and the Rhetorical Work of #NotOkay." *Rhetoric Society Quarterly*, vol. 48, no. 2, 2018, pp. 119–38. DOI: 10.1080/02773945.2017.1402126.

Vianna, Natasha. Personal Interview. 20 Oct. 2020.

Vianna, Natasha, and Christine Soyong Harley. "Long Overdue: A Call to Action for Shame-Free Sex Education." *SIECUS: Sex Ed for Social Change*, www.siecus.org/long-overdue-a-call-to-action-for-shame-free-sex-education/. Accessed 15 Sept. 2020.

Vinson, Jenna. *Embodying the Problem: The Persuasive Power of the Teen Mother*. Rutgers UP, 2018.

Yam, Shui-yin Sharon. "Visualizing Birth Stories from the Margin: Toward a Reproductive Justice Model of Rhetorical Analysis." *Rhetorical Society Quarterly*, vol. 50, no. 1, 2020, pp. 19–34, DOI: 10.1080/02773945.2019.1682182.

"Youth Power, Information, and Rights Month." *Planned Parenthood of the Pacific Southwest*, 1 May 2019. www.plannedparenthood.org/planned-parenthood-pacific-southwest/blog/youth-power-information-and-rights-month. Accessed 15 Sept. 2020.

Youth, Tech, Health. "About." *Youth, Tech, Health*, 2020, yth.org/about/. Accessed 15 Sept. 2020.

5 Brokering Reproductive Justice: Solidarity Rhetoric in Senator Wendy Davis's Texas Filibuster

Jill Swiencicki

> Rooted in our identities, power derives from belonging as well as from exercising control over what we belong to.
>
> —Etienne Wenger, *Communities of Practice*

Reproductive justice work is premised on diverse, inclusive collectives. While the movement originated and coalesced through the SisterSong Women of Color Reproductive Health Collective, it extends outside this network and is practiced by people across all racial, class, sexual, and gendered identities. Loretta Ross, a SisterSong founder, embraces such diversity. She states that instead of focusing on the means of reproductive health, "reproductive justice analysis focuses on the ends: better lives for women, healthier families, and sustainable communities. . . . Using this analysis, we can integrate multiple issues and bring together constituencies that are multi-racial, multi-generational, and multi-class in order to build a more powerful and relevant grassroots movement" ("What Is" 4). This statement reflects the reproductive justice core value of "undivided rights," a value that necessitates "creating an agenda and ultimately a movement that reflects the broad set of needs and concerns which all women face" (Silliman et al. 16).

Managing such diversity well means negotiating the politics of solidarity within the movement. Ross argues that reproductive justice work requires "holding ourselves and our allies accountable to the integrity of this vision. We have to directly address the inequitable distribution of power and resources within the movement, holding our allies and ourselves responsible for constructing principled, collaborative relationships" ("What Is" 5). This chapter supports this goal by identifying the rhetorical features of the acts of solidarity Ross describes. What do "principled, collaborative" acts of reproductive justice solidarity entail, and how might they constitute a rhetoric, or set of persuasive moves that can be named and replicated? Chandra Mohanty, Aimee Carillo Rowe, Kim Marie Vaz, and others have clarified the barriers to feminist solidarity across "power lines," or structured differences in power and privilege (Rowe 2) and have identified the features of impactful, inclusive solidarity. Feminist rhetorical scholarship extends this work by naming the persuasive practices that reveal how power differentials are managed and challenged in reproductive justice work to secure undivided rights.

This chapter identifies features that comprise a solidarity rhetoric on behalf of reproductive justice. These features are best analyzed through the concept of brokering, a key rhetorical feature of allyship. If allyship is a role or category, brokering is the rhetorical mode of action allies use to make change. According to Etienne Wenger, brokering focuses on how figures who occupy "ambivalent spaces of multi-membership" (109) in a community of practice can provoke changes in procedure, knowledge, and policy that enrich learning. A broker is a member of a community with enough status and power to open new possibilities for meaning among differently situated stakeholders (Koliba et al. 210). To do the work effectively, brokers must be experts in the work of rhetorical invention, using the available means to translate and coordinate knowledge, information, and opinions in ways that are comprehensible to diverse and competing stakeholders. The goal of this work is to enhance the possibility for alignment of purpose, action, and meaning. Texas senator Wendy Davis, who was a member of a largely conservative legislative chamber, a feminist, and a reproductive justice activist, engaged the feminist rhetorical strategies of brokering in her thirteen-hour filibuster of Senate Bill 5 (SB 5). The filibuster took place in June 2013 and is captured in the transcript, *Let Her Speak*.

Davis's filibuster was a response to a bill—voted down in a regular legislative session but revived by Governor Rick Perry in a special session—that constrained and in places completely eliminated women's access to reproductive health care, including abortion. Davis did not use the filibuster to run out the clock on a vote, despite its history as being a tool of vacuous speech and a tactic to perpetuate structural racism (Jentleson 6). Instead, Davis used the filibuster to introduce medical expertise, Texas state legislative history, and women's testimony (their epistemic resources and practices) to create a scene of public deliberation where it had been occluded. In her words, Davis used the filibuster to "give voice to the people who were not able to provide their voice as part of the testimony" (*Let Her Speak* 31). Over 180,000 people watched the livestream on *YouTube*, millions followed the events on *Twitter* and contributed their abortion stories, and hundreds filled the capitol rotunda and the senate chamber where Davis held the floor (Stevenson 502). The event was a distributed, networked, and participatory process, as activists and protesters tweeted their stories, their information, and their support to Davis, publicizing the injustice of the bill's contents. It was also a spectacle that was strikingly coordinated through the figure of Davis herself (Harp et al. 228). Hers was a rhetorical performance of solidarity, one in which Davis was acting as broker, or "epistemic agent" (E. Davis 726), aware of the duty of care necessary in representing the stories and knowledge of others who were excluded from the scene of argument and acting in partnership with those protesting in the senate chamber and on *Twitter*, *YouTube*, and *Facebook*.

In the history of how the Reproductive Justice Movement confronted Targeted Regulation of Abortion Providers, or TRAP, laws through interwoven materialist and rhetorical struggles, Davis will have a role, I hope, as more than a failed and vanquished elected official and reproductive justice activist. Current scholarship in the fields of rhetoric and communication emphasize her diminishment. Dana Cloud argues that Davis's efforts in the filibuster offer a "more decorous—and less effective—process" than those of the "unruly" activists in the chamber and capitol building (41). Such binaries of protester/legislator blunt the value of undivided rights so central to the reproductive justice vision: that of multiply situated actors working toward human rights goals. More recently, Davis's work in the filibuster has been minimized by a scholarly emphasis on how conservative forces marshalled sexist media frames, such as "Abortion Barbie," that undermined her political efficacy (Corrigan and de St. Felix 13). Understanding the attack on Davis's ethos is critically important to understanding the constraints on her efforts, and the ways those may have "sealed Davis's identity" as a failed, amoral reformer of abortion legislation (2). Yet to speak of any subjectivity as "sealed," or trapped, distorts the ways in which, as Anis Bawarshi argues, identity, authority, and genre are in constant development in communities of practice, and new, potential selves are available for meaningful action (105). As we historicize efforts to protect reproductive autonomy we need the dialectic of analysis of feminist activist rhetorics and analysis of the forces that seek to diminish it.

In all lawmaking, including TRAP laws, those who are elected can speak and have access to debating legislation in the senate chamber, and those subject to the law are cut off. It is this situation that Senator Davis brokers. She does this not by speaking for targeted women, but by filling the shell of the filibuster with their testimony, expertise, and medical science. The filibuster helped to publicize the contents and effects of TRAP laws like SB 5, but the damage from the bill endures and deepens. Davis indeed "opened a closed rhetorical space about abortion by sharing the stories of sixty-five women opposing HB2" (Corrigan and de St. Felix 2). While Davis did not and could not succeed in stopping SB 5, and restrictive abortion bans have only continued to win court sanction and change the landscape of abortion access in Texas and many other states (Wilkinson), she succeeded in providing a public and replicable model of reproductive justice brokering as she worked to move discourse on reproductive health to progressive outcomes.

Brokering is an act of rhetorical choice-making. It is not just a go-between role; it makes something new. A kind of inventional curation, brokering is the use of one's role in acts of translation, coordination, and alignment of knowledge to create interactions among groups and texts that help to produce new meaning. I examine Davis's acts of translation and coordination of women's testimony, as well as procedural and medical history, which attempts to align stakeholders against the assumptions the bill rests upon. Because of procedural manipulation by the Republican majority to preserve conservative lawmaking, her brokering fails to align her senate colleagues and the Texans protesting this bill. Given these constraints, successful brokering involves adaptation, featuring bold acts of rhetorical invention, and managing epistemic harm and purposeful (mis)alignment of audience and values. These adaptations allow for a new way of thinking about alignment, that of a solidarity that fortifies the larger, majority movement for reproductive justice. Elizabeth Wardle argues that those in communities of practice continually negotiate their identities and authority as they take on new workplace roles, and rhetorical choices help actors construct the social identities they wish to project; what appears to be a brokering failure, then, can be a form of resistance and a making of a different, fortified community.

Davis's filibuster can be read alongside reproductive justice assumptions about what constitutes embodied authority, about who gets to speak and speak for others, and principles of care and listening when delivering structural critique. Davis engaged the sexist epistemology implicit in the bill itself, as well as senate customs of somatic rationality and coherence, with a range of discourse characterized by materialist feminist analysis and acts of personal identification. As Shari J. Stenberg and Charlotte Hogg argue in *Persuasive Acts*, the "impetus for some of the strongest surges of women's voices in the last two decades often comes back to the denial of women's voices, personhood, and agency" (4); contemporary women rhetors, above all, "respond to a problem of lived experience, whether in the community, profession, or one's body" (10). Davis's rhetorical work is powerfully instructive toward these ends, both as she works to halt the loss of reproductive health facilities and procedures throughout the state, but also as she endeavors to represent lived realities that are not her own. In their introduction to their anthology of twenty-first century women's rhetorics, Stenberg and Hogg introduce the concept of rhetorical sway, "rhetorical impact demonstrated through creating or connecting to cultural flashpoints that forward or respond to gendered issues" (14). Rhetorical sway means to "work within and against traditional rhetorical means to invent rhetorics that engage wide audiences, change conversations, and create openings for rhetors to enter" (16). Wendy Davis is emblematic of sway in her filibuster, demonstrating "feminist rhetorical resilience" (19) through a transformative brokering process that may not immediately change oppressive conditions, conditions made through decades of structural misogyny, but may "chang[e] the way a life is lived" for activists seeking principled procedure for the work ahead (Flynn, Sotirin, and Brady 7).

The Rhetorical Situation of Senate Bill 5

In the late twentieth century, prompted by a string of Supreme Court cases, Republican members of US state legislatures began to chip away at what constitutes an undue burden in access to safe, legal abortion. A twenty-four hour waiting period here, a vaginal ultrasound there: patronizing and oppressive, in their proclaimed attempts to protect the safety of women seeking healthcare, the burdens to access began to pile up. Such TRAP laws circulate in numerous states, reduce abortion access (especially for poor women, women of color, and rural women), and force changes to medical protocol, often against the recommendations of national physician's associations. Created in anti-choice thinktanks like the American Legislative Exchange Council (ALEC), conservative legislatures, and anti-choice legal organizations, TRAP laws are not a local effort, but a "calculated and heavily financed piece of a national strategy" (Cloud 40). In the spring of 2013, the Texas legislature was considering one such law, called HB 60, which would continue to restrict access to safe, legal abortion.

One hour after HB 60 was initially voted down in the Texas state house, Governor Perry called a special session to reconsider the bill. This senate version of the TRAP bill, SB 5, aimed to enact the following restrictions: ban abortions after twenty weeks; require doctors performing abortions to have admitting privileges at nearby hospitals; revise the medical method for determining fetal gestation age; and require that all Texas abortion clinics be upgraded to "ambulatory surgical centers." SB 5 aimed to contradict and counteract established science, current medical regulations, women's diverse reproductive, personal, and family histories, bodily needs, and material, temporal situations. SB 5 begins with the medically unfounded fetal pain premise, and from this premise builds a regulating structure for how doctors may conduct health treatment of women seeking reproductive care. From the twenty-week ban, to ambulatory surgical center requirements for the premises, and even to a revision of the calculation of gestational age, it restructures the health service from a point of view unfounded in scientific research, against statistics about the safety of the procedure, and in denial of women's bodies, material realities, and lived knowledge. Texas senator Glenn Hegar and the coauthors of the bill, such as Dr. Robert Deuell, set up norms of female fertility and of medical treatment from their conservative interpretation of Judeo-Christian and Catholic epistemologies.

TRAP laws and their defenders represent a sexist "model of knowledge as power," or system of epistemological assumptions that rest on creating dichotomies (Williams 7). Such a system of knowing "generat[es] a distant and hierarchical relationship between the knower and the known and promises knowledge with a high degree of certainty and generality. In exchange, it exacts from the knower a sense of deep fragmentation both in himself and in the world more generally" (7). During the filibuster the authors of the bill express this sexist worldview to feminist dissenter Davis in predictably patronizing ways, such as feigned advocacy: "You know," Deuell says to her, "this bill is really about women's health" (*Let Her Speak* 87). Another senator attempted to reassure Davis of his intentions: "you know I love women because . . . I have fond memories of my grandmothers, my Mama, who I thank for life" (100). Other senators were more pointed about the real focus of their commitment to the bill: to center "the rights of the unborn" (101).

As the Texas house of representatives' initial vote on HB 60 drew near, hundreds of women signed up to testify against a bill that would constrain reproductive health clinics to the point of closure, limiting and in some places eliminating access to services like abortion (*Let Her Speak* 30). Concerned Texans were ready with their only point of leverage: their personal testimony about their reproductive healthcare needs past, present, and future. Davis recounts that "the chair of the committee hearing testimony . . . made a decision that no longer would testimony be accepted. In his words, 'because it had become repetitive'" (30). The refusal to listen to the women who would be vulnerable to the bill's restrictions is what the philosopher Emmalon Davis would call an act of epistemic marginalization (704). E. Davis examines the varied ethical harms that can happen when the knowledge developed in marginalized communities gets detached from those who produce it. She concludes that, for true feminist solidarity, "Any practice that is developed without centering the participation of those persons whose lives it purports to improve risks distorting those persons and their lives" (727). Speaking directly to their elected representatives, Texas women were aiming for intercommunal uptake of their knowledge, experience, and demands so that policy could be crafted with their human rights in mind. In the decision to end hearing testimony, these women were prohibited from their right to shape "democratic moral inquiry" (707) and were prevented from shaping the very policy that would determine their access to care.

Reproductive Justice Brokering

The Texas senate exemplifies what Wenger, who theorizes about the production of knowledge and identity in workplaces, would call a community of practice. As in any workplace, individuals learn together and develop their identities by pursuing shared endeavors and solving problems using varied expertise. The key is to have a participant who can identify, integrate, and negotiate conflict as new knowledge is moved from outside the community of practice to its center. As Wenger posits,

> The job of brokering is complex. It involves processes of translation, coordination, and alignment between perspectives. It requires enough legitimacy to influence the development of a practice, mobilize attention, and address conflicting interests. It

> also requires the ability to link practices by facilitating transactions between them, and to cause learning by introducing into a practice elements of another. Toward this end, brokering provides a participative connection . . . because what brokers press into service to connect practices is their experience of multimembership and the possibilities for negotiation inherent in participation. (109)

Wenger argues that communities rely on members who do the work of brokering, or "introducing into a practice elements of another" to achieve a purpose, and that their legitimacy emerges from their ability to identify missing knowledge and practices, enact inclusion, and negotiate conflict (109). If this work is done well it achieves a "participative connection," or depth of knowledge that comes from a shared sense of process (109).

Brokering is a form of allyship that can engender epistemic inclusion and transformation, pulling the knowledge of a marginalized or oppressed group into a dominant discursive space to transform lived reality. It offers methods of action that fortify the position of the vulnerable in the scene of potential exploitation or oppression. Of course, as a Texas senator, Davis used her position to prohibit voting on the bill in a special session, one meant to override the failure of the vote through democratic means. Davis's ambivalent relations of multi-membership include blocking her colleagues' attempts to pass a bill that would harm her constituents and harm those shut out from the walls of power where these decisions are unfolding. But she is more than a shield or defense, and the method by which she enacts reproductive justice solidarity can serve as a model for other advocates. This method involves brokering epistemic resources from the medical community, from women's testimony from their own lives, and from the lives of their mothers. They involve invitational rhetorical strategies that expose epistemic oppression and attempt redirection. Brokering, then, is a kind of invention, a making that shifts possibilities for meaning all the while staying legible to diverse participants.

Davis is brokering historical and current realities—competing identities, historical legacies, oppressions, and privileges—to establish and set laws and influence lawmakers. Doing this reproductive justice work as a white woman involves speaking for others in a historical context in which white women have repeatedly ignored the interests of Black and brown women to gain favor in a patriarchal structure that more clearly values white fertility in the service of white supremacy (Ross and Solinger 29). She structures her filibuster primarily with the silenced testimony of Texas constituents who showed up to protest the house bill. Brokering knowledge from one community into another can compromise the agency and power of the knower. One must be able to benefit from one's own epistemic labor. In this work, Davis ran the risk of misappropriating a story, silencing storytellers, and positioning testimony in the filibuster in ways that would mute or de-emphasize. Yet in spaces of exclusion, like the Texas senate, where one must be an elected official to enter and speak, one sometimes needs representation. A danger in this filibuster is that Davis's brokering acts as a Trojan horse, confirming the assumption that, for more marginalized women's stories to "gain intercommunal uptake, they must first unfold via a comparatively privileged epistemic agent," often white, cisgender, middle-class, and privileged (E. Davis 716). E. Davis warns of the epistemic harm in which marginalized "perspectives remain tethered to the dominant" (718). As a way to communicate their experiences and seek advocacy, "the strategy remains limited as long as marginalized knowers are not located at the center of their own stories. Though indicative of progress, this state of affairs must not be confused with justice" (718).

Davis indeed garnered national and even international attention for the thirteen-hour filibuster. As a white, cisgender, feminine presentation of self, her body stands in for the bodies of others, less representing "bodily difference" than reinforcing a civil, normative presentation of the female self (Chávez 244). She was fetishized in fashion magazines like *Vogue* and feminist organizations like Planned Parenthood for her running shoes; for her poise, stamina, and vulnerability; and for her courage as a leader. Much media coverage and coverage in activist circles perpetuates the idea of the lone, heroic rhetor speaking against the odds. Even in her 2020 ad campaign for the United States House of Representatives, Davis herself emphasizes the physical arduousness of standing for thirteen hours unaided. In her role,

> benefits disproportionately advantage the powerful. While relationships that facilitate the exchange or mutual sharing of epistemic resources between dominant and marginalized knowers are potential sources of moral and epistemic transformation, the prevailing structures of power under which such relationships develop threaten to undermine the liberatory potential of these relationships for marginalized knowers. For even as epistemic

> agents struggle against unequal power structures, they operate within them. (E. Davis 715)

As a broker of testimony, facts, and data, Davis works within the constraints of the SB 5 wording, the restrictions of the legislator's deliberative procedures, and her empowered role to represent others more vulnerable to the bill's restrictions in order to limit epistemic harm. To enact this rhetorical event, Davis brokered competing audiences and worldviews: engaging the religious, anti-choice authors of SB 5 with this intersectional, feminist testimony and argument.

Rhetorics of Translation, Coordination, and Alignment

The work of epistemic brokering is that of being the bridge between the vast digital and experiential expanse of reproductive justice stakeholders and the elderly, cisgender, Christian white men who wrote the SB 5 TRAP law and eventually voted it into law. This work requires translating knowledge and perspectives into reference frames that are comprehensible to new communities, work that requires coordination and curation. These actions have the potential to align perspectives, shift alliances, meaning, and material relations. Davis curates the filibuster by selecting and arranging testimonies, letters, tweets, medical research, and journalism. She centers the knowledge of those who are subject to the law so that this knowledge, preserved as recorded testimony, can live on to critique and reshape law going forward.

Before this brokering can happen, a broker must be perceived as a subject with the authority and identity to serve in the role (Wardle). Wenger features *ethos*, or perceived legitimacy, as the key element that shapes the ability to bridge epistemic gaps. To create an *ethos* of multimembership that sustains "principled, collaborative relationships" (Ross, "What Is" 5) is the relational and rhetorical challenge of this work. Davis chooses to minimize her own health history and emphasize her legislative identity. While she occasionally identifies herself as having mothered her daughters in poverty, as having had to terminate a pregnancy, and therefore having been in situations similar to those most vulnerable to SB 5, she mentions these events in crisp declaratives and does not narrativize them, but merely touches upon them as brief moments of identification with the community she is brokering into the scene of power. The subject position she predominantly crafts is that of a legislator and elected official. She frames herself as bringing deliberative democracy into what she calls "a raw abuse of power," where senate business is appropriated by religious and political conservatives (*Let Her Speak* 2).

In the Texas talking filibuster, legislators pride themselves on civility and decorum, and refer to themselves—even while arguing about rules—as being a supportive "family" (156). Davis engages this language of amity and filiality, often declaring feelings of respect for aspects of her anti-abortion colleagues' identity that align with her own. An example is her response to Senator Lucio who, early in the filibuster, interrupts her reading testimony to bemoan that "no one's talked about the rights of the unborn" (*Let Her Speak* 101). Davis responds to Lucio by translating the testimony's reproductive justice claims into his own moral context:

> I believe you have a compassionate heart beyond compare . . . I see you every day reading your Bible on your iPad as you sit here on the senate floor. I know your decision on these issues comes from that very deep place of faith. I also know that you are a man who fights for children in need. I watched you in this session work on the food bill . . . and I saw the sadness and the despair that you had, day after day, as you tried to convince a two-thirds majority of the senate to suspend, so that your bill to feed hungry children in schools could pass . . . I'm sorry that we disagree on this particular issue . . . your hope for what this bill would achieve is that abortion services would decrease in Texas. Um, I don't think that that's been the stated purpose for this bill. (102)

Davis speaks to Lucio and other senators sympathetic to SB 5 as a peer, invoking the fullness of his humanity. She is a witness to his Christian faith, seeing him as he brokers his faith into the context of his senate service. Yet she uses his work on the food bill to translate it into a pro-life stance and coordinates it into reproductive justice concerns relating to the right to parent in conditions of care and health. She ends by declaring that his ethics are actually misaligned with SB 5, and even inaccurate in their purported care for children. Lucio's interruptions are constraints that Davis must manage to hold the floor. She turns them into moments of brokering, reinforcing her status and right to speak. She is perceived as effective, as one anti-abortion senator remarked to her during the proceedings that "people of all persuasions in this body are respecting you now because you've been very statesman-like" (159).

Her rhetorical brokering proceeds like this, through a series of "transactions" and "linking practices," "introducing into a practice elements of another" (Wenger 109). This work is assertive, as the broker must "press into service" an epistemic element that members likely treat with skepticism or perceive as harmful (109). Along with establishing relational amity through language of fullness rather than diminishment of her colleagues, Davis engages in other translation and coordination practices that emerge as set pieces in the filibuster. For example, Davis recenters the procedural and medical knowledge that SB 5 erases and distorts. The first section of the filibuster is a summary of the procedural malfeasance that negates a democratic vote for partisan maneuvering in an omnibus bill introduced in a special session. Using story as a gesture of unmasking, Davis tells the story of SB 5's arrival to the senate chamber to those who brought it there, reframing the narrative of SB 5 from legislation that protects women's health to failed legislation that died in the house (*Let Her Speak* 3) and was reborn through "narrow partisanship" (2). These procedural facts not only enact a civic literacy as they educate non-lawmakers on senate procedure, but they fundamentally diminish the warrants of the bill. Those warrants are diminished further by testimonies from state and national medical associations on the bill, ones she presses into service to show the political rather than medical motives for SB 5.

Her most consistent brokering involves expanding and shifting the epistemic frame of SB 5 with testimony from women against the bill. Although there are a range of topics covered in the dozens of testimonials, over and over again, Davis presses into service stories that feature intergenerational maternal knowledge. Three testimonies feature women who invoke the stories and experiences of their mothers as they argue against the bill. Davis's curation of them promotes a generational brokerage, as women connect their mother's experiences and knowledge with the bill on the senate floor. We see this in Davis's selection of the testimony of "Julie," who imagines what her deceased mother would think of SB 5. Julie opens her testimony by recounting her mother telling her that she had to get clearance from her husband in order for her doctor to be willing to prescribe birth control (*Let Her Speak* 38). Her mother saw a slow march to access to family planning options, and Julie is writing to defend the legacy of her mother's generation's struggle. She states that her mother would

> have been horrified to see . . . the influence of the religious right on reproductive rights. She'd also have tied that chipping away directly to the desire to have a permanent poverty class, a kind of economic slavery class and destruction of our economic safety. . . She would have said that people who are poor and kept from education wind up desperate. They take bad jobs because that's all there is. They find themselves trapped in marriages or pregnancies. The poverty class keeps itself locked in because there aren't policies in place to help. (*Let Her Speak* 39)

To voice a critique of SB 5, Julie references her mother as part of a long fight women have had to wage to achieve reproductive agency. Her mother's analysis is a kind of reproductive justice knowledge that sees the regulation of female fertility as part of a structure of "class" suppression that is linked to other kinds of oppression. Julie says "access is power" (39), arguing that legislators need to reduce abortions through sex education, accessible birth control options, a social safety net with "unions, workers' rights, fair wages, fair and ethical bank practices, health services, state-funded daycare services, insurance, and more" (39). Reproductive justice is premised on the idea that there is no single axis issue, like abortion; that while abortion appears to be a singular issue, it is connected to the rights to choose when and if to parent and to be able to parent in conditions that support human flourishing. Davis includes this testimony, which is artful but not unique. Rather, it is representative of an epistemic of reproductive agency that is linked to enduring class and gender struggles. Here Davis implicitly aligns those senators, like Lucio, who write legislation that helps to feed children in school, with feminist materialist critiques of structural poverty and sexism.

Julie ends her testimony by stating that she expects "all of those points to be rebuffed with anti-choice tropes about loving babies and loving women" (39), and then repeats the haunting phrase, "what a strange kind of love." Anticipating patronizing placation from the bill's authors, this discourse of "loving babies" is actually, Julie argues, a cloak for domination. The examples she provides of this "strange love" include promoting the purity myth, requiring that women bring unviable fetuses to term, and requiring mandatory vaginal ultrasounds, even for rape victims. Revealing the cruelty of SB 5 through these examples, Julie states, "But then it's not about love, is it? It's about economics and a perpetual poverty class and about keeping power from those that have the right to it" (39). Julie lifts the veil behind the stated goal, using her mother's phrasing, revealing the more sinister reality of reproductive restrictions: keeping women economically vulnerable and dependent. As feminist philosopher Mariana Ortega writes, "loving, knowing ignorance is not loving at all. . . . It is a mode of arrogant perception whose alleged aim is not simply to coerce or dominate or turn someone into what we want them to be, but to make knowledge claims that are supposed to further understanding of the object of perception" (61). Reproductive justice is premised on knowing the ways women's bodies have been disproportionately targeted by the state—targeting that is historically woven into other forms of injustice. Ross and Solinger argue that storytelling is a foundational part of building the knowledge and resources of reproductive justice—finding connections, common struggles, and points of privilege to use as levers for rights (59).

Davis selects the testimony of a woman named Lisa to serve as historical corrective to the many moments that white women have used their privilege to protect their interests rather than stay in solidarity with others. Lisa represents herself as post-menopausal, as someone who is beyond the scope of surveillance by the state, but who came to advocate for those still subject to this law. Lisa points out the glaring omission of SB 5, that "this vote requires a lifetime of commitment":

> Texas actually had legislation this past session concerning child-care for teen parents wanting to complete their high school education and referred to it as rewarding bad behavior. When is deciding to become a parent considered bad behavior? The legislature seems to want it both ways, not allowing the woman's human right to choose what happens to their bodies. Then when they decide to choose what these laws intend. They are not supported but shamed . . . (50)

By including Lisa's testimony, Davis is again highlighting the double bind SB 5 places women in. "Reproductive justice" as defined by SisterSong emphasizes the ethic of doing *with* rather than *to*—creating agency for women to make the families they want, not to run an obstacle course around laws that constrain agency. Lisa believes that women have the right to parent in the conditions that best support their notions of family and that material situations must be supportive for the flourishing of those lives.

Naming Epistemic Arrogance

Davis's reproductive justice brokering not only amplifies testimony that is silenced but also engages the silencers themselves to unmask and reframe their erroneous assumptions and strategies. The third strategy of the filibuster involves Davis's direct speech to these colleagues, specifically in her framing of the discourse of Senator Robert Deuell. Deuell is a physician and one of the thirty-one members of the Texas state senate. Throughout the filibuster, Deuell regularly interrupted Davis as she was reading testimony. His approach was to engage Davis in a series of broad questions that asked her to expand on her claims that SB 5 harmed women. His questions and replies reveal him as an interlocutor who is unwilling to comprehend the justice-oriented positions that Davis brings to the chamber in protest of the bill. In her work on epistemic oppression, Katie Dotson draws on the concept of "meta-blindness," an ableist term that nevertheless explains the condition of being unable to detect one's inability to understand certain ideas, positions, or concepts. People who isolate themselves in privileged "social imaginaries" without "epistemic friction" or diversity of standpoints and perspectives are prone to this type of overlooking and "situated ignorance" ("Tracking" 248). Without the propensity to actively search "for more alternatives than those noticed" and to engage those alternatives, one runs a high risk of fostering and maintaining ignorance ("Conceptualizing"). Dotson asserts that "this kind of insensitivity to the limits of one's instituted, social epistemology fosters and maintains poor epistemic habits, for example, epistemic laziness, closed-mindedness and epistemic arrogance" ("Conceptualizing"). This kind of arrogance, when paired with the ability to enshrine one's sexist and racist beliefs into laws, becomes dangerous Texas state policy delivered in an avuncular, placating, commonsensical style.

For example, having just heard Davis read the testimony of medical professionals and of Texas constituents like Julie, Lisa, and others, Deuell asks, "how are women being degraded in this bill?" (81), and "I was wondering what you found in this bill that holds any disregard for a woman facing the tough decision of whether or not to have an abortion?" (81). The presumption is Davis's unreasonableness and the common sense, transparent reasonableness of SB 5. There is a willfulness to Deuell's epistemic arrogance and lack of epistemic resilience; despite hearing statistics in Davis's earlier testimony on the overwhelming safety of medical and surgical abortion procedures, he asks: "Women, as you have pointed out by some of the testimony who are facing this tough decision, are very vulnerable. Do you, given what's happened in Philadelphia and Houston and some other abortion clinics in these squalid conditions, do you think, perhaps, that some of these vulnerable women should not have the state of Texas protect them by setting standards of care for their abortion?" (*Let Her Speak* 87). And when faced with the information that, of the forty-two clinics that serve women's reproductive needs in Texas, only five are ambulatory surgical centers (82) and that requiring those that are not to achieve that status would put thirty-seven of them out of business, he is unmoved. "[T]hey make a lot of money with these abortions" (91), he states, so "I don't see any reasons for these clinics to close" (91). At this point in the transcript, the warrants of Deuell's (and SB 5) include the following: women need protection; the state can do that better than current medical regulations; abortion clinics are often dangerous places; women are being respected through this regulatory process, as are the unborn; abortion is a highly profitable business. Despite being presented with evidence, Deuell refuses to acknowledge Davis's support and counterclaims. While the mark of successful brokering is alignment of information to provoke new knowledge and action, Davis is never able to achieve alignment from senators in this session.

Davis's two approaches to this epistemic arrogance necessitate attention, and both entail framing the narrative to reveal how a minority attempts to hold power. Deuell asked Davis: "You mentioned a raw abuse of power . . . we have a process here . . . how do you feel this bill is a raw abuse of power?" (84–85). Davis replied by stating the undemocratic nature of the procedure:

> The regular session worked to ensure a balance of those opinions, made its way into the bills that passed into law and those that did not. But after we adjourned we were called back by the governor, another single individual, and the Lieutenant Governor chose not to recognize the two-thirds rule as part of the way we would take up and consider legislation in the special session. I believe that when two individuals exercise power in that way, it abuses the power they have been entrusted with, because it denies the minority voices who are represented by Democratic senators on this floor an opportunity to be heard. (85)

Deuell stated that sixty percent of the senators wanted the bill passed, claiming that would "represent a majority of the people in Texas" (86). Davis rebutted that the polling showed otherwise: "you know as well as I do . . . about the consequences of a history of redistricting in the state of Texas" (86). While Deuell may have been unmoved by this unmasking, hundreds of thousands of observers of the filibuster were being educated on senate process and procedure, deciding for themselves if it was just. Over and again, Davis critiqued not only the procedure but the premise of the bill itself: on the claim that SB 5 makes women safer, Davis replies: "I believe that this nexus has not been demonstrated here . . . [and] that there are many women who will lose their access to care as a consequence of this law" (91).

Throughout this engagement, Davis and Deuell enact an epistemic stratification in which, like sedimentary rock, one belief system layers itself atop another without permeating the ones above or below it. But what appears to be a brokering failure might actually be the creation of another kind of brokering, that of the digital and physical presence of so many protesters and observers whose understandings were gaining dimension, and due to their presence, who assisted in new knowledge being developed and shared. Deuell's refusal to understand can be taken up by those who oppose his position as an invitation for others to absorb the exchange and the knowledge Davis brokered and, in the process, deepen their understanding of sexist refusals to know the material conditions surrounding women's reproductive lives. In undercutting powerholders' refusal to know, participants and observers learn how "rhetors respond to and recuperate the inherent limits of scenes of persuasion" (Swiencicki 152).

Later in the filibuster Davis uses another rhetorical tactic to frame the bill and reveal Deuell's epistemic arrogance. While direct questioning of each other yielded no movement, Davis ends deliberation and replaces Deuell's defense of the bill within the larger Republican strategy of restrictive abortion laws. She does this by reading Jordan Smith's 2011 article, "War on Women's Health." In this article, Smith meticulously outlines both how protections and earmarks through Title X require sources of revenue dedicated to women's health services as well as the success Deuell has had in stripping sixty-two million dollars from the family planning and reproductive health state budget. Smith calls this "The Deuell funding scheme," outlining exactly how he shifted ten million dollars of family planning money from Planned Parenthood to federally qualified health centers, "arguing that states should fund comprehensive medical providers" (122). Smith chronicles how this change overloads the healthcare system, where forty-one thousand fewer women were treated, impacting their ability to get well-women checkups, cancer screening, pap smears, and abortions (122). Deuell had inserted himself into the filibuster by asking questions, trying to assert his frame through a purported desire to know in which he simply repeated his own worldview without acknowledgement of the facts. Here Davis uses Smith's text to reposition Deuell's motives within a feminist epistemic frame: Smith showed how "the Deuell Rider" has reduced access to reproductive health services across the board as a sexist "allocation scheme" (123). By renaming such actions a "scheme" and connecting the dots from these actions to SB 5, Davis's brokering uses Smith's reporting to reveal how Deuell and the other authors of the bill care less about the health of women than exacting their ideological agenda. Davis's rhetorical framing moves beyond the audience of the Texas senate to millions who are livestreaming the filibuster, encouraging them to comprehend this entrenched commitment to ideology over medical facts, access, and women's health. Since white women and women of color continue to have unequal access to reproductive dignity and safety (Ross and Solinger 97), it is imperative to identify the rhetorical strategies such as the ones employed by Davis that make up brokering to use the tradition of rhetoric in the service of reproductive justice world-building.

Over the course of the thirteen hours at the podium, Senator Davis made original arguments directly to the authors of the bill, communicated the stories and arguments of the women and the medical professionals impacted by the bill, and leveraged the research and data on the veracity of the assumptions about the procedure that create an undue burden for Texas women. This is distributed cognition, in which all knowledge producers are thanked and given credit for their work. Davis helped to prevent the epistemic oppression of un-naming, where the women speakers were not only detached from their role in the production of knowledge, but focus was misdirected and misattributed (E. Davis 710). Solidarity in reproductive justice spaces is not meant to erase or abdicate one's own subject position and contributions; rather, the strategy of "redirection" of attention to the epistemic source (712) is a crucial rhetorical move to ensure there is no drift in ascribing ideas.

Conclusion: Rhetorical Brokering for Reproductive Justice

As the passage of SB 5 illustrates, even during the decades of protections that Roe offered, TRAP laws passed in state legislatures across the country, slowly eroding abortion access (Wilkinson). For example, according to the Texas ACLU, in 2021, 900,000 people of reproductive age lived 150 miles from a reproductive health clinic that provided abortion; only eight cities in the entire state had locations that provided abortion services. HB 5 and HB 2 have had a devastating impact on access, physician protocols, accurate information, and patient agency. The two-visit requirement before the abortion procedure, including the additional requirements of transvaginal ultrasound and mandatory fetal doppler (to capture heart audio), added psychic and economic costs to the procedure. And now, those TRAP laws have given way to a total abortion ban passed in Texas in July 2022, a permission structure created by the Supreme Court ruling, *Dobbs v. Jackson Women's Health Organization*, in June 2022. In Texas and across the country, reproductive justice activists remain consistently vigilant and creative as they protect what abortion access remains.

This pragmatic, material fight for resources is accompanied by a fight to unmask the language of benevolence, paternalism, and protection of women's standard of care. The distortions in warrants about gestational fetal age and viability and about the mortal danger of the abortion procedure and the impugning of medical practitioners who perform abortions must be confronted and replaced with sound data from leading medical associations, from clinics and their workers, and from women telling us what their lives require, demand, and aspire to. It is in this rhetorical space that reproductive justice brokers can do their work. Their multi-membership is a singular asset in the work of human rights. We certainly need outsiders and insiders. But we need those who can press into service the knowledge from one community to, in the case of SB 5, a community intent on passing mere dogma in legislative fiat. In the case of Davis, a senator and a reproductive rights activist, brokers can use genres—like filibusters—to shed light for those observing the brokerage on the erosion of democratic processes, of norms of deliberation, what counts as fact, and the silencing of lived experience.

Davis's case helps us see the creative use of available means, and what feminist invention can look like. My hope here is that we understand how differently positioned actors exert agency in their multi-membership in adjacent communities. So many examples of feminist brokering come to mind; Rickie Solinger's participation in the *Interrupted Life* exhibit is another example of an activist using genres (poster art, oral and written storytelling, grant writing) and her multi-membership to perform acts of public education "crucial to a real democracy and to offer a challenge to the prison industrial complex, a challenge that started inside its very walls" (Solinger 403). In the case of Davis, an examination of her filibuster transcript shows a masterful, exhaustive fight for women's lives. It could not do the work of fully stopping the TRAP law machine, or the loss of federal protections. But for all of us to do that work, in solidarity with the most vulnerable, we need reproductive justice activists to lift back the curtain. Davis gives legislators an opening, a chance to do better, and they don't. While constrained or/and vilified, Davis's strategies in the filibuster have replicable uptake. Many of us protest for reproductive justice in streets and capitals. More frequently we are invited to look for the moments of feminist invention, moments in our community when we can serve as brokers and use our role and tools to press into service the stories and knowledge from experts and vulnerable groups into the scene of persuasion.

Works Cited

ACLU Texas. "Abortion in Texas." *ACLU Texas,* 10 Dec. 2021, aclutx.org/en/know-your-rights/abortion-texas. Accessed 7 June 2022.

Bawarshi, Anis. *Genre and the Invention of the Writer: Reconsidering the Place of Invention in Composition*. Utah State UP, 2003.

Chávez, Karma R. "The Body: An Abstract and Actual Rhetorical Concept." *Rhetoric Society Quarterly*, vol. 48, no. 3, 2018, pp. 242–50.

Cloud, Dana L. "Feminist Body Rhetoric in the #Unrulymob: Texas, 2013." *Unruly Rhetorics: Protest, Persuasion, and Publics*. Eds. Jonathan Alexander, Susan C. Jarratt, and Nancy Welch, Pittsburgh P, 2018, pp. 27–44.

Corrigan, Lisa M., and Skye de St. Felix. "A New Doll in Texas: A Feminist Media Analysis of Senator Wendy Davis's Rhetorical Framing as 'Abortion Barbie.'" *Feminist Media Studies*, vol. 22, no. 7, 2022, pp. 1602-1619.

Davis, Emmalon. "On Epistemic Appropriation." *Ethics*, vol. 128, no. 4, 2018, pp. 702–27.

Dotson, Kristie. "Conceptualizing Epistemic Oppression." *Social Epistemology*, vol. 28, no. 2, 2014, pp. 115–38.

—. "Tracking Epistemic Violence: Tracking Practices of Silencing." *Hypatia*, vol. 26, no. 2, 2011, pp. 236–57.

Flynn, Elizabeth, Patricia Sotirin, and Ann Brady, editors. "Introduction." *Feminist Rhetorical Resilience*. Utah State UP, 2012, pp. 1–29.

Harp, Dustin, Jaime Loke, and Ingrid Bachman. "The Spectacle of Politics: Wendy Davis, Abortion, and Pink Shoes in the Texas 'Fillybuster.'" *Journal of Gender Studies*, vol. 26, no. 2, 2017, pp. 227–39.

Hegar, Glenn, et al. TX 2013-SB5. "Relating to the Regulation of Abortion Procedures, Providers, and Facilities; Providing Penalties." 83rd legislature, 1st special session.

Jentleson, Adam. *Kill Switch: The Rise of the Modern Senate and the Crippling of American Democracy*. Norton, 2021.

Koliba, Christopher J., Jack W. Meek, Asim Zia, and Russell W. Mills. *Governance Networks in Public Administration and Policy*. 2nd ed. Taylor and Francis, 2018, pp. 210–11.

Let Her Speak: Transcript of Texas State Senator Wendy Davis's June 25, 2013, Filibuster of the Texas State Senate. Counterpath, 2013.

Mohanty, Talpade Chandra. *Feminism without Borders: Decolonizing Theory, Practicing Solidarity*. Duke UP, 2003.

Ortega, Mariana. "Being Lovingly, Knowingly Ignorant: White Feminism and Women of Color." *Hypatia*, vol. 21, no. 3, 2006, pp. 56–74.

"Reproductive Justice." SisterSong Women of Color Reproductive Justice Collective. www.sistersong.net/reproductive-justice.

Ross, Loretta, "What is Reproductive Justice?" *Reproductive Justice Briefing Book: A Primer on Reproductive Justice and Social Change*. Civil Liberties and Public Policy Institute. www.law.berkeley.edu/php-programs/courses/fileDL.php?fID=4051.

Ross, Loretta and Rickie Solinger. *Reproductive Justice: An Introduction*. U of California P, 2017.

Rowe, Aimee Carillo. *Power Lines: On the Subject of Feminist Alliances*. Duke UP, 2008.

Silliman, Jael, Marlene Gerber Fried, Loretta Ross, and Elena R. Gutierrez, eds. *Undivided Rights: Women of Color Organizing for Reproductive Justice*. Haymarket, 2016.

Smith, Jordan. "The War on Women's Health." *The Austin Chronicle*, 22 April 2011.www.austinchronicle.com/news/2011–04–22/the-war-on-womens-health/. Accessed 4 Apr. 2022.

Solinger, Rickie. "Making Art for Reproductive Justice." *Radical Reproductive Justice: Foundation, Theory, Practice, Critique,* edited by Loretta J. Ross, Lynn Roberts, Erika Derkas, Whitney Peoples, and Pamela Bridgewater Toure. Feminist P, 2017, pp. 397–403.

Stenberg, Shari J., and Charlotte Hogg. "Introduction: Gathering Women's Rhetorics for the Twenty-First Century." *Persuasive Acts: Women's Rhetorics in the Twenty-First Century*. U of Pittsburgh P, 2018, pp. 3–22.

Stevenson, Amanda Jean. "Finding the *Twitter* Users Who Stood with Wendy." *Contraception*, vol. 90, no. 5, 2014, pp. 502–07.

Swiencicki, Jill. "Rhetorics of Invitation and Refusal in Terry Tempest Williams's *The Open Space of Democracy*." *Women's Studies in Communication*, vol. 38, no. 2, 2015, pp. 151–66.

Vaz, Kim Marie and Gary L. Lemons. "'If I Call You, Will You Come?' From Public Lectures to Testament for Feminist Solidarity." *Feminist Solidarity at the Crossroads: Intersectional Women's Studies for Transracial Alliance.* Ed. Kim Marie Vaz and Gary L. Lemons. Routledge, 2012, pp. 1–14.

Wardle, Elizabeth. "Identity, Authority, and Learning to Write in New Workplaces." *Enculturation*, vol. 5, no. 2, 2004. www.enculturation.net/5_2/pdf/wardle.pdf. Accessed 4 April 2022.

Wenger, Etienne. *Communities of Practice: Learning, Meaning and Identity.* Cambridge UP, 1999.

Wilkinson, Barbara B., Chiamaka Onwuzurike, and Deborah Bartz. "Restrictive State Abortion Bans—A Reproductive Injustice." *The New England Journal of Medicine*, vol. 386, no. 13, 2022, pp. 1197–99.

Williams, Susan H. "Feminist Legal Epistemology." *Berkeley Women's Law Journal*, vol. 63, 1993, pp. 63–105.

Rhetorics of Practice

6 Advancing Black Women's Maternal Health Using Black Rhetorical Action: Addressing Systemic Racialized Maternal Abuse

Adele N. Nichols

On April 12, 2016, Kira Dixon Johnson and her husband Charles Johnson went to Cedars-Sinai Medical Center for Kira's scheduled cesarean section (United States Congress, *Testimony* 3). Instead of celebrating the birth of her second son, Langston, Kira needlessly died eleven hours postpartum due to substandard maternal care by clinicians (3). Kira's life did not have to end this way. It should *not* have ended this way. When Charles told a staff member that Kira had blood in her catheter, a CT scan was ordered to be completed immediately; however, the CT scan was not performed, and for ten hours, she lay in bed in pain (3). For ten hours Kira's symptoms worsened, yet medical staff told her that her issues did not have precedence over those of other patients (3). For ten hours, Charles listened as Kira repeatedly told him, "Charles, I'm so cold; Charles, I don't feel right" (3). When Kira was finally taken to surgery, there was not one, not two, but three liters of blood in her abdomen (4). The maternal care Kira received was not only delayed but also physically and verbally abusive because her nurse's words were used to physically withhold treatment.

Kira's maternal death is a cautionary tale of what can go wrong medically when a Black[1] woman experiences a blatant display of racism. Since

1. "Black" and "White" have been capitalized when referring to Black women, White women, or White clinicians to differentiate between the colors black and white and the social grouping of Black and White persons. The term Black is inclusive of all Black women, not only those who are American, and the term White specifically refers to persons of European descent who have historically

Kira's death, national attention has focused on the issue of Black maternal death (e.g., Villarosa). Charles has made it his priority never to let Kira's life, story, or name be forgotten. Due to his diligence, the Preventing Maternal Deaths Act of 2018 was signed into law "to save and sustain the health of mothers during pregnancy, childbirth, and in the postpartum period, to eliminate disparities in maternal health outcomes for pregnancy-related and pregnancy associated deaths, to identify solutions to improve health care quality and health outcomes for mothers, and for other purposes" (United States Congress, "Preventing"). While the premise of this law is significant because the policy addresses the present-day problem of Black maternal health and requires solutions to be created to reduce the issue, the law is deficient because it neither addresses systemic occurrences of Black women receiving adverse maternal care nor their connection to current maternal care practice. My use of "systemic" in this chapter references practices that are deeply rooted and widespread in society, and thus are ingrained. For instance, in 1973, after Shirley Brown separated from her husband and became eligible for Medicaid, she experienced verbal abuse when Dr. Pierce, her physician, threatened to have her discharged from the hospital after delivering her third child if she refused to comply with his sterilization policy (Kluchin 162). During the nineteenth century, an unnamed enslaved Black woman was ignored similarly to Kira when she attempted to tell the doctor she was experiencing pregnancy symptoms (Schwartz 131). The doctor dismissed her concerns, and it was not until she went into labor that the doctor claimed he was confused because the woman's symptoms resembled a disease rather than pregnancy symptoms (131). Both Shirley's and the unnamed Black women's maternal care experiences are comparable to Kira's experience. All three women are intergenerationally linked through being denied maternal care services due to clinicians' racialized notions about Black women. Dr. Pierce believed that Black women like Shirley needed to be controlled through sterilization because of their reliance on governmental services, the unnamed Black woman's physician thought that she was too ignorant to know the cause of her symptoms because of her

---

been granted access to social power and privilege. Also, for simplicity and consistency, the word "Black" will be used to describe any Black woman notwithstanding the century she was born. For instance, rather than referring to a Black woman from the nineteenth century as negro and a Black woman from the twentieth century as Afro-American, the term Black or Black woman is used throughout.

race, and Kira's clinician believed that as a Black woman, Kira did not need medical intervention. These examples depict Black women's intergenerational experience of receiving racialized and abusive maternal care by clinicians, which, as these stories demonstrate, is long-standing.

While these experiences are described by scholars like Dána-Ain Davis as "medical racism" when discussing the impact of racism on clinicians' current medical treatment of Black women and maternal outcomes, it is crucial to introduce an alternative term that represents Black women's lived experiences: systemic racialized maternal abuse (SRMA) (202). Because medical racism can happen to any person of color and occurs in all areas of healthcare, there needs to be a distinct term that explains Black women's unique maternal care experience. SRMA highlights how Black women, like Kira, Shirley, and the unnamed Black woman, receive maternal care (prenatal, labor, birth, postpartum) that is physically and/or non-physically violent because of intergenerational negative words or thoughts that are ingrained in society. This violence involves identifying, defining, or describing Black women in ways they did not recognize, explain, or label themselves, such as the idea of Black women as strong, fertile, and angry (Hinson et al. 5). Essentially, SRMA focuses on how racialized ideology, as the root of SRMA, turns into abuse; this premise is what sets SRMA apart from medical racism.

The term SRMA relies on the African rhetorical concept of *Nommo*, where "the generative power of the spoken word" is utilized to accurately *name* Black women's maternal care experiences (Hamlet 27). In short, "Nommo was believed necessary to actualize life and give man mastery over things" (27). In light of the 2022 *Dobbs v. Jackson's Women's Health Organization* decision to rescind the federal right to an abortion, naming SRMA becomes even more paramount. Without accurate terminology to describe the phenomena of SRMA, there cannot be an understanding of how revoking the right to abortion has ramifications beyond abortion care for Black women that stems back to the nineteenth and twentieth centuries where Black women were bred by slave owners and were sterilized against their will or without their knowledge. In the present, the outcome of the *Dobbs* decision will continue to negatively compound Black women's ability to receive adequate maternal care and/or further negatively impact their maternal outcome (Declercq et al.)

Thus, if SRMA cannot be adequately named, the consequence is that the root of it cannot be addressed, and the systemic racialized maternal abuse against Black women will continue to occur at the hands of clinicians sworn to serve, sworn to care, sworn to heal. It should be noted, however, that while this chapter focuses primarily on the interactions between clinicians (doctors and nurses) and SRMA, there are other stakeholders, for example, the government and policymakers, involved in the racialized, violent mistreatment of Black women as evidenced by the *Dobbs* case. Consequently, SRMA needs addressing immediately since it is an exigence: "a defect, an obstacle, something waiting to be done, a thing which is other than it should be" (Bitzer 6). Because SRMA has been described and named, readers will be able to understand how twenty-first century Black women experience the same racialized maternal abuse Black women experienced in the nineteenth and twentieth centuries due to twenty-first century clinicians' acceptance and use of nineteenth- and twentieth-centuries racialized ideas about Black women. Thus, I begin by illustrating why SRMA needs to be addressed now and how change can transpire with a brief history of nineteenth and twentieth century racialized beliefs and the ways they are intergenerationally linked to twenty-first century racialized ideas. After proving how systemic racialized ideas manifested as systemic racialized maternal abuse, I demonstrate how the current discourse of systemic racialized ideas is a social, cultural, and rhetorical issue that can be addressed. Lastly, drawing on what Jonathan Alexander and Susan C. Jarratt refer to as "unruly rhetoric," I articulate my recommendations for addressing SRMA using a socioecological model so that I, a Black woman, can intentionally enter a space where Black voices "nee[d] to be heard" to change a dialogue "in which [Black women's] voice is either actively elided or not yet legible" for the sole purpose of disrupting the current system of SRMA that is harming Black women (13–14).

Nineteenth Century and Twentieth Century Racialized Ideas

In the early nineteenth century, it was common for enslavers not to utilize the services of physicians during childbirth because birthing was believed to be a natural process that did not necessitate a physician's assistance (Schwartz 144). This position on childbirth slowly changed, and physicians in the North and South began to be enlisted to speed up the childbirth process and to help lower the high maternal and infant mortality rate when childbirth complications arose (144). Despite this, enslaved Black women did not always have physicians available to assist in childbirth because of the racialized idea that "female slaves got so much exercise in their field work they 'were not subject to the difficulty, danger and pain which attended women of the better classes in giving birth to their offspring'" (qtd. in D. White 111). When it came to cesarean sections, physicians thought Black women were more robust in comparison to White women and had less chance of dying following the dangerous procedure of a cesarean (Wolf 585).

Because it was believed socially that Black women had easier births due to "a higher pain threshold," any "suffering" experienced in childbirth was by White women (Schwartz 167). This negligence by enslavers considerably impacted Black women's childbirth experience (167). When Black women did receive care from a physician, it was up to the discretion of White enslavers to decide the type of care they received since they were considered property (144). This means Black women could not communicate their health needs, such as if they wanted a procedure done or not. One glaring example of this occurring is between Dr. J. Marion Sims, who is known as the founder or father of modern gynecology; three enslaved Black women, Anarcha, Lucy, and Betsey; and their slave owners. When each of these three women experienced the postpartum complication vesicovaginal fistula, Dr. Sims contacted Mr. Westcott, Anarcha's owner; Mr. Zimmerman, Lucy's owner; and Dr. Harris, Betsey's owner, for permission to provide "treatment" to them (Simms 227–29). In 1845, once Dr. Sims had all three of his subjects to experiment on, he decided how he wanted to proceed with fixing their fistulas through experimentation and the use of various objects, such as a pewter spoon that led to his invention of the speculum (234–35).

At the time when Dr. Sims began his experimentations, anesthesia was not available; nevertheless, he went ahead with attempting to fix Lucy, Betsey, and Anarcha's fistulas. Lucy's procedure was first, which he described as a "tedious and difficult" procedure (237). In spite of this acknowledgment, Dr. Sims claimed Lucy "bore the operation with great heroism and bravery" despite the pain she endured and sickness that followed the insertion of a "little piece of sponge into the neck of the bladder" (237–38). Lucy's pain was so great he thought she would die, yet after realizing he fixed the fistula, he was not deterred from continuing his experimentations on Betsey and Anarcha (238). Dr. Sims did not successfully complete his experiments until four years later in May or June of 1849; this means that for four years all three women, along with other unnamed enslaved women, had to endure numerous, painful experiments until he was satisfied with the results (246). Ultimately, the nineteenth century set the tone for how enslaved Black women would continue to be racialized and adversely treated in the twentieth century.

In the subsequent century, the belief that Black women were able not to feel pain, could endure lengthier labors with fortitude, and could start labor without the assistance of a physician, as well as the belief that they were socially and morally lower than White persons, persisted along with other racializations (Levy and Mayer 418–19). For instance, it was believed that Black women were more apt to give birth prematurely because they had a "higher incidence of syphilis," they gave birth to babies weighing less than White babies did, and they had a lower incidence for birth injuries since their babies were smaller (419). It was also believed that Black women did not seek medical attention until it was nearly too late, that physicians found Black patients to be uncooperative due to incomprehension, and that patients did not, or could not, follow the suggested treatment plan because of their low economic status (419). One distinguishing aspect of twentieth century racialized ideas that carried over from the nineteenth century is that Black women's low economic status and low intelligence was the cause of their poor maternal health. During this time period, according to Rebecca M. Kluchin, some Black mothers were sterilized because they were poor and gave birth out of wedlock, which was the evidence "social workers, physicians, and members of state eugenics boards" needed to support their stereotype of Black women as "idiotic" (92). To further justify racialized beliefs, those in power created racist policies, strategies, and initiatives to control Black women's reproduction since they were thought unsuitable for childbirth (92).

Twenty-First Century Racialized Ideas

As the twentieth century ended, global rates for Black women's maternal outcomes continued to decline between 2000 and 2013 with the United States ranking "second worst in [high Black] maternal mortality among thirty-one Organisation for Economic Cooperation and Development nations" (Owens and Fett 1343). When comparing death associated with pregnancy rates between American Black and White women, Black women were "three to four times" more likely to die than White women (1343). In addition, in my own research I found that twenty-first century clinicians' attitudes and behaviors have been—and are—the same as those of clinicians in previous centuries who believed that Black women did not need attentive maternal care (Harmata) or that Black women did not need postpartum care to prevent complications (Waldman). I also found ongoing perceptions: Black women can give birth without support from a clinician, a partner, or a doula; they do not need medical interventions; and they do not feel pain while giving birth (Garcia). Because some clinicians believe Black women do not feel pain, they believe Black women do not need pain medicine (Cullors). Similarly, maternal care does not need to be discussed with Black women (Cullors). Too often, if a Black woman tries to communicate about her pain, she is ignored by her clinician (Cullors). Even the idea that Black women cannot understand medical procedures is a twentieth century belief that still reigns in healthcare (Cullors). Far too often, when a Black woman expresses concern about her health, she is ignored and/or dismissed, so medical interventions are delayed when clinicians do not believe Black women when they say they have health concerns (Haskell).

Systemic Racialized Ideas to Systemic Racialized Maternal Abuse

Again, the distinguishing factor of SRMA from medical racism is the act of abuse, defined as the repeated course of action a clinician, who has "power and control," uses against Black women to create an environment that induces physical, verbal, psychological, and/or financial abuse (Reach Team). Black women experience this when receiving maternal care that impacts the quality of their health and healthcare because of institutionalized practices based on racialized ideas. When SRMA occurs, it happens simultaneously rather than in isolation. A Black woman, for example, may experience both financial and psychological abuse or dismissive medical professionals and postpartum complications rather than only financial or psychological abuse. While Deirdre Cooper Owens's scholarship explains the history of medical racism and Davis's work focuses on contemporary medical racism with a focus on pregnancy and premature birth, I build on these works by demonstrating how Black women have been experiencing SRMA since the nineteenth century and still are presently through acts of racialized ideologies and beliefs that create a web of violence. SRMA draws from the rhetorical understanding that actions and consequences are part of racialized ways of thinking, communicating (verbally and non-verbally), feeling, acting, and being.

Through reading multiple stories and thinking about racialized maternal violence against Black women across generations, and in broad rhetorical ways, I use SRMA as a tool that urges clinicians to advocate and work as activists for the systemic end to racialized violence.

In order to understand the complexity of Black women's various standpoints and multiple levels of discrimination when experiencing exacerbated maternal health outcomes due to systemic racialized maternal abuse, Womanism and intersectionality are appropriate feminist perspectives to utilize. Womanism values the voices of Black women who have a plethora of common experiences and thoughts on what it is like to live as a Black woman in America where they are routinely disparaged (Banks-Wallace 34). It is through sharing these experiences that Black women's standpoints can be developed and more fully understood. In much the same way, intersectionality works as a supplement to Womanism that resists analyzing Black women's discrimination experiences as exclusively race, gender, or class issues but instead as race and gender and class issues (or any other identities a Black woman may have) that all negatively influence their lives (Keane 182). Accordingly, this central idea of racialized violence against Black pregnant women will be more fully understood when viewing their experience as multilayered rather than singular. In the following stories, I not only highlight the different types of SRMA but how these women experience SRMA due to their various identities.

Amber Rose Isaac

In April 2020, Amber Rose Isaac, a Black and Puerto Rican woman, died after giving birth to her son Elias (Harmata). Although Amber initially detected "that her platelet levels had been decreasing since February," because of the COVID-19 pandemic, she could not see her doctor in person despite being in the third trimester (Harmata). Amber advocated for herself by calling "her doctors at the Montefiore Medical Center in the Bronx" to alert them about her low platelet levels, but her doctor "ignored her" (Harmata). By the end of April, Amber was admitted to Montefiore and diagnosed with HELLP syndrome, "a pregnancy-related complication that can be fatal if left untreated, according to Healthline" (Harmata). Because of Amber's concerns about her low platelet levels being ignored, she was not provided quality maternal care. Amber, dissatisfied with the care she received, expressed her frustrations on *Twitter*: She couldn't "'wait to write a tell all about my experience during my last two trimesters dealing with incompetent doctors at Montefiore'" (qtd. in Harmata). Following Amber's death, her partner, Brian McIntyre III, stated that if she had been White, more attention would have been paid to her concerns (Harmata). What Brian was articulating here is that due to Amber's race and her lowered social standing as a Black and Hispanic woman, he believes her health needs were not addressed with the same urgency and attention they would have been if Amber was a White woman with a higher social status.

According to bell hooks, "[a]s far back as slavery, white people established a social hierarchy based on race and sex that ranked white men first, white women second, though sometimes equal to black men, who are ranked third, and black women last" (52). Thus, it can be argued that Amber's doctor did not see her as a woman in need of assistance but rather as a trope, a Black woman with superhuman strength who did not need medical interventions due to intergenerational racialized beliefs about race and social status. Although "the underlying causes behind the interaction between [Amber] and her [doctor] cannot be confirmed" (Davis 51), one thing can be:

> [T]he fact that she [and Brian] thought racism played a role draws . . . attention to the overall stressors faced by Black women in a society where bias—while not always observable—is indeed an ever-present possibility in the context of a medical structure that has historically failed to fully embrace caring for Black women. (51)

And it is the "medical structure" that Davis references that cost Amber her life. Amber's doctor refusing to listen—and address—her concerns about low platelet levels caused physical abuse to her body since she died due to lack of treatment.

Serena Williams

When Serena Williams gave birth to her daughter Olympia in 2017, she experienced SRMA despite the fact she was a wealthy and famous athlete (Williams). Even though Serena has a higher social status than the typical Black woman who is not famous or wealthy, she still could not escape her status as a Black woman because "[m]ost Americans, and that includes black people, acknowledge and accept this hierarchy; they have internalized it either consciously or unconsciously" (hooks 52). Because Serena is Black, it was easier for her to be dismissed by her nurse as being confused when she tried to tell her that "she needed a CT scan with contrast and IV heparin (a blood thinner)" (Haskell). Serena's nurse's dismissal is an illustration of how "[m]edical racism also includes the sometimes subtle and sometimes not-so-subtle ways in which the medical complex . . . cumulatively dismisses, misdiagnoses, and undermines women's feelings and intuitions about their reproducing bodies and . . . disproportionately undermines Black women's reproduction" (Davis xv). This observation is significant because it is within this bubble of racism that the violent, destructive nature of SRMA hurts and destroys not only poor, financially challenged, working class, or uneducated Black women but also any woman who is Black.

Davis reiterates this point by claiming "[t]o believe that one's educational attainment and insurance coverage will serve as a protective mechanism against adverse birth outcomes in an anti-Black society is ideological pablum and offers a false sense of security" (201). If you are a Black woman, you are a target (susceptible to experiencing SRMA) regardless of education, money, or status. Period. This factor is also evidenced in Kira's case: Her mother-in-law was famed Judge Glenda Hatchett, who "spoke four languages, lived in China and had run several companies," yet Kira still experienced SRMA (United States Congress, Testimony 2). Similarly, Serena's dismissal by the nurse was a form of physical and verbal abuse because the nurse, in a position of power, misused her authority to verbally refuse Serena the care she needed while simultaneously withholding lifesaving care that directly impacted the health of her body (Haskell). It was not until Serena advocated for herself again that she received a CT scan, which revealed she had blood clots and not that she was confused because she just had surgery (Haskell). Serena relentlessly advocating for herself is part of the "negotiating interactions to achieve better care" that Davis claims is the result of Black persons knowing "the consequences of being Black in Medicaid spaces—being dismissed, not being taken seriously, suffering mistreatment, and being misdiagnosed" (69). What happened to Serena would be an example of what Davis terms as a "diagnostic lapse" (the "outcome of medical racism in which professionals make or neglect to make medical decisions, thus exacerbating the vulnerabilities of a racially or ethnically marginalized group") but I would describe it as SRMA (203). Serena's story is more than a diagnostic lapse because of the ingrained racializations in nursing, in healthcare, and in this country that often results not only in Black women being more vulnerable due to racism but in them experiencing physical, verbal, and emotional abuse because of their acceptance of racist racialized ideologies.

Dacheca Fleurimond

Additionally, the geographical and physical location a Black woman receives maternal care can positively or negatively affect the trajectory of her maternal outcome. For Dacheca Fleurimond, the maternal outcome she experienced at a Brooklyn hospital, SUNY Downside, was deadly after a series of three events. First, when going to visit her sons in the neonatal intensive care unit (NICU), Dacheca's compression boots, which lose effect after fifteen minutes, were removed for approximately ninety minutes (Waldman). Second, three anonymous employees stated that she waited at minimum forty minutes before she was returned to her room after the NICU visit (Waldman). And third, there was no record of her being checked on once she was back in her room (Waldman). While an autopsy report revealed that she died from a pulmonary embolism, or "a condition that almost always has a chance of being prevented," it did not reveal that the day after giving birth to twins via cesarean section, she experienced physical and financial abuse that contributed to her adverse birth outcome (Waldman). As evidenced by Dacheca's experience, financial abuse can be a consequence of how a hospital where a woman gives birth can physically harm her life when money that can be utilized to save Black lives is not. As it turns out, it is not uncommon for hospitals that are part of the medical-industrial complex to make decisions based on the amount of money they can make rather caring about their patients (Davis 51). It can, therefore, be argued that the hospital administrators' decision not to use preventive care is financially abusive because resources like heparin are readily available for use but are not used because of racialized beliefs that Black women are lower socially and they do not need lifesaving medical interventions due them since they are biologically robust.

Because of these socially accepted myths, it appears that Dacheca received neglectful postpartum treatment when clinicians neither put her compression boots back on nor gave her heparin, "a blood-thinning medicine used at other hospitals to prevent pulmonary embolism in mothers with high risk factors, for whom compression boots are unlikely to be enough" (Waldman). Dr. Alexander Friedman, an assistant professor of obstetrics and gynecology at Columbia University Medical Center, admits, "There are some experts who feel that it's not worth the time, trouble and cost to avoid relatively rare events" (Waldman). Such rationalizations of these acts of neglect that are physically and financially abusive, and serve as examples of SRMA, contribute to why SRMA keeps occurring to Black women like Dacheca (Waldman). At Maimonides Medical Center, another Brooklyn hospital near where Dacheca gave birth, there are more White patients than there are Black patients and a reduced "complication rate related to hemorrhages" (Waldman). At this hospital, almost all mothers who give birth via cesarean section or have other risk factors are given blood thinners—a stark difference in the medical treatment Dacheca received at SUNY Downside (Waldman). For example, at Brookdale University Hospital Medical Center, Kings County Hospital, and SUNY Downside "more than half of mothers who hemorrhaged during delivery experienced complications" (Waldman). The New York City Department of Health and Mental Hygiene mapped the areas in Brooklyn that showed where the most maternal harm occurs, and the areas in Brooklyn where gentrification had not occurred, "mothers face[d] up to four times the complication rates of neighborhoods just a few subway stops away" (Waldman).

Tammy Jackson

Another group of women in the twenty-first century who experience SRMA are Black women who are considered unfit for mothering/childbearing due to their imprisoned status. The number of Black women who fall under this category is significant with ninety-two Black women out of 100,000 imprisoned in contrast to forty-nine White women out of 100,000 in 2017 (The Sentencing Project 2). Tammy Jackson was imprisoned at Broward County Jail when she gave birth to her baby girl, Miranda, when she experienced the effects of physical and psychological abuse due to SRMA (Perez). Although Tammy repeatedly called for assistance from her isolated jail cell in Florida, no one came; instead, "She was forced to crouch down and just catch the baby." Altogether, it took seven hours for Tammy to give birth, which meant she went "seven hours without medication or seeing a doctor" (Garcia). Her status as an imprisoned Black woman demonstrates not just the complexities of gendered racism but the violence that SRMA causes.[2] This is reminiscent of the

2. In October 2020, a little over a year after Tammy's ordeal in the Florida jail, Tammy died. In June 2020, before her death, the Tammy Jackson Act was enacted. The act mandates that pregnant inmates in labor must be taken to a hospital (Perez). Even though Tammy is no longer physically here, her horrify-

way enslaved Black women gave birth with no assistance from clinicians (Garcia). hooks details this ordeal by stating how African women, who were pregnant before they were taken by force and sold as slaves, "were forced to endure pregnancy without any care given to their diet, without any exercise, and without any assistance during the labor" (18). This way of giving birth was in direct opposition to what African women were used to, for "[i]n their own communities African women had been accustomed to much pampering and care during pregnancy, so the barbaric nature of childbearing on the slave ship was both physically harmful and psychologically demoralizing" (18). Similarly, the way Tammy was barbarically forced to give birth in a jail cell is equivalent to the same way African women, pregnant and non-pregnant, were squeezed into a compartment of sixteen by eighteen feet" upon the slave ship Pongas (18). Tammy's birthing experience unfortunately is not unique as her experience echoes what other Black women like Amber, Serena, and Dacheca have experienced through "condescension, lack of consent, and adverse birth outcomes [that] amount[s] to a form of gender-specific violence" like SRMA (Davis 94).

Patrisse Cullors

Patrisse Cullors, co-founder of the Black Lives Matter movement, is yet another contemporary example of a Black woman experiencing SRMA. Prior to her cesarean section, she was not informed about the procedure (Cullors). To rectify this, before her cesarean section began, Patrisse mentioned to her surgeon, who was White, that the procedure was not discussed (Cullors). His response was "What do you need to know?" in a manner that implied Patresse was "dumb for not knowing or too dumb to comprehend what the procedure would involve" (Cullors). It may have been that the doctor did in fact believe Patrisse was not able to comprehend what her procedure involved due to racializations about Black women's intellect, or it could have been that Patrisse questioning him made her appear disagreeable like women were racialized to be in the twentieth century (Cullors). Regardless of the motivation for her doctor's actions, there is an explanation for him, and other clinicians, "dismiss[ing] the signs, disclosures of fear, sense of endangerment, and knowledge of a woman who is [rightfully] concerned about her health" status (Davis 109). As Davis explains:

---

ing birthing experience paved the way for other women to receive the dignity of birthing in a hospital.

> Racial science, medical racism, ideologies of pathology, and hardiness have been marshaled in ways that mark Black women as both flawed and superhuman. On the one hand, hardiness positions Black bodies as flawed because the "strength" possessed does not register as human, and Black nonconformity is almost always in need of intervention—usually in the form of policing. Simultaneously, the idea that Blacks are impervious to pain enables diagnostic lapses. (100)

Another explanation for Patrisse not receiving the necessary information about her procedure is simply because "blacks are assumed to be more ignorant than whites, they get less by way of explanation of what is happening to them" (qtd. in Davis 51). Patrisse's doctor's failure to provide her with informed consent is a form of psychological and verbal abuse because of the withholding of pertinent information regarding a surgical procedure, which probably caused her more apprehension. Additionally, Patrisse suffered physical abuse from delivering her child by cesarean section while undermedicated (Cullors). Patrisse's account of her cesarean is harrowing:

> I stayed in the hospital for four days after my C-section. Four days of being in excruciating pain because they had under-medicated me. Four days of my mother begging the nurses and doctors to pay attention to me and bring me some much-needed relief, because these doctors like the "Father of Modern Gynecology" before them believed on some level that Black women don't experience as much pain as White women. (Cullors)

The abuse Patrisse experienced due to racializations by White clinicians should be unfathomable and unimaginable, but it is not because it continues to happen repeatedly.

Patrisse's experience, Black women's experience, is a nightmare—one that needs to be identified, named, and comprehended as a pattern of systemic racialized maternal abuse against Black women. The idea that some clinicians believe Black people do not feel pain due to their perceived "endurance," "durability," "hardiness," or even "expendability" morphs into "the justification for forcing [Black] women to withstand pain while at the same time placing them in the position of being violated" again and again (qtd. in Davis 190). Evidence of this pattern is supported in a study that found White medical students and residents "believed incorrect and sometimes 'fantastical' biological fallacies about racial differences in patients," such as that "blacks have less-sensitive nerve endings than whites, that black people's blood coagulates more quickly and that black skin is thicker than white" (Villarosa). Moreover, when it comes to "pain management by medical professionals," it has been revealed that patients who are not White have a smaller chance of having their pain managed, whereas women who are White have a greater chance of being given an epidural when they are in labor compared to "other racial and ethnic groups, due to perceived fragility" (Davis 190). Ultimately, Patrisse's story explains the basis for clinicians' abuse while reinforcing SRMA as a violent occurrence that is rooted in racialized beliefs/ideas about Black women and jeopardizes their maternal care.

The Need for a Socioecological Model to Address Systemic Racialized Maternal Abuse

As a Black woman who has given birth not once, not twice, but three times to Black babies and has experienced SRMA, I *cannot* be silent on this issue of abuse. Hence, this chapter serves as a call to action for clinicians to address SRMA using a socioecological model, defined by Franklin White as "an analytical framework, by which intervention strategies may be designed, implemented, monitored, and evaluated" (107). Another definition of a socioecological model is an interconnected circle of social factors that are analyzed in order to understand how those social factors "put [people] at risk for violence" or can defend [people] from encountering brutality ("The Social-Ecological Model"). Accordingly, I propose using a socioecological model as an intervention strategy to address four social factors—individual, relationship, policy, and systemic—that impact clinicians' education, training, and practice in order to deliver maternal care that is not systemically abusive (see fig. 1). The primary advantage of a socioecological model is the ability to use it to examine how deeply related the factors are and how negatively and positively these factors can affect health outcomes (F. White 107). A secondary advantage is its fluidity to be applied not only to clinicians but to any stakeholder involved in providing maternal care to Black women whether directly or indirectly.

A last advantage of using a socioecological model to address SRMA, or the racist, abusive behaviors of clinicians, is it will push clinicians who have yet to internally "deal with the issue of racism" and the abusive conduct that ensues because of it (Davis 204). Owens and Sharla M. Fett further expound on a point made by Davis:

> as reproductive justice groups such as the Black Mamas Matter Alliance point out, expecting and new Black mothers often find their self-reports of painful symptoms overlooked or minimized by their practitioners. It seems that, rather than addressing systemic racism in obstetrics and gynecology, medical practitioners have instead to some extent emphasized all the ways Black women allegedly make themselves prone to being ill during their pregnancies. Black pregnant women and non–gender binary folks are told their fatness, advanced age, dietary choices, and lack of prenatal care have increased their chances of dying during childbirth. Yet, whereas Black pregnant people and mothers are made into culprits and the initiators of their deaths, doctors, nurses, and the hospitals they run are not looked at as critically as they should be. (1343)

For systemic change to occur, clinicians must confront the systemic racialized ideas that are ingrained in their education, training, and practice and instead use advocacy and activism to address SRMA. Jacqueline Jones Royster uses the online *Oxford English Dictionary* to define activism as "[a] philosophical theory which assumes the objective reality and active existence of everything" and "A doctrine or policy of advocating energetic action" (qtd. in Royster 105). In the same dictionary, advocacy is defined as "1. The function of an advocate; the work of advocating; pleading for or supporting" (qtd. in Royster 105). These definitions are crucial because for advocacy to dismantle systemic racializations, there must be "energetic action," or activism, that occurs in the form of rhetoric/language/words (Royster 105). This energetic action that Royster speaks of can be accomplished by using a socioecological model, an interconnected circle of social factors (individual, relationship, policy, and systemic) that has the ability, when acted upon, to create rhetorical change that is tangible in society (Royster 105).

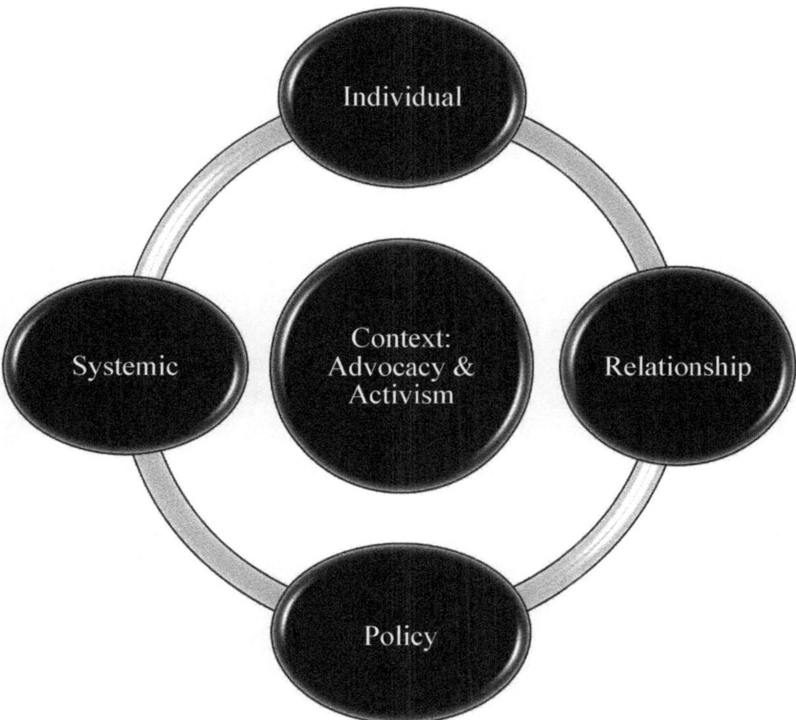

Figure 1. Socioecological Model for Addressing SRMA. Figure created by the author.

Rhetorical Action to Address SRMA Using a Socioecological Model

Consequently, SRMA can only be uprooted by clinicians using a socioecological model, like this one, that requires advocacy (to support the idea for improved maternal outcomes), activism (to form new ideas that are not racialized about Black women according to all four of the social factors—individual, relationship, policy, and systemic—that impact their lives), and action (not abusing Black women when providing maternal care). Otherwise, the cycle of systemic racialized maternal abuse continues. The first social factor, individual, pushes all clinicians, but especially White clinicians, to confront their implicit and/or explicit racialized ideas about Black women and how accepting these ideas as the truth causes maternal abuse. This factor is an example of rhetorical action in that it requires clinicians to change their beliefs about Black women. For example, instead of thinking Black women do not require medical interventions, clinicians should realize that Black women, like Amber, have valid health concerns that necessitate medical intervention. For clinicians to change how they handle maternal care when encountering Black women expressing health concerns, it *is* essential that they recognize White supremacy as a systemic belief that enables White privilege *and* social superiority and *not* because Black women are biologically inferior. This factor is crucial because without clinicians altering how they think about Black women, their behavior continues to be abusive and SRMA cannot be disrupted. This social reframing is a challenge because White clinicians must adjust to "being seen racially" and "sit[ting] with the discomfort of being seen racially" as White and the advantages Whiteness brings (DiAngelo 7). Robin DiAngelo elaborates: "Being perceived as white carries more than a mere racial classification; it is a social and institutional status and identity imbued with legal, political, economic, and social rights and privileges that are denied to others" (24).

The second social factor, relationship, accounts for how the connection between clinicians and Black patients can be established and positively developed. This relationship can be cultivated by clinicians listening to Black women's concerns and then taking action to address them. This factor builds upon the first where the clinician is challenged to actively work, emotionally and mentally, to build authentic, caring relationships with Black women rather than only reflecting on their ideas and behavior about them. While reflection without action is inaction, reflection and action are a form of rhetorical action because of the potential for change based on the clinician valuing what Black women have to say and thereby building a relationship with them. Serena Williams's maternal experience would not have been abusive if her clinician had taken the time to understand why she was asking for a CT scan. Sadly, this issue is not isolated to only Serena and her clinician but is a systemic issue. As a result, clinicians' training should include strategies for relationship-building with their patients (Washington 993). As Deleseo Washington asserts, "no medical school can train students in empathy. But, we have a duty to equip them with the ability to see, to articulate, to grasp, and to comprehend the position of the patient" (993). Training medical students to see the position of their patients rather than to see a Black patient would go a long way in improving relationships and to ending the fragmented relationship between doctors and Black women. Doctors must learn to actively listen to Black women rather than dismissing their concerns as well as developing authentic, caring relationships. The act of listening to patients would be clinicians' way of "partnering" with patients (Davis 205). By partnering with patients, clinicians would invite Black women to take an active role in their care as opposed to not having a say.

The third social factor, policy, examines policy at both the local and government levels. The need exists for clinicians to use written devices, such as policies, research, and toolkits to communicate hospital standards. This factor builds upon the previously mentioned social factors by requiring clinicians to act on behalf of Black women in a way that leads to essential changes to the current problem of an absence of policies protecting Black women, an absence of funded research on Black women, and an absence of written communication on how to effectively provide equity-minded maternal care to Black women through policy. In this way, policies are used as rhetorical action to create codified change to a systemic issue. At the local level clinicians need to support, write, and implement prevention protocols for preventing postpartum complications in hospitals that service predominately Black women like Dacheca. More specifically, these local policies need to require high-risk patients to receive heparin after a cesarean (Prather et al. 256). Doing this would require hospitals to have strategies and practices in place that reduces Black women from experiencing preventable pregnancy-related deaths, like hemorrhaging, hypertension, infection, and cardiovascular conditions (Ozimek and Kilpatrick 183).

To inform effective policy initiatives that are culturally aware and sensitive to Black women's needs, including those women who are imprisoned, increased research funding on Black women's maternal health needs to be established since current research is significantly "white-run and white-oriented" and underfunded (Feagin and Bennefield 12). To ensure Black women's maternal needs are addressed, they need to be included in both the design and implementation of programs for Black women's health (Prather et al. 256). Toolkits would be one way to easily provide information to staff members on how to prevent postpartum complications (Ozimek and Kilpatrick 182). A challenge to this recommendation is getting clinicians to follow the protocol and to see it as "fully applicable to the way they manage their hospitals and treat patients" (Owens and Fett 1344). Other challenges would be receiving sufficient funding to conduct research.

Currently, "People in prison are the only group in the United States with a constitutional right to medical care" even though "[a] pregnant woman in prison cannot choose between a midwife and a doctor; she cannot even choose who will be in the room with her when she gives birth" (Roth 287). This lack of choice is a systemic problem stemming directly from slavery that needs addressing; therefore, at the government level, American Nurses Associations, the American Medical Association, and other healthcare organizations need to advocate and lobby for policies for Black mothers who are pregnant and imprisoned, like Tammy, to give birth with the doctor or midwife of their choice and with social support from a doula, friend, partner/spouse, or family member. Black women, for example, who are imprisoned would benefit from having a midwife like Jennie Joseph. She uses her technique, The JJ Method, which has been "effective in reducing disparities and improving outcomes" (Joseph and Brown). Joseph has achieved effectiveness with her method because rather than seeing Black women as racialized tropes, she believes "every woman wants a healthy baby and that every woman deserves one" (Joseph and Brown).

In addition, doulas of color, who have been trained to provide culturally competent care, comfort measures for physical pain, emotional support, and education, should be considered as essential support persons who advocate for Black women. Katy B. Kozhimannil and co-authors found that "women who received continuous labor support reported greater satisfaction, had higher rates of spontaneous vaginal birth, higher infant Apgar scores, shorter labors, and lower rates of regional anesthesia (e.g., epidural), cesarean deliveries, and forceps or vacuum deliveries" (e341). Challenges to these recommendations could result in the implementation of wide-ranging government policies in "the federal Bureau of Prisons, the federal Bureau of Immigration and Customs Enforcement, state Departments of Corrections, and thousands of local jails" since all those systems currently create their own policies (Roth 288).

The fourth social factor, systemic, is aimed at the eradication of racializations ingrained in clinicians' schooling in order to prevent future Black women from suffering a horrific experience like that of Patrisse Cullors. This social factor supports all the others because of the possibility of a paradigm shift while also reinforcing the other recommendations for rhetorical action: clinicians individually assessing their behavior, judging their relationships with Black patients, and evaluating current policies, or lack thereof, at the federal and local levels. A Black doctor, Jennifer Okwereku, makes the need for an overhaul in what is taught to medical school students clear: "Racism permeates medical education and medical practice, and it has for decades." The only way racist medical education and practice can stop is by those in charge of the curriculum and training to start questioning and rejecting "dominant white racial framing and learn counter-framing from Americans of color" (Feagin and Bennefield 13).

Simultaneously, medical textbooks that have historically positioned White people as biologically and socially superior and women of color as genetically and socially inferior must be rewritten (DiAngelo 23). Medical and nursing school and residency (for both doctors and nurses) need to provide students with the history of gendered racism against Black women from the past and the present while also providing them knowledge about Black nurses and midwives who positively impacted Black women's maternal outcomes. By learning Black women's maternal care history, the bad and the good, clinicians today can learn how to avoid committing the same racialized violence and provide culturally competent care. Another recommendation is to train clinicians how to use their privilege and power to address racialized comments made by patients, faculty, and co-workers (Okwereku). These proposed changes are examples of rhetorical action because of the possibility for change through verbal and written discourse. Challenges to the "systemic" factor include getting clinicians to see that current education and training are based on racist, White standards of care that need to be re-evaluated to acknowledge that the idea of biological/genetic racial differences is a social and cultural construct rather than an actual "distinct" difference (DiAngelo 23).

From Euphemism to Rhetorical Action and Improved Outcomes

It is time for clinicians to acknowledge that what has been termed as "implicit bias" when describing the interactions between clinicians and Black women is not implicit at all. We, Black women, have known for years what clinicians think of us. It is no secret. Implicit bias is nothing more than a euphemism for racialization. For far too long words like "adverse birth outcomes," "health disparities," and "health inequalities," have been used to describe the systemic racialized maternal abuse Black women experience when receiving maternal care. Racialized ideas affect clinicians' behaviors; they have a deadening effect, rhetorically and literally, on Black women like Patrisse Cullors, Shalon Irving, Dacheca Fleurimond, Merowe Nubyahn, Tanesia Walker, Crystal Galloway, Serena Williams, Charity Hines, Sharon Griffith McKnight, Tammy Jackson, Shadae Toliver, Simone Landrum, Amber Rose Isaac, Kira Dixon Johnson, and countless more. Medical professionals need to use evidenced-based research and deracialized practices to address the racialized abuse in their profession.

All clinicians need to consider the part they have played in systemically racializing and abusing a pregnant or postpartum Black woman. Clinicians must begin to form relationships with Black women while fighting for local and governmental policies that benefit Black women the same way enslavers and clinicians for centuries have benefited off Black bodies like mine. Now is the time to address systemic ideologies, language, education, and training that are so ingrained, with impunity, in our country. How many more Black women must die before enough is enough? Now is the time for clinicians to see themselves as activists and advocates who actively work to ensure that all Black women receive the highest standard of maternal care. My positionality as a Black woman, mother, and activist places me in a unique position to offer this model as a radical approach that provides strategies for Black women who are experiencing preventable maternal complications and poor, discriminatory maternal care to receive medical interventions when needed as well as deracialized collaborative maternal care. This model and proposed actions are a blueprint for a future where Black mouths, hands, brains, and bodies, that have socially been labeled as "uncontrollable" or as "other," may reclaim practices that have traditionally been held for White people only (Alexander and Jarratt 10). Black women, who have always been leaders and organizers, have already begun this critical work by becoming doulas, nurses, doctors, and professors, and *now*, more than ever, it is evident that the future is not only female—it is *Black* and *female*.

Works Cited

Alexander, Jonathan, and Susan C. Jarratt. Introduction. *Unruly Rhetorics: Protest, Persuasion, and Publics*, edited by Jonathan Alexander and Susan C. Jarratt. U of Pittsburgh P, 2018, pp. 3–23.

Banks-Wallace, JoAnne. "Womanist Ways of Knowing: Theoretical Considerations for Research with African American Women." *Advances in Nursing Science*, vol. 22, no. 3, 2000, pp. 33–45. *CINAHL Complete*, doi.org/10.1097/00012272-200003000-00004. Accessed 29 Apr. 2023.

Bitzer, Lloyd F. "The Rhetorical Situation." *Philosophy and Rhetoric*, vol. 1, 1968, pp. 1–14.

Cullors, Patrisse. "Protecting Black History Is Protecting Black Mothers: It's Time to Address the Maternal Health Crisis for Black Women in the U.S." *Essence*, 1 Feb. 2018, essence.com/amp/holidays/black-history-month/black-history-black-women-maternal-health-crises-childbirth/. Accessed 15 Oct. 2020.

Davis, Dána-Ain. *Reproductive Injustice: Racism, Pregnancy, and Premature Birth*. Kindle ed., New York UP, 2019.

Declercq, Eugene, Ruby Barnard-Mayers, Laurie Zephyrin, and Kay Johnson. "The U.S. Maternal Health Divide: The Limited Maternal Health Services and Worse Outcomes of States Proposing New Abortion Restrictions." *The Commonwealth Fund*, 14 Dec. 2022, www.commonwealthfund.org/publications/issue-briefs/2022/dec/us-maternal-health-divide-limited-services-worse-outcomes. Accessed 5 Apr. 2023.

DiAngelo, Robin. *White Fragility: Why It's So Hard for White People to Talk About Racism*. Kindle ed., Beacon, 2018.

Feagin, Joe, and Zinobia Bennefield. "Systemic Racism and U.S. Health Care." *Social Science & Medicine*, vol. 103, Feb. 2014, pp. 7–14. *Science Direct*, doi: 10.1016/j.socscimed.2013.09.006. Accessed 16 Oct. 2020.

Garcia, Sandra E. "Ordeal of Woman Who Gave Birth in Florida Jail Cell Prompts Internal Investigation." *New York Times*, 7 May 2019, nytimes.com/2019/05/07/us/woman-gives-birth-jail-cell.amp.html. Accessed 16 Oct. 2020.

Hamlet, Janice D. "Word! The African American Oral Tradition and Its Rhetorical Impact on American Popular Culture." *Black History Bulletin*, vol. 74, no. 1, 2011, pp. 27–31. *JSTOR*, jstor.org/stable/24759732. Accessed 1 Jan. 2021.

Harmata, Claudia. "26-Year-Old Dies Giving Birth During Peak of Covid-19– Family Says It Was Preventable." *People*, 7 May 2020. people.com/health/26-year-old-woman-dies-giving-birth-peak-covid-19-family-says-it-was-preventable/%3famp=true. Accessed 17 Oct. 2020.

Haskell, Rob. "Serena Williams on Motherhood, Marriage, and Making Her Comeback." *Vogue*, 10 Jan. 2018, vogue.com/article/serena-williams-vogue-cover-interview-february-2018. Accessed 17 Oct. 2020.

Hinson, Sandra, et al. "Introduction." Race, Power, and Policy: Dismantling Structural Racism." *Grassroots Policy Project*, pp. 4–5, racialequitytools.org/resourcefiles/race_power_policy_workbook.pdf. Accessed 18 Oct. 2020.

hooks, bell. *Ain't I a Woman: Black Women and Feminism*. 2nd ed. Kindle ed., Routledge, 2015.

Joseph, Lauren L., and Stephan E. Brown. "The JJ Way." *Commonsense Childbirth: Because Every Woman Deserves a Healthy Baby,* Feb. 2020, commonsensechildbirth.org/jjway/. Accessed 2 Nov. 2020.

Keane, Helen. "Feminism and the Complexities of Gender and Health. *Australian Feminist Studies,* vol. 29, no. 80, 2014, pp. 180–88. *Humanities International Complete,* doi: 10.1080/08164649.2014.928192. Accessed 29 Apr. 2023.

Kluchin, Rebecca M. *Fit to Be Tied: Sterilization and Reproductive Rights in America, 1950–1980.* Rutgers UP, 2009.

Kozhimannil, Katy. B., et al. "Potential Benefits of Increased Access to Doula Support During Childbirth." *The American Journal of Managed Care,* vol. 20, no.8, 1 Aug. 2014, e340–e352. *MEDLINE,* ncbi.nlm.nih.gov/pmc/articles/PMC5538578/pdf/nihms881526.pdf. Accessed 24 Oct. 2020.

Levy, Walter E., and Harry Meyer. "A Comparative and Gynecological Study of the White and Colored Races." *New Orleans Medical and Surgical Journal,* vol. 89, no. 8, Feb. 1937, pp. 537–39. archive.org/stream/neworleansmedica89unse#page/418/mode/2up. Accessed 24 Oct. 2020.

Okwereku, Jennifer A. "What Happened When I Talked about What Others Ignore—Racism in Medicine." *STAT,* 27 Apr. 2016, statnews.com/2016/04/27/racism-medicine-lessons/. Accessed 2 Nov. 2020.

Owens, Deirdre Cooper, and Sharla M. Fett. "Black Maternal and Infant Health: Historical Legacies of Slavery." *American Journal of Public Health,* vol. 109, no. 10, Oct. 2019, pp. 1342–44. *CINAHL Plus,* doi: 10.2105/AJPH.2019.305243. Accessed 14 Oct. 2020.

Ozimek, John A., and Sarah J. Kilpatrick. "Maternal Mortality in the Twenty-First Century." *Obstetrics and Gynecology Clinics of North America,* vol. 45, June 2018, pp. 175–86. *Science Direct,* doi: 10.1016/j.ogc.2018.01.004. Accessed 24 Oct. 2020.

Perez, Nicole. "Tammy Jackson, Who Changed Law After Giving Birth in Broward Jail, Has Died." *Local 10,* 27 Oct. 2020, www.local10.com/news/local/2020/10/27/tammy-jackson-who-changed-law-after-giving-birth-in-broward-jail-has-died/. Accessed 26 Apr. 2023.

Prather, Cynthia, et al. "Racism, African American Women, and Their Sexual and Reproductive Health: A Review of Historical and Contemporary Evidence and Implications for Health Equity." *Health Equity,* vol. 2, no. 1, 24 Sept. 2018, pp. 249–59.

Reach Team. "6 Different Types of Abuse." *Reach Beyond Domestic Violence,* 23 Mar. 2017, reachma.org/6-different-types-abuse. Accessed 28 Oct. 2020.

Roth, Rachael. "'She Doesn't Deserve to Be Treated Like This'": Prison as Sites of Reproductive Injustice." *Radical Reproductive Justice: Foundations, Theory, Practice, Critique,* edited by Loretta J. Ross, Lynn Roberts, Erika Derkas, Whitney Peoples, and Pamela Bridgewater Toure, Feminist Press, 2017, pp. 285–301.

Royster, Jacqueline J. "Toward an Analytical Model for Literacy and Sociopolitical Action." *Traces of a Stream: Literacy and Social Change Among African American Women*, U of Pittsburgh P, 2000, pp. 42–107.

Schwartz, Marie J. *Birthing a Slave: Motherhood and Medicine in the Antebellum South*. Harvard UP, 2006.

The Sentencing Project. "Fact Sheet: Incarcerated Women and Girls, 1980–2016." *The Sentencing Project*, 6 June 2019, p. 2, sentencingproject.org/wp-content/uploads/2016/02/Incarcerated-Women-and-Girls.pdf. Accessed 26 Oct. 2020.

"The Social-Ecological Model: A Framework for Prevention." *Centers for Disease Control and Prevention*, www.cdc.gov/violenceprevention/about/social-ecologicalmodel.html. Accessed 5 Apr. 2023.

United States, Congress, House. Preventing Maternal Deaths Act of 2018. *Congress.gov*, congress.gov/115/plaws/publ344/PLAW-115publ344.pdf. 115th Congress, 2nd session, House Resolution 1318, passed 21 Dec. 2018. Accessed 18 Oct. 2020.

United States, Congress, House. Committee on Energy and Commerce. *Testimony of Charles Johnson IV: Better Data and Better Outcomes: Reducing Maternal Mortality in the U.S.*, 115th Congress, 2nd session, 24 Sept. 2018, docs.house.gov/meetings/IF/IF14/20180927/108724/HHRG-115-IF14-Wstate-JohnsonC-20180927.pdf. Accessed 24 Oct. 2020.

Villarosa, Linda. "Why American's Black Mothers and Babies are in a Life-or-Death Crisis. *New York Times Magazine*, 11 Apr. 2018, nytimes.com/2018/04/11/magazine/black-mothers-babies-death-maternal-mortality.html. Accessed 25 Oct. 2020.

Waldman, Annie. "How Hospitals are Failing Black Mothers." *ProPublica*, 27 Dec. 2017, propublica.org/article/how-hospitals-are-failing-black-mothers. Accessed 25 Oct. 2020.

Washington, Deleseo A. "Critical Race Feminist Bioethics: Telling Stories in Law School and Medical School in Pursuit of 'Cultural Competency.'" *Albany Law Review*, vol. 72, no. 4, 4 Nov. 2009, pp. 961–98.

White, Deborah Gray. *Ar'nt I a Woman? Female Slaves in the Plantation South*. Norton, 1995.

White, Franklin. "Primary Health Care and Public Health: Foundations of Universal Health Systems." *Medical Principles and Practice: International Journal of the Kuwait University, Health Science Centre*, vol. 24, no. 2, 2015, pp. 103–16. doi:10.1159/000370197. Accessed 2 Nov. 2020.

Williams, Serena. "Serena Williams: What My Life-Threatening Experience Taught Me About Giving Birth." *CNN*, 20 Feb. 2018, cnn.com/2018/02/20/opinions/protect-mother-pregnancy-williams-opinion/index.html?nost=1556913843. Accessed 24 Oct. 2020.

Wolf, Jacqueline H. *Cesarean Section: An American History of Risk, Technology, and Consequence*. Kindle ed., Johns Hopkins UP, 2018.

7 The Rhetorical History of Choice: Birth Control, Eugenics, and Utopia

Michelle C. Smith

> … so we had the subject up in meeting to settle forever the question.
>
> Shall Mary bear children?
>
> —Sarah Story, qtd. in Fogarty 176–77

In May 2019, Justice Clarence Thomas joined other conservative leaders in summoning a dark historical specter, opining that state intervention is necessary to prevent abortion and birth control from becoming "a tool of modern-day eugenics" (de Vogue). Thomas's remarks were not an isolated instance: three years later, the Supreme Court's decision overturning abortion rights in *Dobbs v. Jackson Women's Health Organization* mobilized the same logic (Ehrlich). Specifically, Thomas insinuated that Margaret Sanger, Planned Parenthood founder, championed birth control to curb the propagation of disabled people and African Americans. Indeed, Sanger's controversial embrace of eugenics late in her career has become a lightning rod for contemporary assessments of her contributions. As Loretta Ross has noted, the "abortion is racist" narrative espoused by Thomas and others "depicts black women as victims of state-sanctioned population control policies by abortion providers; dupes of white elites who provide birth control and abortion; and destroyers of our own people through self-genocide" (61). Liberal voices initially responded to Thomas by refuting the slippery slope argument that birth control leads to eugenics, insisting that, while eugenics removes or constrains reproductive choices, birth control increases individuals' options.[1] In other words, liberal reproductive logics eschew

1. Left-leaning groups have begun to reconsider this stance, as illustrated by the July 2020 decision to remove Sanger's name from Planned Parenthood of Greater New York (Stewart).

the "control" in birth control for "choice." This wishful distancing of control from choice belies the lived experience of reproduction in the past and present.

This chapter contends that control and choice, like birth control and eugenics, are not so easily separated. As Leslie Ruhl notes, the shift in Sanger's thought from "arguments rooted in women's autonomy to eugenic arguments about using birth control to 'improve' the race is a necessary reminder of the slipperiness of attaching a notion of control to processes of conception" (660). Decades before the birth control and eugenics movements, these concerns emerged in a utopian community in upstate New York. The controversial Oneida Community (1848–1881) practiced group marriage, birth control, and communal childrearing—practices that developed into a eugenics experiment. As the above epigraph demonstrates, this phase of the community upended the idea of having children as an individual choice for women and some men, a choice made more meaningful today by the widespread availability of birth control. Thus, the case of Oneida provides a unique opportunity to understand, rather than deny or decry, the historical coincidence of birth control and eugenics. Per Michel Foucault, I propose, in examining Oneida, "to start with these concrete practices and, as it were, pass these universals [i.e., choice, control] through the grid of these practices" (*Birth* 3). Specifically, this rhetorical historiography illuminates how reproductive rhetorics of choice underpin eugenic logics that continue to haunt contemporary reproductive technologies.

I examine Oneida through the lens of reproductive justice, a framework that fuses reproductive rights with social justice. Reproductive justice endorses three main principles: "1) the right *not* to have a child; 2) the right to *have* a child; and 3) the right to *parent* children in safe and healthy environments" (Ross and Solinger 9). Ultimately, I find that the rise of nineteenth-century liberalism and biopolitics undermined all three rights or choices for Oneida women.[2] I locate the rhetorical common ground of birth control and eugenics in their dependence on liberal notions of autonomy, individuality, and the myth of free choice.

2. Though liberalism didn't emerge in Europe until the twentieth century, in the US, "liberalism was appealed to as the founding and legitimizing principle of the state" and thus played a major role throughout the nineteenth century (Foucault, *Birth* 217). Biopolitical impulses can be identified as early as the eighteenth century, as leaders attempted "to rationalize the problems posed to governmental practice by phenomena characteristic of a set of living beings forming a population: health, hygiene, birthrate, life expectance, race" (317).

This common ground has direct implications for reproductive rights in the present, which continue to be framed in terms of neoliberal feminist discourses of choice—and haunted by eugenic logics.[3] Just as explicit eugenic programs aimed to determine "fitness" for reproduction, contemporary contraceptive and reproductive technologies are implemented through an assessment of "fitness" for choice. Moreover, these assessments do not function neutrally, but as a form of "differential biopolitics," Natalie Fixmer-Oraiz's term for "the (micro)technologies of reproductive self-government that are distributed differentially, or otherwise stratified, and that reinscribe a particular (gendered, racialized, classed) social order" (37–38). Behind the rhetorical façade of choice lurks the darker truth that women's reproductive autonomy has been consistently undermined by nineteenth- and twentieth-century eugenics and their twenty-first century descendant: differential biopolitics.

White feminist discourse embraces choice as a personal and political good, a source of women's empowerment. Scholars of reproductive rhetorics trace the rise of choice in feminist discourse from the abortion debates of the 1970s through the ensuing decades, as choice rhetorics extended beyond reproduction to nearly every aspect of women's lives—from work/family "balance" to antidepressants, diets, infant feeding, and prenatal screening (McCarver 21, 26). Indeed, "choice feminism," a term coined by Linda Hirshman in 2005, invokes choice as a metonym for feminism itself (McCarver 35). Challenging this popular discourse, feminist scholars have critiqued rhetorics of choice.[4] As Rachel Thwaites observes, "some seemingly freely made decisions are so influenced by societal practice and opinion that they cannot be considered truly free" (64). Moreover, choice, in practice, is not equivalent for all

---

3. To clarify, in this chapter, I distinguish between a) nineteenth-century liberalism and early biopolitics as an important element of Oneida's *historical context* and b) *a theoretical analysis* of neoliberal feminist discourses of choice. In other words, while one might argue that nineteenth-century liberalism and biopolitics are the historical forerunners of today's neoliberal biopolitics, such an argument is beyond the scope of this piece. Thus, I deploy neoliberalism more as a lens for analyzing contemporary feminist logics rather than applying it to Oneida directly.

4. As de Onís notes, women of color and low-income allies have been problematizing "choice" for decades (1). Similarly, Caeton observes that choice logics do not resonate with individuals with disabilities, thus undermining potential alliances.

women: by glossing over crucial differences in context, the rhetoric of choice "further disadvantages women who confront systemic barriers inhibiting unrestricted, desirable <choices>" (de Onís 4). Specifically, the choices available or marketed to "members of economically and racially marginalized communities" are more likely to be dangerous than those targeting privileged women (Mann and Grzanka 334). Thus, "liberal notions of choice and equity translated into a movement dominated by white middle-class cisgender women" (Derkas 273). While popular discourse celebrates choice as free and unfettered, scholars of reproductive rhetorics find that women's choices are often highly constrained, if not controlled. Working past this binary of choice as autonomous or deterministic requires a better understanding of how the discourse of choice itself upholds this binary by refusing to acknowledge a lived experience where agency emerges in spite of constraint.

The Oneida Community aimed to liberate women by making pregnancy a matter of choice. Founder John Humphrey Noyes's pamphlet on "male continence," an early form of birth control, clarifies this stance: "women shall bear children only when they choose. They have the principal burdens of breeding to bear, and they rather than men should have their choice of time and circumstances, at least till science takes charge of the business" (*Male Continence* 15). Given the community's later foray into eugenics, Noyes's stipulation that women's choice was only necessary until "science" took charge was prescient—and foreboding. Nevertheless, the community identified reproductive choice as the fulcrum of women's autonomy and averred that woman was not meant to drudge away her life as "a mere wife and mother" (qtd. in Dalsimer 80). Such arguments foreshadowed twentieth-century feminist arguments that "women's ability to exercise educational and occupational choices could not be enacted until and unless they also had *reproductive* choice" (S. Hayden and O'Brien Hallstein xxi). Though twentieth-century feminists imagined choice as an inherent right, birth control rhetorics and practices at Oneida illustrate that reproductive choice has always been a right that had to be earned. Again, the epigraph illustrates that Mary, an Oneida member, needed the community's approval before she could "choose" to have a child. Eugenic discourses of "fitness" thus apply not only to reproduction—"who is fit to have a child?"—but also to choice—"who is fit to choose?" In this way, reproductive rhetorics of choice mask spaces and practices of non-choice or incomplete choice, undercutting individual reproductive agency historically and in the present.

In researching Oneida, I have struggled to reconcile the community's stated goal of liberating women from involuntary motherhood with its high degree of surveillance and coercion surrounding sex and reproduction. In particular, I have confronted my own instinctive understanding of birth control and eugenics as ideologically and ethically opposed. Similarly, feminists have reconciled Sanger's endorsement of eugenics with her feminist principles by dismissing her eugenic stance as "opportunistic" and expedient, an "early misstep" (Ross and Solinger 32; Ross 84). As Karen Weingarten explains, "Sanger's more ambivalent positions are often elided; relatively little attention is paid to the element of her rhetoric that is compatible with neither contemporary mainstream feminist arguments nor antiracist nationalisms" (52). In this chapter, I sit with this ambivalence—characteristic of my attitude towards Oneida and scholarship on Sanger—and recognize it as a consequence of a feminist stance grounded in neoliberalism.[5] In Foucault's definition, neoliberalism is characterized by its use of "the market economy and the typical analyses of the market economy to decipher non-market relationships and phenomena which are not strictly and specifically economic but what we call social phenomena" (*Birth* 240). Approaching the social through a market lens means viewing political subjects "as a *population* that a government must manage," a phenomenon that Foucault dubs "the birth of biopolitics" (22). As David Harvey explains, neoliberalism has become hegemonic, "incorporated into the common-sense way many of us interpret, live in, and understand the world" (3). Reproductive rhetorics that adopt a lens of choice—where women must allocate scarce resources to competing ends—thus participate in neoliberal biopolitics. Neoliberalism and biopolitics provide a terminology and framework to grapple with rather than shy away from the ambivalence surrounding reproductive freedom and compulsion, choice and coercion.

Rather than eliding the historical link between birth control and eugenics, this chapter probes this link as an opportunity to examine how rhetorics of individual autonomy (e.g., those of choice) mask the conditions that unevenly constrain women's reproductive choices. First, in considering reproductive practices and politics at Oneida in light of the tenets of reproductive justice, I find that the logic of choice pervades not

5. This approach heeds Ralph Cintron's warning in "Octalog III" that neoliberal paradigms undergird rhetoric and composition, noting that notions of social uplift and empowerment "have been positively used to fight historical injustices but are also seamless with neoliberal agendas" (Agnew et al. 127).

only Oneida's promise to liberate women but also the coercive and eugenic facets of the community's sexual and reproductive life. Next, I analyze the implications of Oneida in light of contemporary discourses of choice feminism and structures of differential biopolitics. This chapter contends that eugenic logics of choice continue from the nineteenth century to the present, dispersed across institutions, practices, and "(micro) technologies of reproductive self-government" (Fixmer-Oraiz 37).

Reproductive (In)Justice in Oneida

Examining women's roles in Oneida is a study in contrasts and contradictions. On the one hand, Oneida endorsed birth control as a means of self-determination, and Oneida women describe themselves as empowered and fulfilled. On the other hand, Oneida was ruled absolutely by a patriarchal leader, and the community's reproductive practices were rife with coercion, surveillance, and abuse. As a feminist rhetorical scholar, I have felt pressure to decide once and for all: was Oneida *more* liberating or *more* restrictive for women? Here, I turn away from this question in an attempt to embrace Foucault's description of nineteenth-century liberalism as a mode of power that "does not divide subjects between an absolutely reserved dimension of freedom and another dimension of submission which is either consented to or imposed" (*Birth* 11). As Harvey, quoting economic historian Karl Polanyi, elaborates: under liberalism, "the idea of freedom 'thus degenerates into a mere advocacy of free enterprise,' which means 'the fullness of freedom for those whose income, leisure and security need no enhancing'" (37). In other words, freedom and submission are balanced, rather than opposed, and are unevenly distributed by not only gender, but also race, caste, class, religion, education, and more.

The early nineteenth-century United States witnessed falling birth rates, rising abortion rates, and increased circulation of fertility-limitation information. New understandings of self-ownership of the body suggested that "sometimes uncontrolled reproductive capacity itself was the cruel master, capable of enslaving and impoverishing both man and woman" (Solinger 58). Noyes combatted this form of "slavery" through the practices of "complex marriage," where each adult male was considered married to each adult female, and of "male continence," an early form of birth control. I explore the rhetorical and material mechanisms through which nineteenth-century liberalism and biopolitics destabilize all three of the rights championed by the later Reproductive Justice Movement, particularly for women rendered vulnerable by Oneida's religious caste system.

1. The Right Not to Have a Child

The first right espoused by reproductive justice is a negative right—a freedom *from* rather than a freedom *to.* Considering Oneida in the wake of the *Dobbs* decision underscores the historical and contemporary similarities of advocacy for and against access to birth control and abortion. From all accounts, Noyes's system of male continence achieved its goal of freeing women from unwanted pregnancy. In all, 135 children were born in or brought to Oneida before 1869, and there were few accidental births (Klee-Hartzell 190). Noyes participated in a wider midcentury discourse involving sex educators such as Frederick Hollick, who redefined female reproduction, observing that "women do not ovulate or become pregnant simply in reaction to male penetration and ejaculation" (Solinger 59). Inspired by Malthusian arguments and rudimentary methods promoted by Charles Knowlton and Robert Dale Owen, Noyes discovered his own method of birth control: male continence, a practice where men avoid ejaculation during intercourse. The efficacy of Noyes's method is incontrovertible: while the general fertility rate in the US dropped from 48.3 annual births per one thousand women in 1840 to 38.3 in 1870 (Haines), the estimated birth rate for Oneida women between 1848 and 1869 was 17.1 (Carden 51).[6]

Despite the success of male continence, the promise that it would increase women's autonomy was undermined by Oneida men's collective and individual control over birth control in practice. First, male continence kept individual men at the center of reproduction. Evident in both the name and practice is an emphasis on male self-control: "this whole process, up to the very moment of emission, is *voluntary,* entirely under the control of the moral faculty, and *can be stopped at any point*" (*Male Continence* 7). As Noyes explains, his discovery of male continence:

6. This number was calculated as follows: roughly one hundred Oneida women of child-bearing age bore thirty-six children—five planned and thirty-one accidental—over twenty-one years (1848-1869) (Carden 51). This figure (children born annually to each woman—.0171) was multiplied by 1000, following the practice used to calculate the national fertility rate.

> was occasioned and even forced upon me by very sorrowful experience. In the course of six years my wife went through the agonies of five births. Four of them were premature. Only one child lived . . . After our last disappointment, I pledged my word to my wife that I would never again expose her to such fruitless suffering. (*Male Continence* 10–11)

Male continence depicted women not as autonomous sexual agents, but as victims freed by Noyes and male partners who would no longer "expose" them. In addition, the community enforced a complicated caste system of ascending and descending fellowship, where younger members were paired with older, spiritually mature partners. This system compounded the power of male elders, who "took full advantage of their superior position within the community to pursue younger women" (Fogarty 133). Together, these elements undermined women's reproductive autonomy: the system "gave women considerable sexual freedom . . . but denied them true choice" (133).

While birth control is often associated with sexual autonomy, male continence most likely did not promote Oneida women's choice and control over their sexual lives. Oneida women were subject to invidious surveillance and control by women leaders. Community "aunts" and "mothers"—such as Harriet Holton Noyes, Mary Cragin, Harriet Noyes Skinner, and Charlotte Noyes Miller—mediated sexual relationships. As Noyes's 1852 lecture, or "home talk," "Practical Suggestions for Regulating Intercourse of the Sexes" explains,

> Proposals for love interviews are best made not directly but through a third party . . . If the third party is a superior, as it should be, one in whom the lovers have confidence, calm wisdom will enter, as it should, to give needed advice and prevent inexpediencies. The third party will also be helpful in arrangements. (qtd. in Fogarty 9)

Through this surveillance, "central authorities were pretty well informed as to what was going on and the general trend of every individual" (La Moy and Cragin 131). As Noyes's talk suggests, the role of the intermediary was also to ward off "inexpedient" pairings: "Neither advice nor help was ever wanting at Oneida, and the fine line that separated an order from 'advice' was not always easy to discern" (Fogarty 41).

Finally, though birth control was presented as giving women "their choice of time and circumstances," it actually functioned as a non-choice, since Oneida women could not choose whether or not to use birth control (Male Continence 15). As Emily Mann and Patrick Grzanka describe, in instances of "non-choice," "proposing a single solution constitutes the freedom to choose" (351). Clearly, such "choice" or "freedom" is highly circumscribed. Freedom from unwanted pregnancy at Oneida did not entail freedom from nonconsensual sex. Girls were introduced to the community's sexual activities at or even before puberty, typically by Noyes himself—a convention starkly termed "Noyes's prerogative." The ideology of ascending and descending fellowship meant that young women who spurned older lovers were seen as less sincere in their faith. As one former member attested, if a woman refused a sexual proposition from an elder, she was "likely to be taken out of any responsible position she held at the time, and not be allowed to do anything until it was thought she had a good spirit and was humble" (qtd. in Van de Warker 790). Furthermore, sexual unwillingness might be interpreted as evidence of a forbidden "special love." One account reports that some women entertained multiple partners "without complaint simply to gain the confidence of those in charge of such things so that she would be allowed to associate with someone she loved" (Van de Warker 789–90). Despite their lauded autonomy, the female refusal rate at Oneida was "probably low," and never "a problem" (Dalsimer 115). The narrative of birth control at Oneida thus supports the concerns of feminist scholars that "'control' in sexual and reproductive matters too often supports a view of 'sex without consequences' that, . . . rather than freeing them to explore their sexuality, actually subjects them to male sexual dominance" (Ruhl 643).

2. The Right to Have a Child

The second right espoused by reproductive justice is positive, establishing the *freedom to* become a parent. At Oneida, however, childbearing was a privilege only available once the "stirpiculture," or eugenics, experiment began.[7] The eugenic phase was instigated by contact with the academic and scientific elite of the day. Noyes's decision to pursue stirpiculture

7. Nineteenth-century eugenics debates are examined in *Evolutionary Rhetoric*. As Wendy Hayden contends, those earlier eugenics arguments, unlike those of the twentieth century, were focused less on class and race issues directly than on women's health, productivity, and notions of ideal motherhood resulting in exceptional children (212-213).

"came at the urging of a dozen or so young men [including Noyes's son, Theodore] who, during the late sixties and early seventies, returned from medical college and scientific studies at Yale and elsewhere" (Fogarty 23–24). The experiment ran from 1869 to the late 1870s, administered first by Noyes and the central committee and later by a Stirpiculture Committee of six men and six women (Fogarty 25). Under the plan, a couple could apply for permission to "try," and the committee would "determine fitness" before accepting or rejecting the proposal. Before and during its eugenics phase, having a child was neither an autonomous right nor choice for women at Oneida.

The patriarchal power dynamics of male continence continued to shape procreation under eugenics. Forty-eight percent of the children born under the plan were fathered by just ten men—including Noyes, who fathered nine children—and "men in the experiment were, on average, twelve years older than the women" (Fogarty 26). Conversely, women needed to surrender their "rights" and "personal feelings," as is demonstrated by the following resolution signed by the women selected to enter "the scientific union." It pledges:

> 1. That we do not belong to ourselves in any respect, but that we belong to God, and second to Mr. Noyes as God's true representative.
>
> 2. That we have no rights or personal feelings in regard to child bearing which shall in the least degree oppose or embarrass him in his choice of scientific combinations.
>
> 3. That we will put aside all envy, childishness, and self seeking and rejoice in those who are chosen candidates; and that we will, if necessary, become martyrs to science, and cheerfully resign all desire to become mothers, if for any reason Mr. Noyes deem us unfit material for propagation. Above all, we offer ourselves 'living sacrifices' to God and true communism. (qtd. in Fogarty 25)

This document suggests that women were chosen on the basis of submission, if not self-immolation. As Fogarty observes, sexual language at Oneida was rife with eugenic hierarchy: "Words like *connection, start, expose, communication* and *service* . . . taken from the language of animal breeding . . . reflect the language of domestication and submission, the language of utility, and the language of master and servant relationships" (43). Eugenics at Oneida, then, operated as a form of differential biopolitics that enacted "reproductive stratification . . . a means of grappling with the complex ways in which women are differentially disciplined into normative codes for behavior" (Fixmer-Oraiz 41). Women higher in the caste system were deemed better candidates for motherhood; less powerful women could only hope to elevate their standing by performing selflessness and submission.

Crucially, the designation of reproductive fitness or unfitness at Oneida depended upon an assessment of an individual's and couple's compliance with social norms, as well as their physical and mental attributes. While many stirpiculture documents have been lost or destroyed, one exception is the diary of a man who fought to have a child at Oneida. Victor Hawley and Mary Jones were two young people in an illicit "special"—read: monogamous—relationship.[8] They were both physically slight, and their families were not seen as strong stock—Mary's father was deaf and epileptic (Fogarty 47). Yet the couple's physical qualities were not the only sign of "unfitness." The leadership deemed "Mary's mind . . . affected," referencing her "inordinate & unsanctified desire" for a child (qtd. in Fogarty 56, 63). Moreover, the community was troubled by Mary and Victor's disobedience. Victor's brother entreats him: "I hope that you will not go directly to Mary and try to arrange the matter between yourselves . . . You will then be more sure of starting right & having the community & a good spirit to back you" (qtd. in Fogarty 62). Tellingly, both Victor and Mary were encouraged to reproduce with other partners, suggesting that their "unfitness" was not essentially physical. After months of resistance, Victor's own mental health is questioned by an elder: "he wanted to make out that I was crazy or something of the sort" (qtd. in Fogarty 194). The couple was deemed not so much unfit for reproduction as *unfit to choose* when, how, and with whom to reproduce. In the end, the committee "decidedly disapproved of our having a baby," and punishment ensued: Mary was banished to another branch of the community and impregnated by Theodore Noyes (qtd. in Fogarty 65).

Mary and Victor continued to leverage liberal rhetorics of choice to fight for their reproductive rights. As members of the younger generation, the couple "had exercised greater choices" and "known prosperity" at Oneida, and their faith in scientific progress contributed to their "desire to exercise choice" in their personal lives (Fogarty 36–37). This stance is evident as they question the committee's decision: "Mary asked

8. For consistency, I follow the primary sources by referring to Victor and Mary by their given names throughout.

Ann why they did not let us have a baby. Ann said on account of stirpiculteral [sic] principles . . . *I said how can that be* for they asked me to have one by Emma [Mary's sister] who is not as well as Mary" (qtd. in Fogarty 89). Mary's resistance becomes particularly clear after the stillborn birth of her child (by Theodore Noyes): "GEC [George Cragin] asked Mary how she did she said real smart I am ready to get up & try it over again" (qtd. in Fogarty 184). The community is taken aback by Mary's assertion of will to a male elder. As Sarah Story recounted:

> she told G.E. Cragin that she was ready to try again. This surprised us all very much & I said to her in a kind way, Mary? That is a great deal to go through and not have a living child. So she sticks to the point with a tenacity that is astonishing . . . She replied, I think that I could have a living child. So you see she sticks to the point with a tenacity that is astonishing . . . (qtd. in Fogarty 176)

Story's (repeated) astonishment is shared by the community. The elder Noyes and the Oneida physician agree—in letters read aloud at community meetings—that "Mary ought not to have a baby" (qtd. in Fogarty 185). Subsequently, as Story narrates, "we had the subject up in meeting to settle forever the question. Shall Mary bear children? And run the risk of bringing sickly children into the community, after we have taken the foremost rank in stirpiculture" (qtd. in Fogarty 176–77). Oneida is unprepared for this young woman to assert her right "in the cliché-worn language of the 1970s," to have "control over her own body" (Fogarty 133). Yet the couple's ability to contest the decision was undermined by their reliance on the same rhetorics of choice through which they had been deemed unfit to choose. Though "it was decided in meeting that Mary could not have another child," Mary and Victor proved tenacious (qtd. in Fogarty 185). The "unfit" couple left Oneida and went on to have five children.

3. The Right to Parent Children in Safe and Healthy Environments

I want to pause on this third principle of reproductive justice to consider its possible interpretations. Depending on where the emphasis is placed, this principle can be understood as focusing either on individual parenting decisions—the right to "parent" (as a verb) in the way one sees fit—

or on the kind of environments parents have access to or are relegated to. In Oneida, I focus more on the individualistic right to parent than on the communal right to do so in a safe and healthy environment. This focus speaks to the racial and other forms of privilege of the primarily white Oneida community. Applying this third principle of reproductive justice to a white community shifts the emphasis from the safe living conditions of a community to the hierarchy within that community. I want to acknowledge that, as a group, all the white members and workers at the Oneida Community were privileged to have a safe environment—one where they were not subject to the racialized violence, unsafe drinking water, hazardous working conditions, jeopardized housing, and inadequate nutrition that communities of color have faced in the past and present. While white communities have largely not faced the same categorically unsafe and unhealthy environments as communities of color, the determination of one's "fitness" to parent is still unevenly applied within white communities.

Indeed, as the experience of Victor and Mary suggests, this final positive right is similarly compromised at Oneida. The couple enacted the third principle of reproductive justice by leaving Oneida, since they could not enact that right within the society. Parents—particularly single mothers—who stayed in the community had little recourse in claiming their parental rights. Indeed, parents were expected to surrender children to be raised by the community. A Children's House document declared: "The essence of our principles is, that children cease to be private property and become property of the Association" (qtd. in Noyes and Foster 54). This system involved physically separating mothers and children, who spent their days at the children's house starting at nine months and lived there full time after eighteen months (Miller). Parents could visit their children but, ultimately, parent-child relationships were subject to the same surveillance as reproductive relations.

Oneida mothers deemed "unfit" in their role were subject to various sanctions, including forced separation from their children. Increasingly, inside and outside Oneida, the assessment of a woman's fitness for motherhood did not stop with pregnancy or childbirth. Mid-century publications asked: "Were women born to be mothers, or was it an office that was to be achieved? Were women suited as they were, or did they have to be changed?" (qtd. in Lewis 62). For his part, Noyes felt that society encouraged women to form obsessive attachments to children, a distortion of the motherly instinct that he referred to as "philoprogenitiveness—the phrenological term for excessive mothering" (Fogarty 52). Discourses of philoprogenitiveness seemingly only applied to women, an interpretation that an unrepentant Mary Jones questioned: "Mary talked to Mr Seymour about some of the men being weak towards their children as well as their mothers Mr said she was thinking evil" (qtd. in Fogarty 149). Compliance with emotional norms of motherhood was enforced through sanctions: Mary Jones's powerful desire for a child was punished by refusing to procure a headstone for her stillborn child (Fogarty 48). Other punishments involved forced separation: Charlotte Leonard's son was removed from her care when she was deemed too attached. In her journal, Leonard works to discipline her affections:

> [Noyes] said he thought that I had a weaned love for Humphrey now, and he thought I was ready to take him back again . . . I feel like taking care of Humphrey as one of God's little children, and not as though he was mine. I do not feel at all like claiming him, for he belongs to God and the Community, and I am only appointed to take care of him for them. (2)

Despite her efforts, Leonard's entries continue to revolve around her son—she routinely writes on the eighteenth of most months, the anniversary of Humphrey's birth. In Oneida as elsewhere, choices surrounding parenthood—like choices regarding sex and reproduction—are only viable for those who meet communal criteria for fit parenting.

In this regard, Oneida's attitude towards communal parenting illustrates on a micro scale the widespread medicalization of the family. As Foucault details in "The Politics of Health in the Eighteenth Century," parenthood was increasingly subject to state interventions not dissimilar to the those imposed on Leonard.[9] Medicalization of childhood and parenthood provided a pretense of individual and private autonomy—parents are obligated to care for their children—while also ensuring that the medical and state apparatus has the final say: "it permitted the articulation of a 'private' ethic of good health . . . upon a collective control of hygiene . . . by a professional corps of qualified doctors recommended by the state" (Foucault, "Politics" 119). Ultimately, parents' supposed autonomy in raising children is a smokescreen for their function as a point of application for state power.

9. Foucault gave two lectures with this title (in 1976 and 1979)—here I cite the 2014 translation of the 1979 lecture.

Though Oneida was one of the first sites where birth control and eugenics coincided, it was not the last. By the early twentieth century, the combination of new reproductive technologies and eugenic ideas about "the race"—an idiom indicating white panic about race and class "impurities" in the social body—gelled into a horrifying amalgam of racism and authoritarianism, the typical connotation for "eugenics" today. But attention to the early coincidence of reproductive technologies and eugenics at Oneida should caution us away from any easy assurance that eugenics is "over." Indeed, present-day reproductive rhetorics and practices are haunted by these histories, a haunting borne out by contemporary practices of differential biopolitics, the process by which "(micro) technologies of reproductive self-government . . . are distributed differentially, or otherwise stratified . . . reinscrib[ing] a particular (gendered, racialized, classed) social order" (Fixmer-Oraiz 37–38).

Unfreedoms of Choice Then and Now

As one of the first communities of men and women to link women's reproductive autonomy to women's full participation in civic and professional life, Oneida is a crucial site in the rhetorical history of choice. Indeed, there were few public advocates of birth control in the mid- and late-nineteenth century, and the fact that Oneida embraced birth control as a means to allow women the *choice* of how to divide their time and energies among a variety of possible roles—factory worker, Christian, citizen, author or editor as well as, perhaps, wife or mother—was forward thinking. Like other intentional communities, Oneida recognized that societal change was needed to support individual self-fulfillment, and its most notable innovations in relation to the society of its time involved the institutions of marriage and motherhood. Liberated from (supposedly) unwanted pregnancies and children, Oneida women were free to explore a wider range of life options than most American women enjoyed.

Yet, the practice of birth control at Oneida did not enable reproductive choice, belying contemporary assumptions coding contraception as synonymous with choice. Choice was something individuals had to qualify for—rhetorics of choice distinguished legitimate and illegitimate sexual partners, women, men, mothers, fathers, and communal subjects. For men to be legitimate, rational choosers, women had to be disqualified as irrational and emotional. For some women to be legitimate mothers, others had to be illegitimate. Choice functioned not as an inherent right but as something one must earn—not once and for all, but over and over again. And this is not only true of Oneida: if Harold Bloom is right that Oneida does not "trouble our imaginations enough," it should trouble us not for its exceptional but for its representative qualities (qtd. in Fogarty 4). Like Oneida, the US government has historically impeded people's ability to enjoy reproductive justice's three essential rights—from nineteenth- and twentieth-century eugenics to contemporary differential biopolitics.

The Right Not to Have a Child

Just as women in Oneida were seen as peripheral to birth control via male continence, US women have continually struggled to enact the choice not to have a child. Historically, African American slave women were denied control of their fertility, and birth control was mediated by doctors, sexual partners, and the law.[10] Oneida is not the only place where birth control promises autonomy for some women while restricting others. As Greta Gaard has noted, advances in contraception unfold along race and class lines, such that "first-world, economically-privileged white women" are offered "technologies with least harm and most freedom of control (i.e., condoms, the diaphragm, the sponge, the cervical cap, the pill)," while "third-world, economically disadvantaged women of color" are offered or coerced to employ "technologies . . . with the least safety and freedoms (i.e., sterilization, hysterectomy, Depo-Provera, Norplant)" (111). The contemporary moment illustrates this vulnerability: a woman's right to an abortion, no longer guaranteed on a federal level, is playing out variously in states across the US, deepening geographical, racial, economic, and rural-urban divisions that were already evident in the uneven access to abortion services and facilities before *Dobbs v. Jackson*. Access to birth control writ large is similarly threatened, as the US

---

10. Under slavery, "owners routinely enforced practices that would enhance fertility" (Solinger 36). In addition, when the American Medical Association endorsed birth control, they insisted that doctors mediate women's access (Solinger 33). Birth control choices are also mediated by women's sexual partners: Schoen's research into eugenic practices in North Carolina found that women seeking sterilization due to mental illness could be overruled by their husbands (133). Tellingly, Schoen also found that black women were more likely to seek sterilization, due to a lack of access to reliable contraceptives and health care (137).

Supreme Court has ruled that employers do not have to provide birth control options in medical insurance coverage.

The Right to Have a Child

Birth control is never simply freeing because contraceptive technologies have repeatedly been deployed to bar particular women from choosing to have children: "pregnancy—and maternity itself—are race and class privileges" (Fixmer-Oraiz 40). Twentieth-century eugenics, in tandem with antimiscegenation and immigration laws, discouraged the reproduction of people of color and individuals with psychological, cognitive, and physical disabilities.[11] The prison industrial complex, welfare policies, and state promotion of long-acting fertility control continue to impede the reproductive rights of women of color. Narratives of individuals being "unfit to choose" participate in neoliberal rhetorics of non-choice. For instance, contemporary discourses surrounding long-acting reversible contraception promote a view of these devices "as agency-promoting" but also "the only viable contraceptive option" (Mann and Grzanka 341). What is deemed responsible for one woman may not be for another, reinforcing the unequal division of resources and options by race and class. Less powerful women are more likely to encounter non-choice: "differential biopolitics imbues some women with a 'right to choice' and reduces others to scripted 'responsible choices'" (Fixmer-Oraiz 31). For the latter group, emergency contraception such as the morning-after pill is framed as a non-choice "between the selection of a regular method of birth control, and the politicized right to an abortion... the inevitable (and responsible) middle ground between one choice eclipsed and another suspended altogether" (Fixmer-Oraiz 39).

The Right to Parent Children in Safe and Healthy Environments

Finally, women's right to make choices about parenting is also subject to intervention. Contemporaries of Oneida who would have been shocked at the separation of white mothers and children proved well able to tolerate such practices when it came to Black, Indigenous, or

11. Women of color suffered involuntary sterilization at alarming rates: thirty-five percent of Puerto Rican women of childbearing age had been sterilized by 1968, and twenty-four percent of Native American women of childbearing age had been sterilized by 1976 (Palczewski 74-5).

immigrant children.[12] While the community's measures were certainly extreme, the US government has endorsed "a variety of laws over time that have separated children from their mothers," allowing the state to define "good motherhood" and "to act against the motherhood of women defined as falling short of that standard, even when that standard might embed and depend on racial and class biases" (Ross and Solinger 15–16). The right to parent also breaks down along socioeconomic lines: poor mothers have been subject to institutionalization or to having their children "rescued" by charities or the state.[13] Under contemporary biopolitics, such interventions have grown more complex as scientific and medical progress have imposed new "choices" on pregnant women. Such "compulsory self-determination" permeates, for instance, prenatal genetic counseling, where pregnant women are forced to make choices regarding their pregnancy (Fixmer-Oraiz 43). Under the model of "informed choice," the pregnant woman learns that "trusting her own senses is deceptive and that she is considered responsible only if she submits to laboratory results, risk calculations, and managerial decision making" (Samerski 756). Silja Samerski concludes, "such professionally imposed self-determination does not empower patients but disables them" (735). Compulsory choice also informs discourses of age-related infertility, where young women are cautioned against "the dangerous consequences of choosing too late" (Bute et al. 57). In this discourse, making "smart choices" means remembering to have children, underscoring the social script of the "inevitability of motherhood" (S. Hayden 278).

Ultimately, under liberal and neoliberal regimes, increased individual choice does not come free. When choice seemingly increases, so too does the biopolitical call for individual responsibility (the need to

12. Enslaved African American children were regularly separated from their parents; the right to mother one's child was "a privilege reserved for white women" (Solinger 38). Indigenous women "lost their pregnancies and children to genocidal wars and forced marches, and then to the boarding school system that aimed to drain Native culture from the minds of children who were being remade as 'Americans'" (Ross and Solinger 13).

13. In the nineteenth and early twentieth centuries, poor white women who had children out of wedlock were often institutionalized, their children sent to "orphan farms" (Ross and Solinger 29). Child-rescue organizations took children from poor mothers if they were "not married or could not afford to stay home all day" (Solinger 68).

make "good" choices) and the social impulse to determine fitness (who is "fit to choose"). Foucault elaborates this hand-in-hand relationship as a hallmark of modern power: "Liberalism must produce freedom, but this very act entails the establishment of limitations, controls, forms of coercion, and obligations relying on threats, etcetera" (*Birth* 64). The history of reproductive choice in America parallels the development of neoliberal biopolitics more broadly, where "the considerable extension of procedures of control, constraint, and coercion" functions as "something like the counterpart and counterweights of different freedoms" (67). The lesson, then, from this rhetorical history of choice, is not just that choice is a myth, but that rhetorics of choice all too often trigger biopolitical infringements in the guise of individual freedom.

Works Cited

Agnew, Lois, et al. "Octalog III: The Politics of Historiography in 2010." *Rhetoric Review*, vol. 30, no. 2, 2011, pp. 109–34.

Bute, Jennifer J., Lynn M. Harter, Erika L. Kirby, and Marie Thompson. "Politicizing Personal Choices? The Storying of Age-Related Infertility in Public Discourses." *Contemplating Maternity in an Era of Choice: Explorations into Discourses of Reproduction*, edited by Sara Hayden and Lynn O'Brien Hallstein, Lexington, 2010, pp. 49–72.

Caeton, D.A. "Choice of a Lifetime: Disability, Feminism, and Reproductive Rights." *Disability Studies Quarterly,* vol. 31, no. 1, 2011, doi:10.18061/dsq.v31i1.1369. Accessed 17 May, 2021.

Carden, Maren. *Oneida: Utopian Community to Modern Corporation*. Syracuse UP, 1998.

Dalsimer, Marlyn Hartzell. "Women and Family in the Oneida Community, 1837–1881." Diss. New York University, 1975.

de Onís, Kathleen M. "Lost in Translation: Challenging (White, Monolingual Feminism's <Choice> with *Justicia Reproductiva*." *Women's Studies in Communication*, vol. 38, no. 1, 2015, pp. 1–19.

de Vogue, Ariane. "Why Clarence Thomas Wrote Over a Dozen Pages on Eugenics." *CNN*, May 28, 2019, www.cnn.com/2019/05/28/politics/clarence-thomas-eugenics-abortion/index.html. Accessed 18 May 2023.

Derkas, Erika. "Retrofitting Choice: White Feminism and the Politics of Reproductive Justice." *Radical Reproductive Justice: Foundations, Theory, Practice, Critique*, edited by Loretta J. Ross, Lynn Roberts, Erika Derkas, Whitney Peoples, and Pamela Bridgewater Toure, Feminist Press, 2017, pp. 272–82.

Ehrlich, Shoshanna. "SCOTUS Claims Abortion Proponents are Motivated by Eugenics and Eliminating the 'Unfit'—But History Says Otherwise." *Ms.*

Magazine, 4 Aug. 2022, msmagazine.com/2022/08/04/abortion-eugenics-black-women/. Accessed 18 May 2023.

Fixmer-Oraiz, Natalie. "No Exception Postprevention: 'Differential Biopolitics' on the Morning After." *Contemplating Maternity in an Era of Choice: Explorations into Discourses of Reproduction*, edited by Sara Hayden and Lynn O'Brien Hallstein, Lexington, 2010, pp. 27–48.

Fogarty, Robert S., ed. *Special Love/Special Sex: An Oneida Community Diary.* Syracuse UP, 1994.

Foucault, Michel. *The Birth of Biopolitics: Lectures at the Collège de France, 1978–1979.* Picador, 2010.

—. "The Politics of Health in the Eighteenth Century." Translated by Richard A. Lynch, *Foucault Studies*, no. 18, 2014, pp. 113-27.

Gaard, Greta. "Reproductive Technology, or Reproductive Justice?: An Ecofeminist, Environmental Justice Perspective on the Rhetoric of Choice." *Ethics and the Environment*, vol. 15, no. 2, 2010, pp. 103–29.

Haines, Michael. "Fertility and Mortality in the United States." *EH.Net Encyclopedia*, edited by Robert Whaples, Mar. 19, 2008. eh.net/encyclopedia/fertility-and-mortality-in-the-united-states/. Accessed Mar. 15, 2020.

Harvey, David. *A Brief History of Neoliberalism.* Oxford UP, 2007.

Hayden, Sara. "Purposefully Childless Good Women." *Contemplating Maternity in an Era of Choice: Explorations into Discourses of Reproduction*, edited by Sara Hayden and Lynn O'Brien Hallstein, Lexington, 2010, pp. 269–90.

Hayden, Sara, and Lynn O'Brien Hallstein. "Introduction." *Contemplating Maternity in an Era of Choice: Explorations into Discourses of Reproduction*, edited by Sara Hayden and Lynn O'Brien Hallstein, Lexington, 2010, pp. xiii-xxxix.

Hayden, Wendy. *Evolutionary Rhetoric: Sex, Science, and Free Love in Nineteenth-Century Feminism.* Southern Illinois UP, 2013.

Klee-Hartzell, Marlyn. "Family Love, True Womanliness, Motherhood, and the Socialization of Girls in the Oneida Community, 1848–1880." *Women in Spiritual and Communitarian Societies in the United States,* edited by Wendy E. Chmielewski, Louis J. Kern, and Marlyn Klee-Hartzell, Syracuse UP, 1993, pp. 182–200.

La Moy, William T. and George Edward Cragin. "Two Documents Detailing the Oneida Community's Practice of Complex Marriage." *New England Quarterly*, vol. 85, no. 1, 2012, pp. 119–37.

Leonard, Charlotte M. *Journals of Charlotte M. Leonard.* Box 63, pp. 1–54, Oneida Community Collection, Special Collections Research Center, Syracuse University Libraries.

Lewis, Jan. "Mother's Love: The Construction of an Emotion in Nineteenth-Century America." *Mothers and Motherhood: Readings in American History,* edited by Rima D. Apple and Janet Golden, Ohio State UP, 1997, pp. 52–71.

Male Continence. Digital ed., Department of Special Collections, Syracuse University Library, 2000, pp. 1–20, library.syr.edu/digital/collections/m/MaleContinence-51k. Accessed 19 Mar. 2019.

Mann, Emily S., and Patrick R. Grzanka. "Agency-Without-Choice: The Visual Rhetorics of Long-Acting Reversible Contraception Promotion." *Symbolic Interaction*, 2018, vol. 41, no. 3, pp. 334–56.

McCarver, Virginia. "The Rhetoric of Choice and 21st-Century Feminism: Online Conversations About Work, Family, and Sarah Palin." *Women's Studies in Communication*, vol. 34, no. 1, 2011, pp. 20–41.

Miller, Tirzah C. "Parentage at Oneida." 25 Dec. 1877, Box 66, Oneida Community Collection, Special Collections Research Center, Syracuse University Libraries.

Noyes, George Wallingford and Lawrence Foster. *Free Love in Utopia: John Humphrey Noyes and the Origin of the Oneida Community.* U of Illinois P, 2001.

Palczewski, Catherine H. "Reproductive Freedom: Transforming Discourses of Choice." *Contemplating Maternity in an Era of Choice: Explorations into Discourses of Reproduction*, edited by Sara Hayden and Lynn O'Brien Hallstein, Lexington, 2010, pp. 73–94.

Ross, Loretta J. "Trust Black Women: Reproductive Justice and Eugenics." *Radical Reproductive Justice: Foundations, Theory, Practice, Critique*, edited by Loretta J. Ross, Lynn Roberts, Erika Derkas, Whitney Peoples, and Pamela Bridgewater Toure, Feminist Press, 2017, pp. 58–85.

Ross, Loretta J. and Rickie Solinger, *Reproductive Justice: An Introduction*. U of California P, 2017.

Ruhl, Leslie. "Dilemmas of the Will: Uncertainty, Reproduction, and the Rhetoric of Control." *Signs,* vol. 27, no. 3, 2002, pp. 641–63.

Samerski, Silja. "Genetic Counseling and the Fiction of Choice: Taught Self-Determination as a New Technique of Social Engineering." *Signs,* vol. 34, no. 4, 2009, pp. 735–61.

Schoen, Joanna. *Choice and Coercion: Birth Control, Sterilization, and Abortion in Public Health and Welfare.* U of North Carolina P, 2005.

Solinger, Rickie. *Pregnancy and Power: A Short History of Reproductive Politics in America.* New York UP, 2004.

Stewart, Nikita. "Planned Parenthood in N.Y. Disavows Margaret Sanger Over Eugenics." *New York Times*, 21 July 2020.

Thwaites, Rachel. "Making a Choice or Taking a Stand? Choice Feminism, Political Engagement and the Contemporary Feminist Movement." *Feminist Theory*, vol. 18, no. 1, 2017, pp. 55–68.

Van de Warker, Ely. "A Gynecological Study of the Oneida Community." *American Journal of Obstetrics and Diseases of Women and Children,* vol. 27, no. 8, 1884, pp. 785–810.

Weingarten, Karen. *Abortion in the American Imagination: Before Life and Choice, 1880–1940*. Rutgers UP, 2014.

8 Choice, Shame, and the Neoliberal Affective Politics of Nurx's App-Based Reproductive and Sexual Healthcare

Melissa Stone and Zachary Beare

> To achieve reproductive justice we must . . . center the most marginalized. Our society will not be free until the most vulnerable people are able to access the resources and full human rights to live self-determined lives without fear, discrimination, or retaliation.
>
> —SisterSong, Inc., "Reproductive Justice"

> Choice, or the illusion of choice, is central to contemporary feminism. Easily aligned with activism aimed at empowering women to make decisions about their own lives and bodies, choice is ubiquitous, rhetorically powerful, and highly portable.
>
> —Carly S. Woods, "Repunctuated Feminism: Marketing Menstrual Suppression Through the Rhetoric of Choice"

The epigraphs opening this chapter speak to the affective dimensions of reproductive health and rights; they also point to the problems of examining these goals through the lens of "choice" alone. Though perpetually appealing to and rhetorically powerful for some, "choice" is often illusory, and even when present, it tends to be inequitably distributed, inaccessible, or dubious to many, especially in the context of reproductive healthcare. The illusory and limited nature of choice has been brought into sharp focus in the aftermath of the *Dobbs v. Jackson Women's Health Organization* decision. Still, the promise of choice continues to shape the discourse of reproductive health and the marketing of reproductive healthcare solutions and technologies, especially those seeking to intervene and provide access to reproductive and sexual healthcare and access to emergency contraceptives and abortion pills. This chapter examines one such venture—Nurx, a telehealth medicine platform that presents itself as a liberating technology, providing users with a sense of empowerment and expansive options for reproductive and sexual healthcare. We argue Nurx operationalizes neoliberal values promoting individual choice and personal responsibility. We analyze Nurx by employing what Shui-yin Sharon Yam describes as a "reproductive justice model of rhetorical analysis" as an attempt to resist an "individualistic and consumeristic framework of choice" (20). This approach encourages rhetoricians and technical communicators to consider how reliable access to reproductive and sexual healthcare is inseparable from "experiences of people who are disenfranchised by intersecting power structures" (20).

Choice is often centered in progressive reproductive and sexual health, rights, and justice movements; however, rhetorics of choice are frequently co-opted by for-profit ventures (like Nurx) to sell products *seemingly* aligned with activism and empowerment. The co-option of rhetorics of choice often hides regressive notions of individual responsibility. Additionally, we tie Nurx's neoliberal values to its rhetoric, for it relies on and reactivates long standing tropes of shame surrounding reproductive and sexual health as a means of recruiting users, rather than confronting or realigning these affects. To illustrate this point, we situate Nurx in relation to historical examples of technologies, showcasing the extended legacy of promoting affects of shame regarding reproducing bodies and marginalized sexualities. The chapter concludes by highlighting lessons that might be gleaned from Nurx, which could benefit both traditional face-to-face and technologically mediated approaches to reproductive and sexual health and by emphasizing what rhetoricians and technical communication specialists can learn from this case study and what future work is warranted.

Founded in 2015 by tech entrepreneur Hans Gangeskar and physician Edvard Engesæth, Nurx is an American web- and app-based telehealth platform focused on providing access to contraceptives, sexually transmitted infection (STI) testing and treatment, and pre-exposure prophylaxis (PrEP) to prevent the spread of HIV. Nurx provides medical care and writes prescriptions for patient-users in thirty states. Nurx is a mission-based, values-forward company, leveraging language of the reproductive rights and reproductive justice movements and articulating a clear mission to empower users and increase access to reproductive and sexual healthcare. As of August of 2020, Nurx reports having over 300,000 monthly users, and that number has been increasing dramatically as COVID-19 has encouraged more individuals to seek out options for reproductive and sexual healthcare that do not rely on traditional in-person office visits (Shieber).

Nurx addresses a clear need, estimating that "there are nearly twenty million women in the U.S. who live in areas without easy access to contraception" (Nurx). This aligns with the increased concerns about access to reproductive healthcare and fears about expanding and multiplying "contraception deserts" across the country (Kreitzer and Watts Smith; McClurg and Lopez; Varney). Following the election of former president Donald Trump and the installation of a conservative majority in the US Supreme Court, lawmakers at all levels have been emboldened to push through legislation restricting access to and decreasing funding for reproductive and sexual healthcare. As we first drafted this chapter in July of 2020, the US Supreme Court upheld the Trump administration's regulations allowing employers with religious objections to avoid providing contraception as part of their employer-provided health insurance packages. Roughly two years later while this collection was still in development, the Supreme Court handed down the landmark decision to overturn *Roe v. Wade* (1973). Judicial action has clearly run parallel to strategic defunding of reproductive and sexual health clinics across the country. This trend is deeply troubling, given that medical experts have made clear that defunding reproductive and sexual health clinics negatively impacts public health (Ciccariello; Hillard; Lawrence and Ness; Slusky).

Rhetoricians and technical communication specialists should play an important role in the research and theorization of app-based mHealth (or mobile health) technologies. Such technologies are rapidly growing (Agnihothri et al.; Fiordelli, Diviani, and Schulz; Marcolino et al.). Nurx and similar mHealth platforms are prime examples of what Erin Frost and Michelle Eble refer to as "technical rhetorics." The term "technical rhetorics" "highlights the persuasive nature of specialized information and content that influences public audiences to think, *feel*, or act a certain way" and in so doing "complicates notions of objectivity and neutral views of technical communication" (Frost and Eble, emphasis added). Elsewhere, Frost has elaborated on this definition, explaining that "technical rhetorics persuade us daily to act, talk, behave, legislate, resist, argue, and think in particular ways. As such, these communications must be considered as part of the technology in question anytime we look to better understand the cultural uptake of a medical technology" ("Ultrasound" 3). The term "technical rhetorics" is a reminder that there is no neutral position when it comes to the design, use, and implementation of technologies, especially those designed to intervene in issues regarding sexual and reproductive healthcare. Communication practices and rhetorical moves made to provide sexual and reproductive care to certain populations not only influence the way individuals discuss these issues but also how they construct specific identities, experience agency, and understand responsibility.

App-Based Models of Reproductive and Sexual Healthcare

The proliferation of app-based healthcare, such as Nurx, has been dramatic, and numbers of mHealth apps are rising. According to the most recent report from IQVIA, a firm dedicated to healthcare data and analytics, over 318,000 health apps are available for download in the top mobile app stores, and approximately two hundred are added each day (3). From counting steps, to monitoring fertility, to managing water intake, to tracking health conditions, diets, and medications, users can find a mobile app for managing any aspect of their health. IQVIA explains that "while the majority of mobile health apps available are general wellness apps, the number of health condition management apps—those often associated with patient care—are increasing at a faster rate, and now represent forty percent of all health-related apps" (3). Some of these apps connect users to physicians for general primary care and the management of a variety of health concerns, while others are targeted for the management of particular healthcare issues. There are apps for managing hair loss, for psychotherapy and the prescribing of psychiatric medications, for erectile dysfunction, and even for opioid addiction; and, of course, there are apps like Nurx, which specialize in reproductive and sexual health.

Due to the pervasiveness of mHealth apps, scholars have turned to them as artifacts for analysis. For instance, Deborah Lupton argues mobile apps are sociocultural products "located within pre-established circuits of discourse and meaning" (610). Lupton explains mobile health apps are shaped by the cultures in which they are produced and often work to reinforce dominant ideologies and social arrangements of those cultures. These apps become active participants shaping users' emotions, their orientation to their bodies, and their performance and interaction within networks of individuals and technologies. They can create new practices and new forms of knowledge. In viewing mobile health apps as "sociocultural artifacts," Lupton positions mobile apps as a generative and "productive form of power" serving political purposes and supporting established forms of dominance and authority (610). Scholars interested in mobile healthcare apps are also concerned about data security and surveillance implications. For example, Les Hutchison and Maria Novotny argue critical digital literacies resisting ubiquitous, non-consensual surveillance of users' bodies are necessary for engaging with emerging technological issues in health and medicine. While Nurx is approved under the Health Insurance Portability and Accountability Act (HIPAA), the service does not guarantee privacy protection. By utilizing Nurx, patient-users are willing to risk exposure of private health information, whether knowingly or not, to enjoy a particular affective experience, and, as Hutchison and Novotny argue, this choice likely has affective consequences.

Key to the design and use of Nurx as a platform is asynchronous communication. Patient-users can seek services either through Nurx's website or their mobile app. Both are sleekly designed, utilizing bold pops of color, modern sans serif fonts, and faux Sharpie-written headings indicating a youthful and approachable DIY ethos designed to appeal to their target demographic of women between the age of twenty and forty (Shieber). New patient-users seeking birth control begin with a "telehealth session" consisting of answering a series of questions (regarding medical history, sexual history/activity, purpose of birth control). Questions are primarily answered by checking boxes or selecting options from drop down menus. Patient-users are walked through the process of uploading scans or photos of their IDs and any medical insurance cards. The information is submitted and then reviewed by a medical provider who provides prescription options and makes a recommendation. The process can take three to five days for information to be submitted and reviewed and for a prescription to be sent. Prescriptions can be filled at local pharmacies or sent via the mail to patient-clients. Patient-clients can communicate with providers through a messenger on either the website or app. Depending on the question, it may be answered by a nurse or a physician (though not necessarily the original prescriber). Unlike some other mHealth apps offering reproductive healthcare, Nurx does not require synchronous video-based telehealth sessions; all contact occurs asynchronously. In addition to the channel of asynchronous communication, Nurx publishes a blog on topics connected to sexual and reproductive health and maintains an extensive FAQ section to answer questions patient-users may have.

The asynchronous nature of the healthcare offered by Nurx is key to its design and success and is central to the affective experience it is meant to deliver. In a *Medium* article from 2019, Nurx extensively quotes from clinicians working for the company who specifically discuss this affective dimension:

> I was honestly afraid that communication would be compromised without face-to-face patient contact, but it turns out that messaging patients through the platform often removes the inhibitions that some patients feel talking in person. I spent a number of years working in an outpatient internal medicine practice, and rarely did patients ask many questions about potentially embarrassing topics. People feel much freer when sending an essentially anonymous text. (Dr. Nancy Shannon qtd. in Nurx, "Setting the Record Straight")

Here, Shannon directly acknowledges the affective contexts shaping reproductive and sexual healthcare. She showcases how asynchronous communication provides users a means of avoiding the shame often experienced and how it can lower inhibitions and increase honesty, which, she argues, leads to better healthcare.

Limits of the App-Based Model of Reproductive and Sexual Healthcare

Nurx's asynchronous reproductive and sexual healthcare is, in many ways, trading in privilege. Nurx provides a way for users to obtain services without ever having to step foot in a reproductive health clinic, thus decreasing the potential for feelings of shame and lessening risks of being seen by someone in the community at a clinic or facing judgment from a medical practitioner. However, while platforms like Nurx might be helpful in providing access for people without reproductive and sexual healthcare clinics in their area or for those who lack a healthcare plan, it is not a sweeping solution. Nurx, while helpful in providing a wider opportunity for access for some people, can never fully replace a reproductive health clinic. Certain types of birth control like intrauterine devices (IUDs) and other implants are only available through visits to reproductive health clinics. Further, preventive and life-saving services like Papanicolaou tests (often colloquially refer to as "pap smears"), cancer screenings, and breast exams are only possible through access to brick and mortar reproductive health clinics.

Nurx claims to be focused on expanding access to reproductive health and offering an affordable product, but it is best designed to support individuals who have health insurance and likely could seek out birth control through more traditional means. Although Nurx does offer relatively low-cost consultation and prescription rates for the uninsured, cheaper alternatives exist through public health and nonprofit healthcare clinics. The affective product Nurx is seeking to sell is one that most likely benefits affluent consumers, individuals who are willing to pay for a particular affective experience of seeking healthcare. The privilege associated with choosing to seek sexual and reproductive health through Nurx is further magnified when one considers that access and successful navigation of the platform is reliant on access to technology and powerful wireless networks, infrastructure often lacking in the rural spaces where access to healthcare is insufficient (Bommakanti et al.; Martin; Struminger and Arora). Nurx is also dependent on users possessing several technological, sexual, and embodied literacies, which may be lacking in the communities the company claims to serve.

While the experience of going to a gynecologist is often associated with felt experiences of shame, the traditional visit and exam has affordances that cannot be duplicated in a telemedicine environment. Physicians use the visual and tactile exam to screen for evidence of serious medical issues and are trained to rely on the office visit conversation for clues about patient affect and state of mind, clues that might not be as readily visible in crafted asynchronous communication. Further, as mentioned, the forms of contraceptives available through Nurx and other similar platforms are limited, and this may result in individuals choosing contraceptive methodologies that are less than ideal for them. Individuals reliant on platforms like Nurx may also miss out on comprehensive lab work (measuring blood count, glucose levels, kidney and liver functions, and lipid levels). This may prevent individuals from discovering serious health concerns (especially diabetes and high cholesterol, leading contributors to death in the United States). There is danger, too, in the platform's reliance on self-reported health indicators like blood pressure and weight, both of which often shape physicians' recommendations for contraceptives. While Nurx has partnered with Lab Corps for STI testing using self-collected specimens, it has not developed a way to duplicate traditional blood panels. Even with the STI testing, limitations still remain. The success of those mail-based lab tests is reliant on users' understandings and abilities to conduct their own swabs and specimen collections.

Nurx's Neoliberal Rhetorics of Choice and (Failed) Affective Realignment

Despite the limitations and risks described, Nurx is appealing; it is efficient, private, and on-demand, all qualities privileged in the neoliberal marketplace. Anne Teresa Demo discusses how logics of neoliberalism have shaped the business of reproduction and motherhood. As Demo explains, neoliberalism embraces free-market solutions to social problems, seeing them as more agile than traditional governmental or community-based social programs. Nurx clearly works within this tradition, a for-profit venture designed to address a genuine societal need for better access to sexual and reproductive care and more expansive and comprehensive sexual and reproductive education. Demo argues such neoliberal ventures often engage in forms of commodification, what she describes as a "reductive process that transforms an experience, activity, or event into a purchasable commodity" (9). We see Nurx as commodifying a particular affective experience, a way of seeking reproductive healthcare "discretely . . . and without judgment." Indeed, purchasing and/or investing in affective experiences is another common trope of neoliberalism. Davi Johnson Thornton links this to neoliberalism's privileging of "emotional management" (400). Thornton argues, "in the context of neoliberalism, individuals are habituated to economic modes of thinking and acting, conditioned to feel, live, and think their lives as 'self-entrepreneurs'" (405). The freedom to choose positive or managed emotional experiences, then, becomes positioned as a form of self-investment and even empowerment, as demonstrated in Nurx's rhetoric of empowering patient-users to "take control of [their] own health."

Nurx's neoliberal approach does little to change the systemic problems associated with reproductive healthcare access. Nurx and its embrace of a rhetoric of choice works within a tradition of activist rhetorics that have privileged *choice* over *justice* or *freedom*. As Sara Hayden and D. Lynn O'Brien Hallstein make clear, discourses of choice tend to overlook difference, histories of inequities, and the complexities of intersectional identities shaping choice making. Similarly, Catherine H. Palczewski argues rhetorics of choice often rely on the "assumptions that all women have the same interests and needs" (83). Palczewski favors the language of "reproductive freedom" over "choice," arguing "reproductive freedom as articulated by women of color and poor women provides an excellent mechanism by which the limited agendas of apparently radical groups can be challenged for their failing to account for privilege" (89). We see Nurx as failing to account for that dimension of privilege. While it provides an option for accessing reproductive and sexual healthcare, its product relies on both technological infrastructure and literacies and best suits individuals who already have insurance and who could access this healthcare through other means. Nurx does not expand access to reproductive and sexual healthcare for people who need it as much as it provides existing healthcare consumers the *choice* for a particular affective experience of reproductive and sexual healthcare.

The tradition of critique offered by the reproductive freedom and justice movements can also help showcase how Nurx both aligns with feminist exigencies and how the company falls short of enacting a radical re-envisioning of the healthcare system by privileging individual freedom and choice and by operationalizing feelings of shame. While Nurx may offer its patient-users a positive affective experience, it does not engage in an affective realignment that benefits all individuals. Affective realignment for Heather Brook Adams represents a "significant rhetorical goal," one that is predicated on creating affectively attuned health literacies (582). Affectively attuned health literacies should help audiences recognize and contend with the fact that much of the reproductive and sexual healthcare texts and technologies of past and present teach people to feel ashamed of their bodies, sexual knowledges, and sexual desires (582). Nurx does not effectively challenge or reverse this tendency. In fact, the marketing Nurx engages in, both in its commercials and its website messaging, actually works to reinscribe the affects of shame. It recruits users through the operationalization of that shame, and even those who do not (or are not able to) utilize its services have those affects triggered.

Nurx's Marketing as a Culture of Shame and Stigma

Nurx's current marketing campaigns maintain longstanding cultures of bodily shame and reproductive and sexual stigma that are still prevalent. There are varied reasons for the shame and stigma associated with reproducing bodies, and Nurx attends to at least two of these reasons—the stigma of reproducing bodies invoking disgust (e.g., shame associated with the menstruating body) and the shame related to feelings of sexual desire and sexual behavior. It is important to illuminate how the effectiveness of operationalizing shame is indebted to the pathologizing of reproducing bodies that pervades histories related to reproductive and sexual health technologies.

Product advertisements, for example, often emphasize concealment as a selling point. An example of this appears in a menstrual education pamphlet produced by Tampax in the 1970s and 1980s. This example informs the reader (the presumed menstruator) to act regarding their menstrual cycle to prevent experiences of shame. Consider the pamphlet's answer to the question "How should you act on a date when you have your period?":

> This is the time to be particularly neat and well groomed—so you will look and feel your best. If you are overly concerned about your period, this may be obvious to others. So, it's up to *you* to prevent embarrassment. Change your protection as often as necessary. Keep extras in your handbag. When you must excuse yourself, do so simply and without embarrassment. Eventually, boys learn to accept and respect the menstrual cycle as a normal, natural part of a girl's life. Your own naturalness, poise and discreetness will help them, too. (Tampax Incorporated 23)

The focus on individual responsibility in preventing a shame-inducing experience—assumed here to be a moment when visible menstrual leakage is detected—is both highly emphasized and problematic. The passage implies that if the menstruator just does as they should (i.e., stay "neat" and "well groomed"), change their protection often, and manage their own potential for shame, men will eventually "accept and respect" the menstrual cycle. This passage shows how a company like Tampax is less concerned with sociopolitical aspects of menstrual health and education and more concerned with capitalizing on that shame to sell a mass-produced product. Its market success is, in fact, predicated on shaming particular bodies. Decades later, similar discursive moves are present in Nurx's branding. For example, one passage from Nurx's website reads:

> Nurx is built to deliver on the three things everyone needs from their healthcare. Choice, so you can make positive decisions about your own body. Control, so you can plan ahead and look after yourself without complication. And freedom, so your access to medication is never blocked by cost, bureaucracy, geography, stigma, or anything else. (Nurx, 2020)

This messaging exemplifies what Carly Woods calls a rhetorical paradox—one that holds a promise of individual agency while simultaneously co-opting it to promote "controversial choices that reinforce sexist stereotypes" (267). At face value, Nurx's promise aligns with feminist values of the autonomy of choice, the ability to control one's own body, and the freedom to access safe and nonjudgmental reproductive healthcare. However, under the surface of this advertisement is Nurx's regressive neoliberal approach to providing accessible reproductive and sexual healthcare, one which operationalizes shame to sell products. Nurx's branding participates in the "rhetorical process of gendering" (Adams; Enoch; Hallenbeck; Jack), and it fails to consider the lived experiences, knowledges, and rhetorical practices of those who are often excluded from dominant narratives of reproductive health. Jessica Enoch describes the rhetorical process of gendering as "the rhetorical work that goes into creating and disturbing the gendered distinctions, social categories, and asymmetrical power relationships that women and men encounter in their daily lives" (115). Adams builds on this rhetorical concept through her notion of affective realignment. She explains that "affect as a nondiscursive, embodied, and everyday emotional engagement" (548) plays a significant role in rhetorical processes of gendering and through rhetorical artifacts like that of reproductive healthcare texts and technologies.

Nurx and the Operationalization of Shame

Nurx's rhetorical choices—across its platforms, social media, and advertising—address and operationalize shame as a means of recruiting and keeping patient-users. Shame, both as an individually experienced emotion and as a circulating affect shaping the social field, has garnered increasing attention from cultural critics and rhetoricians. One of the most extensive theorizations of shame comes from Elspeth Probyn. Drawing on anthropologist A. L. Epstein, Probyn argues shame can easily be harnessed and used to control and manipulate individuals so that it can be "put to use in the management of human interaction" (30). Probyn explains, "shame teaches us about our relations to others. Shame makes us feel proximity differently, understood as the body's relation to itself, the self to itself, and comprehended within a sphere that is human and nonhuman, universal and particular, specific and general" (35). Probyn's discussion of shame as a force mediating our relations and proximity to both human and nonhuman others is especially significant for understanding the appeal of a platform like Nurx. Nurx, with its asynchronous, text-based communication structure, changes the relationship between medical provider and patient; it facilitates both spatial and temporal distance to alter the emotional experience of seeking reproductive healthcare, with the goal of allowing the patient to feel less shame.

The shame associated with seeking reproductive healthcare is part of a larger dynamic of gendered shame associated with reproducing bodies and marginalized sexualities. As Probyn explains, "Common facts of women's lives (menstruation and so on) are framed as shameful," (85) which may make shame a repeated feature in women's lives. Similarly, Shari Stenberg explains that "while all humans experience shame, some subjects face repetitive shaming, relentless breaks in connection, and resultant social isolation" (122). Stenberg specifically discusses how women, especially women of color, and members of the LGBTQ community are likely to experience shame. As she argues, "the accumulation of shame is particularly significant for marginalized groups . . . who have been repeatedly marked—through language, legislation, social exclusions—as inherently shameful" (22). The accumulation and repetition of these experiences function as what Lynn Worsham describes as a "dominant pedagogy of emotion" (221) and showcases why Adams argues that shame can be seen "as a learned type of gendered experience" (586).

The rhetoric found on the Nurx platform illustrates the company's awareness of the power and impact of affects of shame. On their FAQ page, in a section answering the question "Why Nurx?" the company explains, "We make it easy for you to get your medication quickly, discreetly, affordably, and without judgement. By removing the pain points around access to emergency contraception, we've got you covered when it really counts" (Nurx, "About Us"). The language of discretion and "without judgement" suggests that one of the primary "pain points" in seeking reproductive healthcare is emotional—largely associated with affects of shame. While Nurx works to address individually felt pain through a message of personal empowerment, it simultaneously relies on and designs advertisements to trigger that emotion.

This dynamic is demonstrated in one of Nurx's early commercial campaigns called "Stories from the Gynecologist" from 2018. Two episodes of this advertisement exist. The first one, entitled "Is She Judging Me About My Number?," opens on a woman who appears to be in her late twenties lying on an exam table in a doctor's office. The gynecologist, a woman who appears to be in her sixties, wearing half glasses low on her nose and speaking with a strong New York accent, enters and asks, "In for birth control, are we?" She lowers her glasses, smiles and winks as she asks the question. She loudly smacks her hands together and applies hand sanitizer. She sits down on the squeaking rolling doctor's stool and dramatically puts on rubber gloves, stretching and snapping the latex. She encourages the patient to scoot down on the exam table and "assume the position" which the woman does, appearing very uncomfortable. The doctor then says, "Now, I need you to tell me how many sexual partners you've had this year. I need you to be perfectly honest because I'm not here to judge." The camera closes in on the patient's face as she thinks. Descriptors of sexual partners appear in text around her face—Alex, Sam's housemate, Harry, The French Guy . . . Antoine?, Bryan. The doctor interjects, "Ooh, it's taking you a while, huh?," a comment that only adds to the sense of shame experienced by the patient seeking birth control in the commercial. The patient finally answers "Seven," to which the doctor replies, with apparent judgment, "SEVEN?!?" The patient is obviously uncomfortable and experiencing shame. With a face revealing disgust, the doctor then declares "this is going to feel cold" as she inserts a speculum into the patient, who cringes in pain. The commercial cuts to a message from Nurx encircled with a heart explaining "We wouldn't dream of judging you for your number!" The second video in this campaign follows a nearly identical structure, only instead of a shame-inducing discussion about the patient's number of sexual partners, it presents the patient having to explain being in an open relationship, allowing Nurx to reference the sexual shame associating with transcending the bounds of heteronormativity.

This advertising campaign illustrates the rhetorical power of shame and how Nurx intentionally draws upon that power. As Probyn argues, "shame is deeply related not only to how others think about us but also to how we think about ourselves" (45). There is, to use a phrase from Adams, "a sociality of shame" (585); it is interpersonal, relational, and rhetorical. As Stenberg explains, "often, shame arises because one has failed, or refused, to adhere to a societal expectation" (123). This dynamic is explicitly represented in the commercial. The patients seeking birth control in these campaigns experience shame when their sexual histories fail to align with the expectations of the gynecologist. Adams argues, "the intimacy of shame relates to its visibility and its performance on bodies that are looked upon; experiencing shame makes us seen but also confirms that we know we are seen as wrong or less than" (585). These issues of visibility, of being a body on display, are directly represented in Nurx's advertising campaign. The videos repeatedly show the "awkward gynecologist" between the patient's legs looking at them. The insertion of the speculum, too, draws special attention to the gynecological visit as a moment of heightened visibility and vulnerability.

In many ways, what Nurx is selling is a decrease in visibility and an alternate relationality between birth control seeker and birth control prescriber. In one of Nurx's asynchronous birth control consultations, the birth control seeker does not have to undress or slide down an exam table. They do not have to be looked at or waited on while calculating numbers of partners or dates of recent sexual contact. That potential for felt shame is largely eliminated with the temporal and spatial distance facilitated by the app. Those feelings are not completely eliminated, of course. Individuals may still feel shame typing or clicking a response to a question about sexual partners, but the model is designed to attenuate those feelings.

Nurx positions itself as a radical and revolutionary platform (explicitly using that language of revolution). On their homepage, they explain, "We're on a mission to transform healthcare" (Nurx), and a central part of that "transformation" seems to be focused on affect. In addition to saving time and money, they explain that part of what they offer is "peace of mind" (Nurx). Nurx offers an emotional product as well as a medical service and access to pharmaceuticals. Given the emotional service that Nurx describes, it may be tempting to see their platform as engaged in the progressive and feminist project of "affective realignment" theorized by Adams, but we argue that the exact opposite is true. Nurx does not realign the affects surrounding seeking reproductive and sexual health; it capitalizes on them; it utilizes them for marketing purposes. Probyn argues, "It is undeniable that repeated exposure to scenes of shame reactivates and feeds the individual's capacity to experience shame" (85). This is what these marketing campaigns do. Despite the company's slogan work and messages of empowerment, Nurx's business model relies on the gendered dynamics of shame.

Even more troubling, by scripting sexual shame as personal pain in this advertisement, Nurx minimizes the larger political exigencies shaping the need for more accessible birth control and sexual healthcare. The centering of individual pain and individual choice in this campaign and elsewhere in their marketing materials works to the detriment of the political project in which Nurx claims to be engaged. Rather than sponsoring increased awareness about the consequences of sexual shame, the company follows the neoliberal tendency to individualize these issues and offers an individual, consumable solution, rather than a systemic one. Rather than offering a meaningful realignment of the cultural affects surrounding the reproducing and sexual bodies, it relies on them to establish their product as universally appealing. It is not a revolution; it is a maintenance, a reproduction—and a capitalization—on the status quo.

Lessons Learned from Nurx: A Conclusion

While this chapter critiques Nurx for operationalizing affects of shame, the effectiveness of its marketing campaign and the rapid growth in its patient-users makes clear the power of those affects in shaping the context of seeking reproductive and sexual healthcare, especially as neoliberal solutions to healthcare issues proliferate. Thus, it is incumbent on physicians, healthcare communicators, and mHealth technology developers to investigate how their practices and rhetorical choices might reinforce or realign those affects. It is also important that current and potential patient-users be vigilant in assessing how traditional medical providers and mHealth technologies operationalize affects associated with reproductive and sexual healthcare by designing services and tools to trigger or attenuate those affects. We encourage current and potential patient-users to engage in public critique and experience-sharing around existing practices and technologies and to engage in knowledge making and the work of imagining what future, more reproductive justice-oriented practices and technologies might look like.

Additionally, while we see limitations associated with Nurx's asynchronous communication practices, especially if they are the *only* forms of contact between patient and provider, we know traditional face-to-face sexual and reproductive healthcare might benefit from some of Nurx's practices. For instance, clinicians might utilize asynchronous communication tools to invite patients to provide histories (especially surrounding sensitive topics like numbers of sexual partners, their genders and anatomies, etc.) in advance of the face-to-face visit. The application of such tools might also provide opportunities for individuals to ask questions of their providers. Having the time to draft such questions might be an especially helpful alternative to the feeling of being put on the spot during an office visit or needing to respond to heteronormatively framed questions. We also see potential benefits to offering patients the option to self-collect swabs for STI testing. Such a strategy may afford patients a greater sense of control and ease. Practices allowing self-collection of swabs are increasingly common (Dangerfield et al.; Gaydos; Purcell, Gaydos, and Widdice), and some scholarship shows it might be especially valuable in helping LGBTQ patients feel more comfortable seeking sexual and reproductive healthcare (Bell et al.; Goldstein et al.; Reisner et al.).

In addition to offering potentially useful insights for healthcare providers, our case study of Nurx offers valuable lessons for rhetoricians and technical communication specialists interested in mHealth technologies, especially those focused on reproductive and sexual healthcare. While it may appear that Nurx is offering convenience and efficiency, our closer analysis of the platform and its rhetoric reveals that their primary product is an affective one. Such affect management is likely a feature of other neoliberal technological solutions to these and other social problems. Our study of Nurx makes clear that scholars invested in technical rhetorics need to consider the affective and emotional contexts inspiring the development of mHealth technologies and that are triggered by those technologies. Our project also illustrates that understanding these affective contexts often necessitates analyzing the technological platforms, their marketing, and their relationships to earlier technologies and discourses. Finally, in drawing on an intersectional reproductive justice approach to rhetorical analysis, our project showcases how neoliberal for-profit ventures, ostensibly inspired by and addressing feminist causes, can espouse a progressive rhetoric of revolution, transformation, and empowerment while at the same time reaffirming the status quo and reactivating the regressive politics they claim to resist.

Works Cited

Adams, Heather Brook. "The Legacy and Future of *Our Bodies, Ourselves.*" *Peitho,* vol. 21, no. 3, 2019, pp. 580–98.

Agnihothri, Saligrama, et al. "The Value of mHealth for Managing Chronic Conditions." *Health Care Management Science*, vol. 23, 2020, pp. 185–202.

Bell, Stephen, et al. "Acceptability of Testing for Anorectal Sexually Transmitted Infections and Self-Collected Anal Swabs in Female Sex Workers, Men Who Have Sex with Men, and Transgender Women in Papua New Guinea." *BMC Public Health*, vol. 18, no. 776, 2018, pp. 1–7.

Bommakanti, Krishna K. "Requiring Smartphone Ownership for mHealth Interventions: Who Could Be Left Out?" *BMC Public Health*, vol. 20, no. 81, 2020, pp. 1–9.

Ciccariello, Chloe. "Defunding Planned Parenthood: The Stakes for America's Women." *JAMA Internal Medicine*, vol. 177, no. 3, 2017, pp. 307–08.

Dangerfield, Derek T., et al. "Acceptability of Self-Collecting Oropharyngeal Swabs for Sexually Transmissible Infection Testing Among Men and Women." *Sexual Health*, vol. 16, no. 3, 2019, pp. 296–98.

Demo, Anna Teresa. "Reframing Motherhood: Factoring in Consumption and Privilege." *The Motherhood Business: Consumption, Communication, and Privilege*, edited by Anne Teresa Demo, Jennifer L. Borda, and Charlotte Kroløkke. U of Alabama P, 2015, pp. 1–27.

Enoch, Jessica. "Finding New Spaces for Feminist Research." *Rhetoric Review*, vol. 30, no. 2, 2011, pp. 115–16.

Fiordelli, Maddalena, Nicola Diviani, and Peter J. Schulz. "Mapping mHealth Research: A Decade of Evolution." *Journal of Medical Internet Research*, vol. 15, no. 5, 2013, pp. 1–14.

Frost, Erin A. "Ultrasound, Gender, and Consent: An Apparent Feminist Analysis of Medical Imaging Rhetorics." *Technical Communication Quarterly*, vol. 30, no. 1, 5 June 2020, https://www.tandfonline.com/doi/full/10.1080/10572252.2020.1774658. Accessed 3 Aug. 2020.

Frost, Erin A., and Michelle F. Eble. "Technical Rhetorics: Making Specialized Persuasion Apparent to Public Audiences." *Present Tense: A Journal of Rhetoric in Society*, vol. 4, no. 2, 2015, https://www.presenttensejournal.org/volume-4/technical-rhetorics-making-specialized-persuasion-apparent-to-public-audiences/. Accessed 3 Aug. 2020.

Gaydos, Charlotte A. "Let's Take a 'Selfie': Self-Collected Samples for STIs." *Sexually Transmitted Diseases*, vol. 45, no. 4, 2018, pp. 278–79.

Goldstein, Zil, et al. "Improved Rates of Cervical Cancer Screening Among Transmasculine Patients Through Self-Collected Swabs for High-Risk Human Papillomavirus DNA Testing." *Transgender Health*, vol. 5, no.1, 2020, pp. 10–17.

Hallenbeck, Sarah. "Toward a Posthuman Perspective: Feminist Rhetorical Methodologies and Everyday Practices." *Advances in the History of Rhetoric*, vol. 15, no. 1, 2012, pp. 9–27.

Hayden, Sara, and D. Lynn O'Brien Hallstein. Introduction. *Contemplating Maternity in an Era of Choice: Explorations into Discourses of Reproduction*, edited by Sara Hayden and D. Lynn O'Brien Hallstein, Lexington, 2010, pp. xii-xxxix.

Hillard, Paula J. Adams "Adolescent Reproductive Health without Planned Parenthood." *Journal of Pediatric and Adolescent Gynecology*, vol. 30, no.4, 2017 pp. 445–46.

Hutchison, Les, and Maria Novotny. "Teaching a Critical Digital Literacy of Wearables: A Feminist Surveillance as Care Pedagogy." *Computers and Composition*, vol. 50, 2018, pp. 105–20.

IQVIA Institute for Human Data Science. "The Growing Value of Digital Health: Evidence and Impact on Human Health and the Healthcare System." *IQVIA Institute of Human Data Science*. 7 Nov 2017 https://www.iqvia.com/-/media/iqvia/pdfs/institute-reports/the-growing-value-of-digital-health.pdf.

Jack, Jordynn. "Leviathan and the Breast Pump: Toward an Embodied Rhetoric of Wearable Technology." *Rhetoric Society Quarterly*, vol. 46, no. 3, 2016, pp. 207–21.

Kreitzer, Rebecca, and Candis Watts Smith. "'Contraception Deserts' Are What You Get When You Cut Off This Little-Known Federal Program." *The Washington Post*. 26 Sept. 2016, www.washingtonpost.com/news/monkey-cage/wp/2016/09/26/contraception-deserts-are-what-you-get-when-you-cut-off-this-little-known-federal-program/. Accessed 3 Aug. 2020.

Lawrence, Hal C., and Debra L. Ness. "Planned Parenthood Provides Essential Services that Improve Women's Health." *Annals of Internal Medicine*, vol. 166, no. 6, 2017, pp. 443–44.

Lupton, Deborah. "Apps as Artefacts: Towards a Critical Perspective on Mobile and Medical Apps." *Societies*, vol. 4, 2014, pp. 606–22.

Marcolino, Milena Soriano, et al. "The Impact of mHealth Interventions: Systematic Review of Systematic Reviews." *JMIR mHealth and uHealth*, vol. 6, no. 1, 2018, e23. doi: 10.2196/mhealth.8873.

Martin, Thomas. "Assessing mHealth: Opportunities and Barriers to Patient Engagement." *Journal of Health Care for the Poor and Underserved*, vol. 23, no. 3, 2012, pp. 935–41.

McClurg, Lesley, and Ashley Lopez. "Birth Control Apps Find a Big Market in 'Contraception Deserts.'" *National Public Radio*. 26 March 2018, www.npr.org/sections/health-shots/2018/03/26/595387963/birth-control-apps-find-a-big-market-in-contraception-deserts. Accessed 3 Aug. 2020.

Nurx. "About Us." 2020. https://www.nurx.com/team/. Accessed 3 Aug. 2020.

Nurx, "Setting the Record Straight." *Medium.* 26 April 2019. www.medium.com/nurx/setting-the-record-straight-34d01beffa37. Accessed 27 Jan. 2021.

Palczewski, Catherine H. "Reproductive Freedom: Transforming Discourses of Choice" *Contemplating Maternity in an Era of Choice: Explorations into Discourses of Reproduction*, edited by Sara Hayden and D. Lynn O'Brien Hallstein, Lexington, 2010, pp. 73–94.

Probyn, Elspeth. *Blush: Faces of Shame.* U of Minnesota P, 2005.

Purcell, Hillary N., Charlotte Gaydos, and Lea Widdice. "Preference for and Acceptability of Self-Collection of Pharyngeal Swabs for Sexually Transmitted Infection Testing." *Journal of Adolescent Health*, vol. 62, no. 2, 2018, p. S81.

Reisner, Sari L., et al. "Comparing Self- and Provider-Collected Swabbing for HPV DNA Testing in Female-to-Male Transgender Adult Patients: A Mixed-Methods Biobehavioral Study Protocol." *BMC Infectious Diseases*, vol. 17, no. 1, 2017, p. 444.

Shieber, Jonathan. "Nurx Has $22.5 Million in New Money." *Tech Crunch.* 11 Aug. 2020, www.techcrunch.com/2020/08/11/nurx-has-22–5-million-in-new-money-a-path-to-profitability-and-new-treatments-for-migraines-on-the-way/.

SisterSong, INC. "Reproductive Justice." 2020, www.sistersong.net/reproductive-justice. Accessed 14 Oct. 2020.

Slusky, David J. G. "The Impact of Women's Health Clinic Closures of Preventive Care." *American Economic Journal: Applied Economics*, vol. 8, no. 3, 2016, pp. 100–24.

Stenberg, Shari J. "'Tweet Me Your First Assaults': Writing Shame and the Rhetorical Work of #NotOkay." *Rhetoric Society Quarterly*, vol. 28, no. 2, 2018, pp. 119–38.

Struminger, Bruce Baird, and Sanjeev Arora. "Leveraging Telehealth to Improve Health Care Access in Rural America: It Takes More Bandwidth." *Annals of Internal Medicine*, vol. 171, no. 5, 2019, pp. 376–77.

Tampax Incorporated. "Accent on You…Your Personal Questions Answered About Menstruation." New York: Tampax Incorporated, 1972.

Thornton, Davi Johnson. "Neuroscience, Affect, and the Entrepreneurialization of Motherhood." *Communication and Critical/Cultural Studies*, vol. 8, no.4, 2011, pp. 399–424.

Varney, Sarah. "'Contraception Deserts' Likely to Widen under New Trump Administration Policy." *Kaiser Health News.* 29 Sep 2018. www.khn.org/news/contraception-deserts-likely-to-widen-under-new-trump-administration-policy/. Accessed 3 Aug 2020

Woods, Carly S. "Repunctuated Feminism: Marketing Menstrual Suppression through the Rhetoric of Choice." *Women's Studies in Communication*, vol. 36, no. 3, 2013, pp. 267–87.

Worsham, Lynn. "Going Postal: Pedagogic Violence and the Schooling of Emotion." *JAC*, vol. 18, no. 2, 1998, pp. 213–45.

Yam, Shui-yin Sharon. "Visualizing Birth Stories from the Margin: Toward a Reproductive Justice Model of Rhetorical Analysis." *Rhetoric Society Quarterly*, vol. 50, no. 1, 2020, pp. 19–34.

9 Rhetorical Visions of Vasectomy: How Television and Film Representations Influence Reproductive Lives

Jenna Vinson

Long before protestors held signs calling attention to vasectomies at rallies against abortion bans, feminist and public health advocates across the world called for a cultural shift so that men are equally involved in preventing unwanted pregnancies (Arditti 130; Boston Women's 204; Terry and Braun 478; United Nations *Report* 27). Yet, most available contraceptives remain targeted for women's bodies, and in the US, as well as many other countries, female sterilization is the leading method of pregnancy prevention.[1] In fact, since the United Nations called for men's active and equal contribution to pregnancy prevention measures, the worldwide rate of male sterilization declined—dropping from three percent to .8 percent between 1994 and 2019 (United Nations *Contraceptive* 5).[2] In the US, approximately six to seven percent of men eighteen to forty-five years old have had vasectomies (Ostrowski et al.; Sharma et al.). Sociologist Andrea M. Bertotti, drawing on data from the 2006 and 2010 National Survey for Family Growth, writes that "only fifteen percent of married and cohabiting couples in the United States rely on vasectomy for contraception, compared to forty percent who rely

1. Australia, Bhutan, Republic of Korea, and the United Kingdom are the only countries where the rate of male sterilization is the same or higher than the rate of female sterilization (United Nations *Contraceptive* 12).

2. A note on terms: "Female sterilization" is used by the UN and other major health organizations to refer to tubal ligation, the procedure that sterilizes fertile bodies with ovaries and uteruses. "Male sterilization" is used to refer to vasectomies, the procedure that sterilizes fertile bodies with testicles. For nonbinary and trans people these terms may be inaccurate, alienating, or pathologizing; further research on the rhetoric of sterilization is needed.

on female sterilization" (13). She asserts, "Like other forms of domestic labor, the time, attention, stress, and physical burden associated with avoiding pregnancy lies primarily on the shoulders of women" (13).

In response to this persistent gendered imbalance, I offer a feminist rhetorical critique of fictional television and film representations of vasectomies. These texts reflect and shape the cultural meaning of vasectomy, influencing thinking and action around this means of pregnancy prevention. Vasectomies are simpler and safer outpatient procedures than tubal ligation and, thus, should be an equally viable if not more popular option.[3] Yet the *way* the procedure is represented in mainstream US television series and films reifies status quo negative attitudes about vasectomy, fails to promote reproductive justice and, ultimately, reinforces white supremacist patriarchal gender roles. Informed by the reproductive justice framework, I conducted a feminist rhetorical analysis of thirty-seven representations of vasectomy from 1972 to 2020. This analysis surfaced troubling patterns that prompt men to reject vasectomies and to accept women shouldering the burden of fertility management. First, language and dramatic conventions perform a pedagogy of fear, encouraging attention to and empathy for men's fear of pain while normalizing women's pain, labor, and fear of pregnancy. Second, vasectomy is depicted as a means of emasculation, compromising its cultural acceptance. Finally, homogenous representations obscure how intersections of race, class, and age shape men's experiences with, and access to, sterilization. Altogether this chapter contributes to reproductive justice work by identifying rhetorics that obstruct a dignified vision of men as people who actively manage their fertility.

Reproductive Justice and Sterilization

The three key principles of reproductive justice are that people have the inherent right to "have children, not have children, and to parent the children we do have in safe and sustainable communities" (SisterSong).

---

3. There are risks associated with vasectomies and, like tubal ligation, public health practitioners emphasize that sterilization methods are permanent solutions for people who do not want to have (more) children. In their article "Vasectomy: the Other (Better) Form of Sterilization," medical experts and a Planned Parenthood representative review rigorous studies and find, "Compared with vasectomy, tubal ligation is twenty times more likely to have major complications" (Shih et al. 311).

As a procedure that can help people exercise their right to *not* have children, sterilization is a reproductive justice issue, falling under the scope of fertility management. Thus, it is important to ensure that all people can access a safe, dignified, and voluntary sterilization procedure. However, as reproductive justice scholarship demonstrates, the history of sterilization in the US is intertwined with racism and eugenics. Sterilization has been deployed to dehumanize and obstruct the rights of people to have children including Indigenous people, people of color, immigrants, people with disabilities, people with mental illness, people who are incarcerated, and people in poverty (O'Connell 305; Ross and Solinger 50–54). Contemporary reports surface that people are still coerced into sterilizing their bodies, particularly those trapped in the criminal justice system (Flores; Ross and Solinger 89, 217). At the same time, white, able-bodied women with private insurance have struggled to access sterilization procedures on their terms—particularly when they are young, single, or childfree (Davis and Dubisar).

The white supremacist patriarchal structure of the US often renders feminized bodies the target of reproductive oppression, yet men have also been targets—particularly men of color, men in poverty, and men who are institutionalized. In fact, vasectomy's emergence coincided with the emergence of the eugenics movement. The first human vasectomy was performed in 1893 in London and just six years later Harry Sharp, a physician in Indiana, used the procedure on young male inmates to solve the "problem" of masturbation. By 1907 Sharp performed vasectomies on "176 masturbating minors" and that year his state introduced "the world's first eugenic sterilization act" (Wolfers and Wolfers 196). This law allowed for forcibly sterilizing a wide range of "socially inadequate persons" (Ross and Solinger 30). Other states followed suit and since then the US has struggled to ensure that people who terminate their ability to procreate are doing so consciously and free from coercion.

Keeping this horrific history of forced sterilization in mind, this chapter reckons with the misogynistic cultural expectation that it is women's responsibility to endure the pain, labor, and risks of fertility management. It is important to address the unequal role men and women play in preventing pregnancies. Reproductive justice activists have rightly critiqued white feminist scholarship on reproductive politics for focusing narrowly on women's access to birth control and abortion without much attention to the social structures that repeatedly deny poor women and women of color the right to experience pregnancy or raise the children they have in safe and healthy environments. In attempting to convey the need for access to birth control and abortion, many feminist advocates implied that some women should *not* have children—namely young women and those in poverty. Thus, as a white feminist scholar, I am wary of what I am doing here—calling, again, for academic attention to fertility management and implying that some men should consider sterilization. Yet, I feel impelled to wrangle with this: cisgender heterosexual men who do not want (more) children do not often voluntarily sterilize their bodies, even though vasectomies are safer and simpler than tubal ligation. This abnegation of fertility management reifies the gendered ideology that posits interventions on women's bodies as the best solution to unwanted pregnancies. For cisgender heterosexual men who co-created children, this is particularly troubling as their partners already underwent considerable risk, pain, and unpaid labor to produce those children. Where is the justice in this?

Men's (in)actions are part of the conditions that shape women's reproductive decisions and lives. While men are most certainly included in the reproductive justice framework, which is carefully articulated as being about human rights (Ross and Solinger 6–7), less attention has been given to how men are involved in the project of reproductive justice. This chapter contributes a feminist rhetorical analysis of language and symbolic structures that shape what men do. Loretta Ross and Rickie Solinger encourage reproductive justice scholars to focus on how "social institutions, the environment, economics, and culture affect each woman's reproductive life" (69). Feminist rhetorical analysis is a helpful method in this regard because it surfaces how particular symbolic cultural representations affect women's reproductive lives by challenging or reproducing ideologies of domination based on sex and gender—while remaining attentive to the intersection of gender, sex, race, class, age, and ability (hooks, *Feminist Theory* 33). I critically interrogate texts that construct public understandings of men's role in fertility management, and, for the purposes of this chapter, I focus specifically on television and film representations of heterosexual, cisgendered men's role in preventing unwanted pregnancies when these men do not want to parent (more) children. My close reading of texts is feminist and rhetorical in that I am responding to the existing gendered imbalance in rates of voluntary sterilization by breaking down the visual and verbal signs of shows/films that persuade people to imagine which bodies should (or should not) be sterilized.

Looking for Patterns across Films and Television Shows

Ross and Solinger explain that reproductive justice illuminates how "the state and other entities create unequal power relations," in part, by marking "different groups of people . . . for reproductive management differently" (139). Film and television are "entities" that contribute to the gendered power relations that disproportionately mark women's bodies for fertility management and that encourage the public to see men's bodies as off-limits. As cultural studies scholars attest, fictional representations in everyday media reflect, reproduce, and/or challenge cultural norms and beliefs. Studying such texts can provide important insights into the cultural logics proliferating in the moment and can be points of intervention and critique when seeking to change the status quo. Of course, viewers do not passively absorb the signs and underlying messages in television and film (Hall 170–73). However, such texts are rhetorical in that they influence thinking and potential action in response to social/political issues—particularly when patterns of representation emerge across multiple and divergent texts, prompting viewers to accept such thinking as common or "the way things are." Moreover, fictional texts structure our thinking about social norms in powerful ways because they are less likely to be thought to be doing so.

From a reproductive justice perspective, everyday media are part of the "social context in which individuals live and make their personal decisions" (Ross and Solinger 117) and, thus, the insidious messages about gender, race, age, class, sexuality, and reproduction underlying fictional media need questioning and critique. Investigating patterns of representation also maintains a focus on *structures* rather than *individuals*—an important move when engaging with issues of reproductive justice because the "reproductive options that fertile people have are always structured by the resources they have—or do not have" (Ross and Solinger 11). The provision of these resources is enabled by policies, laws, and shared attitudes created by human action and beliefs. As such, media representations, which disseminate broadly and influence human action and belief, are an important point of intervention in the "racial, gender, and class prejudices" that may "interfere with . . . reproductive decision making" (10).

Overall, I studied thirty-seven representations of vasectomy—including three shows with vasectomy storylines that extended over two episodes—beginning with the 1972 sitcom *Maude* and ending with the 2020 series *Sex Education*. I analyzed the visual, verbal, and audio cues (like laugh tracks) during scenes about vasectomies. Common themes surfaced in how the procedure was represented and how characters reacted to the procedure; I focused, in particular, on patterns that reproduced/challenged gendered inequalities and reproductive justice.

Following Shui-yin Sharon Yam's important call for rhetoricians adopting the reproductive justice framework to address "the cis-heteronormative assumptions" in reproductive discourses (21), I note first that these texts exclude queer and trans bodies from vasectomy plotlines. One film, *Happy Endings* (2005), features a gay cisgendered man who briefly mentions his vasectomy; otherwise, all representations focus on cisgendered heterosexual men and women, often spouses. Many representations also reinforce heteronormative and transphobic thinking by suggesting that being a man requires testicles and procreative sex. Not only do these representations of vasectomy exclude particular genders and sexualities, in the following sections I show how patterns across these texts dissuade viewers from envisioning men as taking an active role in fertility management.

Pedagogy of Fear: Dramatizing Men's Pain and Dismissing Women's

"Snip, snip" surfaced repeatedly across television and movie representations as a way to describe or reference vasectomies. In many cases, female characters used the trope to emphasize the simplicity of the procedure when asking their partners to get one. For example, Gloria from *All in the Family* (1976) tells her husband that a vasectomy is "as easy as 1-2-3, snip, snip, snip." Jay from *My Wife and Kids* (2005) rejects her husband's assertion that she "just get [her] tubes tied" by emphasizing that tubal ligation is "major surgery" but "a vasectomy is just a little snip, snip." Debra from *Everybody Loves Raymond* (1998) uses "snip" metonymically to reference vasectomy when discussing possible contraceptive options with her husband: "There is another option . . . a little snip, snip." "Snip, snip" reduces public understanding of the overall procedure to certain steps: 1–2 small incisions on the numbed scrotum (in the scalpel method) and the cutting of the *vasa deferentia*, tubes that carry the sperm to the other fluids that comprise semen.

Although the phrase emerges across these narratives—and broader discourses of vasectomy—as an attempt to assuage men's fears about pain, "snip, snip" actually provokes fear. Many of the male characters stiffen, agonize, and take issue with the "snip." Eddy from the sitcom *'Til Death* (2008) replies to Joy, "A little snip, snip? That's the biggest snip, snip there is!" The husband from *According to Jim* (2004), exclaims, "Snip, snip? Owwww! No, no!" The mere mention of "snip" prompts many male characters to grab their groins, crouch in pain, and moan. Charlie, from *Two and a Half Men* (2004) critiques the metonymy when his brother suggests Charlie could avoid impregnating the many women he sleeps with if he just gets "snipped." Charlie finds "snipped" belittling, unrefined even: "It is what you get at Supercuts for $12." For Charlie, as for many of the other male characters, "snip" does not do justice to the pain they associate with sterilization. Fear of pain, it is suggested again and again, keeps men from accepting women's proposals to share in fertility management work.

Interestingly, by associating "snip" with a haircutting salon, Charlie's comment highlights how effective this rhetorical choice is in helping those who are not in pain imagine the sensorial experience. "Snip" is an onomatopoeia—it sounds like the cut it references and in doing so enlivens or dramatizes our understanding of the cut. Although "snip" sounds more like cutting paper than the incisions made during vasectomies, this figure of speech evokes an image of scissors, a rather effective way of communicating pain to others. Literary and cultural theorists have long acknowledged the difficulty in communicating pain to people who are not in that pain themselves (Gilman 663; Scarry 4). Elaine Scarry finds that one complicated yet effective means of communicating pain is a "language of agency" that conveys pain by naming a material object capable of inflicting pain (15). Such language, I add, encourages audiences to fear that material object and the experience of pain it creates. Thus, rather than conveying the simplicity of the procedure, "snip, snip" actually emphasizes physical discomfort and, therein, participates in a gendered pedagogic performance of fear and pain. What I mean by this is that the trope and the character reactions to the phrase/procedure teach viewers something about pain—when to fear it, when it is warranted, and whose really matters. Sensory symbolic references to men's pain, in conjunction with comparatively abstract references to women's, encourage public fear and rejection of one and routine acceptance of the other.

As figurative language, the "snip" stands in stark contrast to the colloquial phrase for women's sterilization procedure: "tying your tubes." Yet both procedures involve tubes. Both procedures often involve cutting.[4] *Vasa deferentia* may even be tied, depending upon the doctor's preferred method (other options are cutting or searing the ends of the tubes) just as the fallopian tubes may not be tied at all but instead cut or seared. According to the *Oxford English Dictionary*, vasectomy involves ligation, the medical term for operations that tie up something: "Excision of the *vas deferens* or a portion of this; ligation of one or (more commonly) both *vasa deferentia*, usually performed to render the subject infertile" ("Vasectomy, n."). So why is one called "tying" while the other is a "snip" when both are likely steps of human sterilization? What are the effects of these different colloquialisms? Well, pain is not often associated with tying. Tying conjures images of knots, bows, shoelaces, braids—harmless, useful, even beautiful, human arts that require skill but rarely pain. Certainly, one can be bound or tied up in negative situations, but "tying" does not have the same effect as a "snip" that prompts vicious visions of cuts and scissors. "Tying" minimizes the pain of this procedure and naturalizes it as women's work.

When male characters reject the idea of the vasectomy by saying, "Why don't *you* tie your tubes?" female characters do not grab their abdomens and moan, though they certainly could. Women in these shows often counter that their sterilization procedure is "major surgery" or "invasive," but these words are rather abstract; they do not draw attention to the visceral—the drugging, cutting, bloating, and penetrating of muscle and flesh involved. As an "invasive" surgery, sterilization of bodies with ovaries and uteruses involves cutting the skin of the stomach, piercing the abdominal wall, and then—after inserting surgical tools

4. There is a "no scalpel" form of vasectomy that includes clamping the *vas deferens* and making a minor puncture in the scrotum to lift the tube out to seal or cut it (Boston Women's Health Book Collective 242). Since there are no cuts made to the scrotum, stitches aren't needed. For people with ovaries and uteruses, there were no-cut sterilization options like Adiana (from 2009–2012) and Essure (from 2002–2018) that required the insertion of metal coils (Essure) or silicone implants (Adiana) through the vagina and cervix into the fallopian tubes where, three months later, the devices and tissue combine to block the tubes. Production of these products ceased, presumably because of the adverse effects reported, so these methods are no longer available. Thus, for people with fallopian tubes who seek sterilization, "snip, snip" is always an apt description even if we don't use this phrase to discuss tubal ligation (*Essure*; Stacey).

inside the body—cutting, binding, or searing the fallopian tubes. To do this work—again, *inside* the body—the doctor often inflates the abdomen with gas. These physical manipulations and sensory experiences are obscured within the language of a "tube tie." As rhetorician Jenell Johnson demonstrates, "visceral feelings (that is, when they are shared) serve to intensify the certainty of feelings and magnify conviction in their truth" (4). The visceral language used to describe the visceral experience of vasectomy intensifies viewers' gut feelings that this procedure is just not right. In comparison, the non-visceral language used to describe the visceral experience of tubal ligation functions to keep viewers calm about this procedure. Moreover, the abstract language used in reference to tubal ligation does nothing to magnify the risks women of color face each time they enter a racist healthcare system that may neglect them or conduct unnecessary interventions on their bodies (Gutiérrez; Roberts).

An emphasis on pain, and men's fear of feeling pain, was the most common theme I identified. Many representations included language, character reactions, and other conventions to dramatize the cutting and pain of a vasectomy. For example, in *According to Jim* (2004), a low angle camera shot of Jim sitting on the medical table emphasizes the ridiculously huge size of the needle in the foreground—prompting viewers to empathize with Jim's sheer fear of the instrument used to numb the scrotum. In *My Wife and Kids* (2005), the morning of Michael's vasectomy appointment, a series of events exaggerate and ridicule Michael's fear of the procedure—his wife chopping a carrot, his son carving wood, his daughter cutting thread and accidentally making pieces of fabric "too small" and "useless." In an episode of *Modern Family* (2012), Phil's son cracks nuts at the kitchen counter on the day of Phil's procedure. Many characters run out of the waiting room (or attempt to) and have to be coaxed back in by companions—e.g., *Modern Family* (2012), *Big Bang Theory* (2017), *Raising Hope* (2011), *Shameless* (2019). This pedagogy of fear constructs an ethos of anxiety for men considering the procedure. Scenes of cutting, chopping, and scary objects prompt audiences to wince along with the male characters and forgive the half of them that ultimately refuse the procedure.

While the pain of a vasectomy is highlighted through these means, women's physical pain, labor, and fears are continually naturalized, minimized, or dismissed. Jim tells Cheryl, who gave birth to their three children, that since they decided to stop having children, "You do whatever it takes and call me, and I'll pick you up from the doctor's office" (*Ac-*

cording to Jim 2004). If attention is given to the pain and labor women went through to previously prevent a pregnancy and/or give birth to the couple's children, it is because the woman speaks to it, the man is unmoved by the appeal, and the show moves on. Women, it seems, are supposed to suffer. When Dre, of *Black-ish* (2015), finally admits to his wife, Bow, that he did not get the vasectomy he promised he would because "this is my balls, *my* balls," Bow points out, "We decided we were done." The show flashes back to that chaotic moment, depicting Bow simultaneously breastfeeding newborn twins while her dancing daughter requests her attention and her son pukes at her feet. She turns to Dre, who is sitting on the couch, and says to "snip it" to which he replies in agreement, "copy that." The comical scene highlights the less comical gendered imbalance of reproductive labor. Bow carried the children to term, breastfed them, and in this scene, paid attention to their needs. Dre's passive position next to her symbolizes the comparatively little labor he put into these tasks. This makes his refusal to have the procedure (and his willingness to risk impregnating Bow as he continues to have sex with her while he is—unbeknownst to her—still fertile) all the more infuriating. Again, representations of vasectomy in television and film perform a gendered pedagogy. Viewers are not prompted to fear the pain, risks, and labor that feminized bodies are subjected to.

Unexpected Pregnancies and "Scares": What It Takes to Get Men Involved

This gendered pedagogy of fear is furthered illustrated by the fact that most episodes that foreground vasectomy as a key plot point featured a pregnancy "scare" or an unexpected pregnancy as the catalyst of the vasectomy story. Several shows open with a scene of a husband and wife waiting nervously for the results of a pregnancy test, a woman experiencing (and dealing with) an unexpected pregnancy, or a wife hearing about a much older woman unexpectedly getting pregnant.

This generic convention is meant to get us to the vasectomy plotline, yet it also continues the trend of smoothing over women's undue burdens in a white supremacist patriarchal culture of reproductive health. Pregnancies are significant, and often scary, physical and emotional events. Considering whether to carry a fetus to term is complicated in a culture centered on surveilling, disciplining, medicalizing (to the point of unnecessary intervention), neglecting (to the point of maternal or infant death), and/or profiting off women's bodies. For women in poverty and women of color, the decision to carry to term is particularly complicated due to systemic racism and economic inequalities. In much the same way, abortion and adoption are difficult personal, political, and resource-demanding options—even more so since the 2022 *Dobbs v. Jackson Women's Health* ruling.[5] Thus, in these scenes that comically position men and women waiting with the same bated breath for the pregnancy test result, the representation problematically situates the moment as equally troubling. Moreover, the fact that it takes a pregnancy "scare" or unexpected pregnancy to engage men in a discussion of contraceptive options suggests that, again, women's physical and emotional pain are just par for the course. This pattern does not help people envision heterosexual men more actively involved in fertility management.

In fact, in scenes that feature the couple's discussion of "what to do now?," men are often depicted as ridiculously irresponsible about matters of pregnancy prevention. In some cases, the characters boldly claim that it *is* the woman's responsibility. Richard, from *The New Adventures of Old Christine* (2008), encourages his partner to stop taking the birth control pills that make her sick but states that he is unwilling to use "condoms or abstinence or anything else that I have to be responsible for [audience laughter]." When Debra, of *Everybody Loves Raymond* (1998), cannot find contraceptive "stuff" when she and her husband, Raymond, want to have sex, Raymond is baffled, "Stuff?" He, somehow, does not know which contraceptives they use to prevent pregnancies. When she explains what she is looking for, he blames her for being out of supplies: "Nice going." The episode ends with Raymond refusing to get a vasectomy but promising to stockpile and use condoms—something that he ultimately fails to accomplish. Thus, audiences are encouraged to be amused by these men's inability to do the labor of fertility management.

Few male characters are shown as choosing, of their own volition, to get a vasectomy. Several of the ones that do can hardly be described as furthering reproductive justice or helping to address patriarchal gender ideologies as they are motivated by a desire to have sex with a new woman or to have affairs without accountability. Both the drama series *Nip/Tuck* (2010) and family sitcom *Reba* (2003) feature characters who have secret vasectomies after impregnating women they are having affairs with. As a more lighthearted example, in a *Seinfeld* (1996) episode,

5. *Maude* (1972) and *Happy Endings* (2005) explore adoption and abortion but they both focus on white middle-class women's experiences.

several characters consider or get vasectomies to attract a woman they have just recently met who does not want to have children. At one moment, Elaine, a main character rejecting cultural pressure to have a baby, walks into a urologist's office with her new boyfriend (who already got a vasectomy to impress her) and is startled to find many of her male friends sitting in the waiting room. She asks, "What are you guys doing here?" Jerry Seinfeld responds matter-of-factly, "We're getting vasectomies [laugh track]." Audiences are prompted to laugh at silly sex-driven men making ridiculous decisions rather than see them as accessing a safe, effective, and dignified way of preventing pregnancies.

"Cutting off My Manhood": Vasectomy as a Castration Threat

Social constructions of masculinity demand that men perform certain actions, attitudes, and emotions in order to affirm their manhood. As the previous section illustrates, men are often depicted as compulsively sexual, uncaring, and reverent of their genitalia. Furthermore, bell hooks writes that white patriarchal constructions of masculinity conflate manhood with having power, dominating others (particularly women and children), and producing (but not actively parenting) offspring (*We Real* 4). From my analysis, I found that vasectomy was frequently constructed as a comedic-but-nonetheless-real threat to such constructions of masculinity.

For instance, in the film *You, Me, and Dupree* (2006), a father named Mr. Thompson feels threatened by his new son-in-law, Carl Peterson. Mr. Thompson takes several courses of action to ruin their relationship. He asks Carl to take his daughter's last name rather than have her take Carl's last name—the custom of the patriarchal institution of marriage. Carl asks, "What about my name? I want my kids to have my name," and Mr. Thompson suggests that they might hyphenate Thompson-Peterson. Later, Mr. Thompson calls Carl into his office to ask him to get a vasectomy. While Mr. Thompson accurately explains the procedure and shares that he had one, it is clear that this request is meant to rattle Carl and effectively does so. Carl is visibly out of sorts and tells his wife that her father is "trying to emasculate and sterilize me." When she dismisses this notion, he asks his friend, Dupree, what he would do if asked to get a vasectomy, and Dupree, similarly, freaks out: "Cutting off my manhood? I think it is barbaric. No one is getting near my parts down there except a woman and, even then, she better not have a scalpel." In a climactic scene, Carl confronts Mr. Thompson: "You asked me to hyphenate my name! You asked me to get a vasectomy!" Vasectomy, in this way, is represented as a drastic attempt to dominate another man and (though assumed natural and not questioned) by extension a daughter/wife. By asking that Carl give up his ability to procreate, Mr. Thompson attempts to subvert Carl's patriarchal power to beget children that carry his name. Vasectomy is presented as the castration threat.

Many shows include a phrase or character that equates vasectomy to castration—a completely different procedure that removes the testicles. For example, Rogelio, of *Jane the Virgin* (2017), tells his wife, Xiomara, that he refuses to be "neutered." A "fixed" man is a subordinate man, and these representations suggest men are anxious about appearing subordinate to others. As another example, in *Everybody Loves Raymond* (1998), Raymond's brother, a cop, tells a story about an officer who "got fixed" and was "never the same." The sterilized officer did not like "firing blanks" and, it is implied, could no longer achieve an erection. The brother laments that now this man is a "mall security guard." This story of an impotent man prompts Raymond to cancel his vasectomy appointment. Vasectomy is represented as emasculation—terminating a man's ability to impregnate a woman challenges his ability to dominate, to physically overpower, to shoot bullets.

The troubling trope, "firing blanks," constructs violence as part of men's reproductive behaviors. If ejaculating semen without sperm is "firing blanks," then the penis is always a weapon and semen with sperm are potentially lethal. Unfortunately, this figurative language makes sense within the context of a white supremacist capitalist patriarchy that perpetuates rape culture and limits women's reproductive agency. Within such constraints, women may be forced to bear the burden of pregnancy, childbirth, and childcare without reasonable compensation or support.

A couple of characters associate being sterile, and thus voluntary sterilization, with aging. Aging, which includes physical degeneration, poses challenges to men's sense of self if that sense of self is built upon patriarchal masculinity's mandate of physical potency and dominance. For instance, Jim, of *According to Jim* (2004), cries that he is already losing hair and has "a gut" so the idea of being "sterile," too, troubles him deeply. The ability to impregnate women is one of his few means of self-esteem. Tim, from *Home Improvement* (1996), says, "When Jill first told me she was pregnant, I never felt more like a man . . . I don't want to have any more children. I just like knowing that I can." It is only after his neighbor and wife both assure him there are other ways of being a man that he consents to the procedure. Not only does this conflation of manhood with impregnating women reify a biological determinism that supports transphobia, but it also reveals the threadbare fabric of patriarchal masculinity that offers men few opportunities for development of self-esteem or self-love and sets up men for continual feelings of unworthiness and dissatisfaction (hooks, *Feminism* 70).

Further supporting the construction of virile, dominant manhood that obstructs a dignified vision of vasectomy is a pattern of using references to the procedure to further characterize men as odd, feminine, or dominated by an overbearing woman—as in the character of Michael from *The Office* (2008) who gets three vasectomies (and two reversals) at the whim of his demanding girlfriend's desires. Other examples include a loving, stay-at-home father in *Meet the Fockers* (2004) who randomly boasts that he had a vasectomy and the silly cuckolded character, Charles Boyle, from *Brooklyn Nine-Nine* (2014) who announces his vasectomy to the precinct when the sergeant considers getting one. The sensitive and caring character Al—an ongoing counterpoint to the brazen "tool-man" Tim—on *Home Improvement* (1996) is feminized and told to "shut up" when he tells the men bullying Tim for considering a vasectomy, "A vasectomy is a noble way for a man to take responsibility. Tim is making a very loving choice." Viewers are not encouraged, by such ridiculing representations, to support voluntary vasectomies.

"Manhood Is Not between the Legs": Better Visions of Vasectomy

Perhaps viewers need these representations of a conscious, loving, responsive, and unconventional manhood (ridiculed or not). Indeed, the cultural shift to balance the gendered labor of fertility management requires a reckoning with "manhood." Access to safe and dignified vasectomies, and potentially new means of male contraception, requires that men advocate for themselves as reproductive beings, and to do so requires them to see the suppression of fertility as just as much integral to their sense of personhood as expressing it (Ross and Solinger 164). Moreover, representations of vasectomy in line with the reproductive justice framework would present voluntary sterilization as a complicated decision, one that bears different weight based on the intersectional positionality of the person considering it as a means of enacting their right to not have a child. A couple of texts illustrate the messy potential of such a vision.

The first is a film called *Claudine* (1974) that features the experience of a Black single mother, Claudine, who is raising her six children. She is forced to deal with the racist, sexist, and impossible requirements of welfare programs to support her household—confronting stereotypes of "welfare moms" head on. The story begins around the time Claudine begins to date a man who is on the run from his own parenting obligations, engaging with stereotypes of Black absentee fathers. The film's representation of vasectomy is brief but worth exploring in depth. It revolves around Claudine's oldest son: Charles. Charles is often situated as observing the family chaos and skeptical of his mother's situation. He is involved in activist efforts to empower the Black community and struggles with his mother over this. She is fearful for his safety as he prepares to protest for jobs, welfare, and dignity. Despite his mother's concerns, Charles is committed to addressing racism and to avoiding what he sees as his mother's troubling circumstances.

When Claudine's new boyfriend abruptly leaves her, Charles confronts Claudine—blaming her for dating another man at all when she has been impregnated and left alone to deal with it so many times. She dismisses his critiques, "My son the black revolutionary . . . you're nothing but a snot-nosed coward." Charles replies that if she had really loved him, she would have killed him like the women on the plantations did to avoid their children enduring slavery. He sees procreation, for African Americans in a white supremacist society, as a problem because it means you "have nothing" and then you have to share it. After this tense confrontation, a subsequent scene shows Charles lying in bed. His mother comes in to ask what's wrong and he explains he had a vasectomy—a couple "snips" and now "no babies." His mother is upset and sees Charles' decision as succumbing to white supremacist society's dehumanizing tactics: "That's what Mr. Whitey does to the black man, he cuts off his manhood. But you did it to yourself!" Charles replies, "Awww, mama. Manhood is not between the legs."

While Charles gets a vasectomy as a means of control in a nation where he does not feel free, his mother sees her kids as "all I got"—a means of asserting personhood and claiming joy in a world that causes so much grief. The film is set (and released) in the 1970s, a time of intense backlash to the gains of civil rights movements, the revelation of the Tuskegee experiments on African American men in Alabama, and systematic coercive sterilization of women of color—women who were repeatedly stigmatized by politicians and journalists as the cause of their own poverty (Solinger 190). Thus, this exchange between mother and son highlights the complicated position of vasectomy in actual lived situations. Charles enacts his right to not have children, resisting a pronatalist life script in the context of racism and participating in fertility management work as called on by feminists at the time. Yet, Claudine's point about "Mr. Whitey" adds another layer of meaning to young Charles' course of action as white supremacism wields sexual and reproductive oppression—including experimentation on and sterilization of Black bodies (Roberts 260). As bell hooks writes, Black boys "bear the weight of a psychohistory that represents black males as castrated, ineffectual, irresponsible, and not real men" (*We Real* 82–83). It is within this racialized context that Charles envisions a different manhood—something more than between his legs, something related to his community-building actions as an activist and son.

No easy conclusions are drawn. *Claudine* is a representation of vasectomy as a dignified but politically loaded means of fertility management used by men who challenge the status quo. It is also a representation that acknowledges the varied meanings of reproductive health options depending on one's position in a white supremacist capitalist patriarchy. While my analysis shows that similar patterns surface across representations of vasectomy, only *Claudine* suggests that race matters. In other words, the Black father from *Black-ish* (2015) replies with similar comments and reactions as the Latino father from *Jane the Virgin* (2017), who reacts similarly to the white father in *Everybody Loves Raymond* (1998). Such representations help to obscure a history of racialized reproductive oppression and conflate all men's anxieties with the white upper-class male privilege of feeling secure in patriarchal masculinity until "threatened" with an outpatient medical procedure.

Furthermore, the only show I found that tackles the economic implications of fertility management—as a vasectomy is often a significant upfront cost—was *Raising Hope* (2011), a television series centered on a white working-class teenage dad raising his daughter with the help of his parents (former teenage parents themselves) and grandma. They live together in the grandmother's house and care for her—as she has dementia—while laboring as landscapers (the men) and a domestic worker (the woman) to pay the bills. When the parents experience a pregnancy scare, the family discusses it. The son and grandmother encourage the parents to elect a permanent means of pregnancy prevention. After a coin toss determines the dad has to be the one to get sterilized, the father and son work together to figure out how to afford it. They barter with a local doctor to clean his pool for a year in exchange for the vasectomy. Much like *Claudine* (1974), this episode highlights different markers of manhood. The men are emotionally articulate and actively loving fathers. The dad who gets the vasectomy is not affronted by the women and children's decisive input on courses of action for the family and for his own body. The dad struggles to summon the courage to endure the pain and wrangles with his sense of self. However, it is not his inability to impregnate women that troubles him but, rather, his fear that he will no longer be needed by his son and then unable to have a new child who may need him. His vulnerability is visible, and it is his adult son who helps him work through it. Like *Claudine*, it is a representation that acknowledges the varied experiences of reproductive health options depending on one's position in the socioeconomic context and offers a vision of manhood that challenges the status quo.

Why Do These Representations (Still) Matter?

Reproductive justice activists encourage scholar-activists to resist focusing on individual "choices" and instead study the structures and resources around reproductive health and rights to better understand and address the contexts in which people must make reproductive decisions. While individual viewers may engage with each fictional show/film in different ways, my analysis spanning decades of representation surfaces longstanding tropes circulating across multiple texts, demonstrating how these patterns structure the audience's thinking about vasectomies. This repetition matters, particularly in a context where there is no other systematic way of prompting people to know or think about vasectomies. And yet, this chapter is just a start. I did not focus on the specificities of representation in particular genres or periods (e.g., the 1970s versus the 1990s). Furthermore, as anthropologist Matthew Gutmann writes, "There are a host of 'outside' factors—from the media to the church to public health institutions and campaigns—that influence the wrangling within couples over such decisions" (162). Future research could focus on other structures that prevent wider participation in this means of fertility management including but not limited to insurance coverage, healthcare systems, and contraceptive counseling.

Rhetoricians know representations matter. The words ("snip" versus "tie"), images (*huge* needles), sounds, and gestures people use to represent reproductive health practices are pedagogic, teaching viewers what those things are and how they impact people's lives. My feminist rhetorical analysis reveals enduring patterns, repeated over time across multiple texts, that reify gender ideologies that position fertility management as women's work and obscure the pain and risks women, particularly women of color, face when doing reproductive labor or seeking reproductive healthcare. Sensory rhetorical appeals and dramatic conventions represent vasectomy as a painful, problematic (rather than welcomed) challenge to white patriarchal norms of manhood. Though often packed as comedic moments, vasectomy scenes normalize that men are just too inept or goofy to handle fertility management. Furthermore, few texts engage with the racism and economic inequalities that actually determine whether men can freely access vasectomies. Finally, as I write this conclusion, I cannot help but think about how troubling the pattern of the "pregnancy scare" that begins many of these vasectomy plotlines is, particularly as post-Dobbs journalistic attention to a yet-to-be-confirmed "vasectomy revolution" proliferates (e.g., Rodriguez). Why must a public discussion of vasectomy use require, first, the precarity and fear of people who can become pregnant?

Representations of vasectomies have the potential to improve the public appeal of the procedure. For instance, psychology scholars Gareth Terry and Virginia Braun interview men with vasectomies in New Zealand—a country with one of the highest rates of male sterilization—and find that "Positive accounts, suggesting an interest in responsibility and care, can act as a useful rhetorical/discursive base from which to strategically reshape the imbalances created by the processes of hegemonic masculinity" (491). In other words, representations of vasectomy could create new understandings of shared responsibility in a complicated world leading to collective actions, policies, and resources that address/enable men as people with the right to manage their fertility. Voluntary vasectomies are potentially liberating, loving, and responsive to the existing gendered inequalities of fertility management even as the procedure has risks, requires vulnerability/pain, and stems from a history of racism and eugenics. As my close reading of *Claudine* suggests, there is messy potential in presenting vasectomy as a difficult decision that boldly challenges conventional understandings of "manhood" and white patriarchal norms. Thus, I write as feminist rhetoricians often do, with the hope that identifying troubling tropes initiates a conversation that fosters change.

Films and Television Episodes

According to Jim, "A Vast Difference," created by Tracy Newman and Jonathan Stark, season 3, episode 29, ABC, 25 May 2004.

All in the Family, "Gloria's False Alarm," created by Norman Lear, season 7, episode 14, CBS, 18 Dec. 1976.

Big Bang Theory, "The Proton Generation," created by Chuck Lorre and Bill Prady, season 11, episode 6, CBS, 2. Nov. 2017.

Black-ish, "Sex, Lies, and Vasectomies," created by Kenya Barris, season 1, episode 18, ABC, 1 Apr. 2015.

Brooklyn Nine Nine, "Chocolate Milk," created by created by Dan Goor and Michael Schur, season 2, episode 2, NBC, 5 Oct. 2014.

Claudine. Directed by John Berry, Third World Cinema Co., 1974.

Everybody Loves Raymond, "Halloween Candy," created by Phil Rosenthal, season 3, episode 6, CBS, 26 Oct. 1998.

Happy Endings. Directed by Don Ross, Artisan/Lionsgate, 2005.

Home Improvement, "The Vasectomy One," created by Matt Williams, Carmen Finestra, and David McFadzean, season 5, episode 16, ABC, 6 Feb. 1996.

Jane the Virgin, "Chapter 69," created by Jennie Snyder Urman, season 4, episode 5, the CW, 10 Nov. 2017.

Maude, "Maude's Dilemma," created by Norman Lear, season 1, episodes 9 and 10, CBS, 14 & 21 Nov. 1972.

Meet the Fockers. Directed by Jay Roach, Universal, 2004.

Modern Family, "Snip," created by Christopher Lloyd and Steven Levitan, season 4, episode 3, ABC, 10 Oct. 2012.

My Wife and Kids, "The 'V' Story," created by Don Reo and Damon Wayans, season 5, episode 26, ABC, 17 May 2005.

The New Adventures of Old Christine, "Unidentified Funk," created by Kari Lizer, season 4, episode 11, CBS, 10 Dec. 2008.

Nip/Tuck, "Dan Daly," created by Ryan Murphy, season 6, episode 11, FX, 6 Jan. 2010.

The Office, "The Dinner Party," created by Greg Daniels, Ricky Gervais, and Stephen Merchant, season 4, episode 13, NBC, 10 Apr. 2008.

Raising Hope, "Snip, Snip," created by Gregory Thomas Garcia, season 1, episode 15, FOX, 1 Mar. 2011.

Reba, "The Vasectomy," created by Allison M. Gibson, season 2, episode 13, The CW, 17 Jan. 2003.

Seinfeld, "The Soul Mate," created by Larry David and Jerry Seinfeld, season 8, episode 2, NBC, 26 Sept. 1996.

Shameless, "The Hobo Games," created by Paul Abbott and John Wells, season 9, episode 11, *Netflix,* 17 Feb 2019.

'Til Death, "Snip/Duck," created by Josh Goldsmith and Cathy Yuspa, season 2, episode 12, FOX, 23 Apr. 2008.

Two and a Half Men, "Can You Feel My Finger?," created by Chuck Lorre and Lee Aronsohn, season 1, episode 24, CBS, 24 May 2004.

You, Me, and Dupree. Directed by Anthony and Joe Russo, Universal, 2006.

Works Cited

Arditti, Rita. "Have You Ever Wondered About the Male Pill?" *Seizing Our Bodies: The Politics of Women's Health*, edited by Claudia Dreifus, Vintage Books, 1977, pp. 121–30.

Bertotti, Andrea M. "Gendered Divisions of Fertility Work: Socioeconomic Predictors of Female Versus Male Sterilization." *Journal of Marriage and Family*, vol. 75, no. 1, 2013, pp. 13–25. *JSTOR*, www.jstor.org/stable/23440758.

Boston Women's Health Book Collective. *Our Bodies, Ourselves*. Touchstone ed., Simon & Schuster, 2011.

Davis, Sara, and Abby M. Dubisar. "Communicating Elective Sterilization: A Feminist Perspective." *Rhetoric of Health & Medicine*, vol. 2, no. 1, 2019, pp. 88–113, doi: 10.5744/rhm.2019.1004.

Essure. Bayer, 13 Jan. 2020, www.essure.com/. Accessed 18 May 2023.

Flores, Jerry. "ICE Detainees' Alleged Hysterectomies Recall a Long History of Forced Sterilizations." *The Conversation,* 28 Sept. 2020. www.theconversation.com/ice-detainees-alleged-hysterectomies-recall-a-long-history-of-forced-sterilizations-146820. Accessed 15 May 2023.

Gilman, Sander L. "Seeing Bodies in Pain: From Hippocrates to Freud." *The International Journal of Psychoanalysis*, vol. 92, no. 3, 2011, pp. 661–74, doi: 10.1111/j.1745–8315.2011.00451.x.

Gutiérrez, Elena R. *Fertile Matters: The Politics of Mexican-Origin Women's Reproduction*. U of Texas P, 2008.

Gutmann, Matthew. *Fixing Men: Sex, Birth Control, and AIDS in Mexico*, U of California P, 2007.

Hall, Stuart. "Encoding/Decoding." *Media and Cultural Studies: Key Works*, edited by Meenakshi Gigi Durham and Douglas M. Kellner, Blackwell, 2006, pp. 163–73.

hooks, bell. *Feminist Theory: From Margin to Center*. 2nd ed., South End P, 2000.

—. *Feminism Is for Everybody: Passionate Politics*. 2nd ed., Routledge, 2015.

—. *We Real Cool: Black Men and Masculinity*. Routledge, 2004.

Johnson, Jenell. "'A Man's Mouth Is His Castle:' The Midcentury Fluoridation Controversy and the Visceral Public." *Quarterly Journal of Speech*, vol. 102, no. 1, 2016, pp. 1–20, doi:10.1080/00335630.2015.1135506.

O'Connell, Katie. "We Need to Talk about Disability as a Reproductive Justice Issue." *Radical Reproductive Justice: Foundations, Theory, Practice, and Critique*, edited by Loretta J. Ross et al., Feminist P, 2017, pp. 302–05.

Ostrowski, Kevin A., et al. "Evaluation of Vasectomy Trends in the United States," *Urology*, vol. 118, 2018, pp. 76–79, doi:10.1016/j.urology.2018.03.016.

Roberts, Dorothy. *Killing the Black Body: Race, Reproduction, and the Meaning of Liberty*. Pantheon Books, 1997.

Rodriguez, Jesús A. "How Dobbs Triggered a 'Vasectomy Revolution,'" *Politico,* 2 Dec 2022, www.politico.com/news/magazine/2022/12/02/how-dobbs-triggered-a-vasectomy-revolution-00070461. Accessed 18 May 2023.

Ross, Loretta J. and Rickie Solinger. *Reproductive Justice: An Introduction*. U of California P, 2017.

Scarry, Elaine. *The Body in Pain: The Making and Unmaking of the World*. Oxford UP, 1985.

Sharma, V., et al., "Vasectomy Demographics and Postvasectomy Desire for Future Children: Results from a Contemporary National Survey," *Fertility and Sterility*, vol. 99, no. 7, 2013, pp. 1880–85, doi:10.1016/j.fertnstert.2013.02.032.

Shih, Grace, et al. "Vasectomy: The Other (Better) Form of Sterilization," *Contraception*, vol. 83, no. 4, 2011, pp. 310–15, doi:10.1016/j.contraception.2010.08.019.

SisterSong. "Reproductive Justice." www.sistersong.net/reproductive-justice. Accessed 9 Mar. 2022.

Solinger, Rickie. *Pregnancy and Power: A Short History of Reproductive Politics in America*. New York UP, 2005.

Stacey, Dawn. "Adiana Permanent Birth Control: No Longer Available." *verywell health,* 10 June 2021, www.verywellhealth.com/adiana-permanent-birth-control-906804. Accessed 17 May 2023.

Terry, Gareth, and Virginia Braun. "'It's Kind of Me Taking Responsibility for These Things': Men, Vasectomy and 'Contraceptive Economies." *Feminism & Psychology*, vol. 21, no. 4, 2011, pp. 477–95, doi:10.1177/0959353511419814.

United Nations. *Contraceptive Use by Method 2019*, Department of Economic and Social Affairs, Population Division, 2019, Data Booklet (ST/ESA/SER.A/435).

United Nations. *Report of the International Conference on Population and Development*, 1994, (A/CONF 171/13). Cairo.

"Vasectomy, n." *OED*, Oxford UP, June 2020, www.oed.com/view/Entry/221654. Accessed 6 July 2020.

Wolfers, David, and Helen Wolfers. "Vasectomania." *Family Planning Perspectives*, vol. 5, no. 4, 1973, pp.196–99. *JSTOR,* www.jstor.org/stable/2133967.

Yam, Shui-yin Sharon. "Visualizing Birth Stories from the Margin: Toward a Reproductive Justice of Rhetorical Analysis," *Rhetoric Society Quarterly,* vol. 50, no. 1, 2020, 19–34, doi:10.1080/02773945.2019.1682182.

10 Doula-Rhetors for Childbirth: Strategic Leading Questions and Reproductive Justice

Sheri Rysdam

I began thinking about rhetorical strategies for improving consenting exchanges in the childbirth setting while serving as a doula and as a doula coordinator in a free volunteer doula program in a large university hospital. It was through this experience that I first came to realize the critical role doulas, who provide nonmedical labor support, can play in reproductive justice. Over time, I came to understand that doulas could be discursive and material rhetorical agents, or doula-rhetors, in the childbirth setting. The advocacy that doulas do as part of their work, the way they interpret encounters with language and touch, and the rhetorical devices they use, such as strategic leading questions, can empower people giving birth. Such work, considered in individual encounters and also systemically, is more important than ever as covert institutional barriers reduce reproductive rights and, in the case of *Dobbs v. Jackson Women's Health*, as overt laws work against bodily autonomy (United States).

I gained the majority of my experience in a volunteer doula program that is housed in a research university hospital and is comprised of both new and experienced doulas. It serves the community by providing free childbirth support for those who otherwise might not have access to a doula. I joined the hospital's volunteer program—with a red t-shirt embroidered with the volunteer service's insignia in hand and a tender spot in my arm from a flu vaccination—in 2013, shortly after its inception. I became increasingly involved in the volunteer program, and I enjoyed my time as a volunteer doula and found the experience to be an intense and meaningful way for me to support women in my community.

So much of my academic work was cerebral and somewhat removed from the physicality of life. However, the opposite was true of doula work. When I got called into a birth as a volunteer, I entered the room, walked to the bed, and held a woman's hand while introducing myself and describing just what, exactly, a doula does. I had the quick conversation to learn about that person's hopes and wishes for their birth. A conversation that usually takes weeks and months to unfold in a traditional doula relationship happened in mere minutes. I then pushed on hips (applied counter pressure), I rubbed feet, I offered water, and I offered encouragement. Tears rolled down the cheeks of the midwives, and of new parents, and down my own cheeks as precious new life emerged on the outside, sometimes crying, sometimes silent and watchful. Women were pushed to extremes. Their bodies stretched and broke, some like it was easy and others like it was unbearable. New love was placed in arms or carted down the hall for Neonatal Intensive Care Unit (NICU) treatment, but each birth I attended was beautiful and profound. It was work that combined my desire to volunteer in the community with my personal feminist mission to help people who are in need, especially in the childbirth setting where they are vulnerable to sexism and oppression.

During my experience as a doula, I supported a wide variety of people: women who were not sure they wanted a doula, women who were desperate for a doula, young women, women without family or other support people, women giving birth without medication, women being induced, women who used epidural anesthesia, women who primarily spoke a language other than English, and more. Each birth I attended was memorable. In her book *Birth, Breath, and Death: Meditations on Motherhood, Chaplaincy, and Life as a Doula*, Amy Wright Glenn writes about the sacred nature of this work. She states, "Doulas stand at the doorway of life" (17–18), and indeed I felt the gravity of the work with each person who I supported as a doula. I became one of the most experienced doulas in the program and began working as a volunteer doula coordinator, which entailed planning events, helping train new doulas, organizing the doula calendar, and other tasks. For my day job, I worked as a professor of writing at a public university, where I studied and wrote about rhetoric. Over time, the two worlds began to merge, and I started to find rhetorical strategies that doulas could use to improve the childbirth experience. By combining my experience as a doula and my experience as a rhetorician, I was also able to integrate some training content about clear communication and some of the rhetorical interventions available to doulas in my capacity as volunteer doula coordinator, all supportive of a reproductive justice mission.

The work left me with a deep sense that I was helping people during childbirth have better experiences in the medical setting and helping other doulas facilitate better experiences for the people they worked with. Once I experienced how doulas could help facilitate improved birth experiences, I realized that women of color, poor women, trans men, non-binary people, incarcerated people (pregnant state prisoners deliver at the University of Utah Hospital), and young people—in other words, those who are or who are thought to be most at risk for negative birth experiences—can all be better served thanks to this free volunteer doula program. I began to see myself working with goals similar to the doulas described in Dána-Ain Davis's *Reproductive Injustice: Racism, Pregnancy, and Premature Birth.* These "radical birth workers seek to ensure that birthing parents are treated respectfully and understand the consequences of the procedures to which they might be subjected. Along with working toward facilitating informed decisions, they actively engage in advocacy, care . . . " (170). I saw myself working within a hospital system to enact positive change.

Doula work, in broadest terms, aligns with the inclusive, human-rights advocacy of reproductive justice activists who support the safety, dignity, and "fairer [reproductive] outcomes based on justice and equity" of all people (Ross et al. 23). As Jennifer C. Nash argues in relation to her specific research on Women of Color doulas, "in the wake of a new public attention to the Black maternal mortality crisis, birth workers, particularly birth doulas, have become increasingly visible agents of birth justice" ("In the Room" 17:24–17:35). Although a doula's role in childbirth is primarily in administering nonmedical comfort measures, doulas are also in a position to use clear communication and rhetorical strategies, such as strategic leading questions, which help facilitate individuals in making more informed choices during their childbirth experience. Shui-yin Sharon Yam refers to some of the rhetorical devices available to doulas as "soft advocacy," which can include "creating deliberate space, cultural and knowledge brokering, and spatial maneuvering" ("Complicating Acts" 200). By facilitating effective communication in the childbirth setting, doulas are able to function as activists in their own right, helping to create more positive and consenting interactions in the childbirth setting.

Doulas, whether renumerated or free, can be activist rhetors in a specific type of rhetorical situation—childbirth. As such, they operate rhetorically by listening to and responsively negotiating for the birthing parent. Also, they can interject themselves into the rhetorical flow of medical providers. This interruption and use of strategic questions can slow or pause medical intervention so that the birthing person has space to understand what is happening, weigh possible options, review their previously stated wishes, provide or decline informed consent, and/or express their emotional responses to the situation. This liminal role makes a doula a doula-rhetor. The potential importance of a doula-rhetor is suggested by reproductive justice scholars Loretta J. Ross and Rickie Solinger, who explain a key instance of birth injustice—coercive medicine:

> Reproductive justice/birth justice activists assert that women have the right to determine their own birth plans, use midwives and doulas if they choose, and have home births or use free-standing birthing centers if they prefer. The fact is that pregnant women are vulnerable to many birth injustices, harms that we can define as 'obstetric violence'—for example, forced Caesarians and other unnecessary medical procedures—some of which have resulted in women being imprisoned for poor birth outcomes if they resist this treatment. Indeed, many women report that they have been bullied in hospitals into accepting aggressive medical interventions they did not want or necessarily need. They are often denied midwifery services, and hospital staff members often ignore a woman's birthing plans. (188)

A doula-rhetor is in a position to ask questions and solicit information to be communicated between the healthcare providers and the person giving birth. In doing so, doulas can facilitate a more just and comforting birth experience, both in terms of what happens in a birthing room and, potentially, the more long-term wellness of a parent and child.

The rhetorical power dynamics that people experience while giving birth and the effects of this power are real. These power dynamics and their implications are why individual doula-rhetors, especially those working collaboratively in a volunteer program in a university hospital dedicated to free doula care, can be so critical to reproductive justice and why rhetorical approaches could be used to move toward greater justice in birthing contexts. Based on my own experience and my research, I first situate this discussion of doula work in contemporary scholarly and activist efforts to reclaim stories of birthing. I then further describe doula work before detailing my concept of strategic leading questions as a cornerstone of doula-rhetoric. Together, these stories and perspectives convey my concept of doula-rhetors as discursive and material rhetorical agents who are uniquely situated to use their insights, knowledge, and access to advocate in service of reproductive justice goals, both in individual cases and to address related, structural concerns. Dwelling in this possibility, this chapter ends with a call for free doula programs as well as questions for further discussion about the potential complications of such programs.

Recent Rhetorical Interventions in the Experience of Birthing

While the medicalized version of "childbirth as difficult" dominates popular culture, those experiences are not the only reality. In response to the medicalized "difficult" narrative, stories have circulated more widely and in emerging forms to provide alternative narratives/counter narratives to the childbirth experience. Ina May Gaskin, a key figure in childbirth advocacy (especially among white practitioners), works to normalize childbirth, in part, through storytelling. She does this by sharing stories of childbirth that show multiple possibilities that are not frightening, that are not dangerous, but that are actually positive, empowering, and sometimes even pleasurable. *Ina May Gaskin's Guide to Childbirth* is largely composed of birth stories, which in and of themselves can serve powerfully to teach and promote empowering narratives. As an act of "centering," such storytelling demonstrates "placing oneself in the center of the lens in order to discover new ways of describing reality from a particular standpoint," an act of awareness building that reproductive justice activists employ and encourage others to use to further learn from perspectives of those who have been rhetorically silenced (Ross and Solinger 64).

Similarly, in the past few decades, scholarly approaches to understanding childbirth support as rhetorical have frequently turned to the rhetorical importance of storytelling for the purposes of teaching and defining. In *The Rhetoric of Midwifery: Gender, Knowledge, and Power*, Mary M. Lay argues that the rhetorical power of birth stories improves understandings and connections between people giving birth and healthcare providers. Kim Hensley Owens, in *Writing Childbirth: Women's Rhetorical Agency in Labor and Online*, illustrates the ways people use stories to regain power in spaces where power has been lost. She shares the story of her own birth in a Volkswagen bus in order to illustrate her point. She maintains, "Women absorb, respond to, and share many kinds of childbirth stories, with a variety of rhetorical and material effects that extend far beyond childbirth itself" (x). For Owens, this story serves to teach and to share information about what is possible in childbirth, and she demonstrates how the story can function rhetorically.

Making a similar but distinct move, Yam has written about the *Instagram* account @empoweredbirthproject, which shares explicit images and videos of people giving birth, often at home and/or in nonmedical settings. Yam argues that by sharing these depictions, the *Instagram* account does work in the "retraining of the audience's gaze [and] paves the path toward helping viewers achieve critical access to birthing technologies, which have historically been made inaccessible to those who lack the cultural capital to navigate dominant medical institutions" ("Birth" 81). Because of the visual nature of the platform, the account shares birthing possibilities even more immediately than some longer-form stories that have more traditionally been shared about childbirth with the purpose of educating the viewer on what is possible. More recently, Yam analyzes a *YouTube* series entitled *Doula Diaries* through a reproductive justice lens, which relies on an intersectional methodology "to also pay attention to the voices that have been omitted . . . the voices of queer, trans, and gender nonconforming birthing people who may rely on assisted reproductive technology to become pregnant" ("Visualizing" 30). Stories on social media and online are yet another way to center birthing people from various communities and with different life experiences in order to imagine and work toward more just birthing practices.

Advocacy through birth stories and other alternative narratives seems to have gained traction across birthing sites and experiences, but such uptake does not result in equity of access. While historically people have always performed doula work for each other during childbirth, more recently, in more medicalized settings, and with the increase in formal doula training, access to a doula can be limited due to expense—rendering it a service for the privileged. In many communities "red tape" prevents people from receiving any kind of care outside of a traditional hospitalized medical practice, so gaining access to those spaces can be challenging. People like Jamarah Amani, executive director of Southern Birth Justice and founder of the National Black Midwives Alliance, are working to improve birth experiences, especially for people of color. Much of Amani's activism is through information sharing and storytelling, as she shares accounts of Black women giving birth in birth centers, with midwives, sharing that other sometimes more supportive birthing alternatives are available (Mayer). All stories about birthing can result in more diverse ways of understanding who is giving birth under what conditions and how these birthing experiences happen. As Ross and Solinger affirm, "it takes many lenses to provide a full range of possibilities" (59).

These scholars, activists, and scholar-activists focus on the rhetorical acts of sharing unique types of stories in varied ways. Considered together, the stories remind that "childbirth is difficult" is only one of many experiences, and that the details of each story are linked to the person's lived and "crucial" contexts (Ross and Solinger 164). Listening to individual experiences expands upon the available ways of thinking about childbirth and, at the same time, can help all people understand how different communities might experience birth in more just or less just ways. Sharing stories also can help people giving birth recognize how they might be able to shape their own story. This chapter reflects my experience of being a doula to emphasize how the work of managing one's own experience of childbirth—writing one's own story—can be difficult but can be a supported possibility for *all* birthing people through a free doula program.

How Doulas Further Support Birth Experiences on Birthing People's Terms

Understanding the role of the doula is critical to understanding how they can function rhetorically within a childbirth space. The definition of roles in the childbirth setting is widely discussed in the field and that is particularly true of doulas. Doulas of North America (DONA) International, the oldest and largest doula training organization in the world, and incidentally also the organization through which I was certified as a doula, defines a doula as "a trained professional who provides continuous physical, emotional and informational support to a mother before, during, and shortly after childbirth to help her achieve the healthiest, most satisfying experience possible." DONA International emphasizes "continuous physical, emotional and informational support" ("What Is," *DONA*).[1]

For a doula, physical support could be the use of "counter pressure," which is a technique that usually involves applying pressure to a laboring

1. Recent scholarly and journalistic accounts of women of color birth workers expand upon how doulas consider their work to be paraprofessional, spiritual, and political (Nash "Birthing"; Olsen).

person's back, hips, or knees. Emotional support might be offering words of encouragement. A doula might say to a person giving birth, "You are strong. You are capable." Informational support could include educating a pregnant person on the three (or four) stages of labor. Even seemingly "low impact" interventions such as using lavender oil for relaxation during labor is considered outside of the scope of practice for many doulas. (Applying scented oil to the body is not generally recommended in this setting because it is hard to remove if necessary but sniffing oil or using a diffuser is generally permitted and considered to be within a doula's scope of practice.) Significantly, midwives are medical professionals trained to monitor labor, childbirth, and postpartum care, and OBGYNs do the same, but also can perform surgery such as cesarean sections. The doula role, however, is nonmedical, as they attend to the comfort and emotional care of the person giving birth.

Yet another definition of "doula" from WebMD emphasizes the doula's "nonmedical" role:

> A doula is a person who provides emotional and physical support to you during your pregnancy and childbirth. *Doulas are not medical professionals. They don't deliver babies or provide medical care.* A certified doula has taken a training program and passed an exam in how to help pregnant women and their families during this exciting *but challenging experience.* ("What Is A Doula," *WebMD*; emphasis added)

The WebMD definition carefully and accurately delineates doulas from medical personnel. At the same time, it refers to childbirth as a "challenging experience," whereas much of doula culture tends to avoid the use of negative language when describing childbirth. This language choice is a rhetorical strategy used to recenter the person giving birth as a powerful agent in the experience and to build a narrative around capability and strength that normalizes and naturalizes childbirth. Rhetorically considering these various definitions of the term "doula" shows how more medicalized texts tend to emphasize childbirth as a medical process that necessitates intervention in support of a successful birth. To be clear, childbirth is often challenging, and medical interventions are sometimes needed to improve outcomes, but sometimes birth is easy and oftentimes it requires no medical intervention. Either way, a healthy baby is not the only important outcome in childbirth. For a birthing parent, who is a human being with feelings, emotions, and agency, feeling physically and emotionally well is important too.

People should not have to make sophisticated rhetorical moves to advocate for themselves during childbirth. For many people, childbirth is an intensely physical, personal, and spiritual experience. Families are expanding, parents are meeting their children, and bodies are tested, sometimes to the limit. Ideally, the experience is positive, leaving the people involved with a sense of wellness. Too often, people giving birth have to engage in complex arguments and navigate a difficult set of scenarios at a time when they are least capable of making those arguments. For example, Kimberly Turbin won a lawsuit against her doctor, who forcibly gave her an episiotomy against her wishes in 2013 ("Kimberly"). The lawsuit was won, in no small part, because the exchange was captured on video. What viewers may notice in that video is just how calm, focused, and communicative Turbin has to remain throughout the verbal exchange, even while she is experiencing the most intense final stages of labor. In fact, doula friends of mine report having witnessed doctors threaten to (and even) tear the patient's body with their hands when a person giving birth argues against getting an episiotomy.

Unfortunately, doulas witness these exchanges all too often, and unsurprisingly, women of color, poor women, trans men, non-binary people, incarcerated people, and young people are particularly at risk for negative birth experiences. Ideally, the typical childbirth experience would not require this kind of argument and rhetorical savvy from people while they are directly in labor and giving birth. While doulas can use the strategic leading question to help offset that work for the person giving birth, hopefully, these kinds of complex rhetorical maneuvers will become less necessary and less common over time as birth culture and practices improve. However, in the meantime, people giving birth, especially those who do not have access to a doula, continue to be at risk for worse childbirth experiences and even outcomes. Organizations like DONA International must negotiate between promoting work that is most supportive of people in childbirth, while also working with the hospitals and care providers in those settings and supporting the doulas who have certified with them. DONA's website states, "Our doulas serve as a bridge of communication between women and their providers, lifting them up to help them find their voices and advocate for the very best care" ("Benefits"). They indicate that communication and advocacy does play a role in the doula experience, but there is a careful line between improving communication and "working with" versus "arguing against."

Strategic Leading Questions as a Rhetorical Intervention—The Rhetoric of Doulas

Rhetorical approaches can be used for the purposes of reproductive justice, and as a doula, one of the most important rhetorical strategies that emerged for me as an activist doula was something I came to refer to as *strategic leading questions.* Strategic leading questions include the following range of rhetorical actions:

- Disrupting medically based scripts (with emphasis on timing)
- Creating space for birthing people to think about wishes
- Discussing medical discourse and procedure with birthing people
- Attending to emotional aspects of the experience of the birthing person
- Timing communication for desired outcomes

Strategic leading questions used by doulas during childbirth help improve agency, although such rhetorical empowerment is complex. It should be a site of listening, responsiveness, and negotiation among those participating in a birth. These questions are rhetorical in that they function to create new information. At the same time, they are performative, meaning that they function, in part, to elicit an utterance that improves the agency of the person giving birth. For instance, when a birthing person is told by their care provider that they need to begin a Pitocin drip, as a doula I might say, "Your birth plan states that you want to avoid Pitocin." Then I might pose the question, "Do you want to talk to your care provider about your concern or other alternatives that might be available to you now?" In this way, questions are not exactly transactional or directive. Instead, they serve the purpose of creating space as needed to allow the person giving birth to verbally state their intentions, hopes, and ultimately advocate for themselves during the birth experience. Yam explains that doulas can "help create time and space for their clients to exercise more agency and autonomy in making medical decisions" ("Complicating Acts" 206). Strategic questions, a rhetorical strategy for questioning, which creates an opportunity for the person giving birth to verbally state their preferences, is critical because doulas are nonmedical support people. Doulas exist in a somewhat liminal space and must ensure that their work does not become medical advice or practice. This means they do not make medical decisions, and they do not perform any medical procedures.

Activist strategies for doulas, such as using strategic leading questions, are needed in childbirth. Hospitalized childbirth makes those giving birth vulnerable to cultural injustice such as sexism, transphobia, and/or misogynoir, or specifically anti-Black misogyny (Ross and Solinger 78). Doula-rhetors, using intentional rhetorical strategies, can help personalize and humanize the experience in a space where people can easily become objects/subjects in the childbirth setting. While the use of "subject" and "object" to refer to people in childbirth may seem jarring, it illustrates the power differential that is so often at play within the typical white supremacist capitalist patriarchal (hooks) medical industrial complex (Ehrenreich), wherein the birthing body is so frequently acted upon, despite being the source of the action and despite the culture's supposed valuing of agency and autonomy.

The strategic leading question is one of the most effective rhetorical strategies I use as a doula—and one that helps subvert the objectification of people during childbirth. Strategic leading questions require at least three people in order to complete the exchange: the first is usually the healthcare providers (the "subject"), the second is usually a person giving birth (the "object" in the worst, most restrictive childbirth settings), and the third is an intermediary, who in this case is a doula. An audience (or witness) may also observe or participate, and these people might be partners, attending friends and family members, and other healthcare providers, such as nurses. In the exchange, the subject/doctor or midwife initiates the terms or phrasing. For example, they might say, "We need to do an episiotomy," or "Let's go ahead and section her." While this sort of direct statement may seem somewhat surprising to readers, variations of these phrases are commonly used and heard in the childbirth setting. Note that they are statements or commands and are not communicated as questions or possibilities. In part, this rhetorical approach helps maintain or establish the healthcare provider's power and control in the situation. Of course, in many cases, the healthcare provider is there as the expert. However, sexist practices embedded in the US medicalized childbirth culture often prevail, and doctors have primarily been men and people giving birth have mostly been women. It is important to note that this power differential certainly exists with female medical practitioners as well, and all people can enact existing practices. That is why rhetorical strategies for justice, such as strategic questioning, in the medical setting are needed to help circumvent these power differentials and better facilitate fully consented procedures.

In the exchange leading up to the strategic leading question, the subject (usually the doctor or midwife) has stated that a procedure (or any action where the "object" is acted upon) is about to occur. The "object" is the person who is giving birth. This is the person who, according to the two previous examples, may get an episiotomy or a cesarean section, according to the seemingly mandated statement from the subject/doctor or midwife. The intermediary is the doula, who can then implement strategic leading questions, by integrating the relevant keywords or phrases stated by the doctor or midwife to ask the "object"/person giving birth a question that helps the potential recipient of the procedure to state their preferences and provides an opportunity to ask questions and/or expand or minimize time. The doula, acting as intermediary, assembles the strategic question(s) by combining the influencing factors of the situation. For example, the doula might turn to the person giving birth and say, "It sounds like the doctor wants to do an episiotomy. When we discussed this earlier, you indicated that you did not want an episiotomy. Do you want to discuss this further, get more information, or wait? Or, maybe you want to have the procedure done now? Tell us what you're thinking." In answering the doula's question, the patient has an opportunity to state (or restate) their preferences and an opportunity for a more in-depth dialogue emerges. Preferably, in this situation, the patient can then have a conversation with the healthcare provider. Oftentimes, family members and nurses join in on this conversation as well. The resulting conversation ideally allows the patient to reach a decision—a decision that is not coerced and not made under duress. It has been my experience that the patient often feels better about the medical outcome (whether or not they initially wanted the procedure) because they have made (or at least have helped contribute to) the decision.

In the Pitocin example provided earlier, this might play out as follows. The birthing person is told by their care provider that they need to begin a Pitocin drip to augment their labor. Frequently, this is a directive the care provider states to the nurse, "Let's start her on Pit." Without an intermediary, the person giving birth is, indeed "started on Pit" without conversation or question. However, if a doula is present, they might say,

"Your birth plan states that you want to avoid Pitocin. Do you want to talk to your care provider about your concern or about other alternatives that might be available to you now?" This strategic leading question disrupts the medical script and, as needed, interprets medicalized language so that the birthing person can understand what is being said in relation to their body. The question thereby enables a conversation to be had between the care provider and the person giving birth. The strategic leading question also functions to create space for the birthing person to think about and communicate their feelings, concerns, and/or birth wishes. This approach helps attend to the emotional aspects of the person giving birth, allowing them to communicate and make decisions (opposed to being acted upon with the Pitocin).

What follows is usually a conversation involving the care provider, the doula, and the person giving birth about options for augmenting labor. The doula and care providers might suggest alternatives to Pitocin, which include activities such as walking, sitting on a birth ball, laughing, or nipple stimulation. In this case, the strategic leading question can be a tactical tool, timing communication for a desired outcome. The person giving birth may decide to try forty-five minutes of walking. In the process, labor picks up and Pitocin is avoided. Conversely, the person giving birth might walk for forty-five minutes with no change, at which point another conversation can ensue about Pitocin or other methods for inducing labor, which is when the doula-rhetor's strategic leading question facilitates a discussion of medical discourse and procedure with birthing people. In this example, the care provider did not ask permission or ask the person giving birth, but rather directed the nurse to begin the drug, as is common practice. If the person giving birth ultimately needs to start Pitocin because alternatives were ineffective, they often feel better about starting Pitocin because they have had the opportunity to try alternatives. Throughout the exchange, the doula has facilitated the necessary strategic leading questions to create the exchange.

Reaching a kind of agreement can play an important rhetorical role in consenting medical exchanges. Judy Z. Segal calls this agreement reached in a medical setting "concordance," which is an ideal outcome of navigating the healthcare system and results in more fully bringing the patient into decision making (134). Segal's concordance provides a space for the patient to be persuaded. Marleah Dean relatedly writes about "[p]atient empowerment," which "refers to patients' personal goals and autonomous choices in the management of their healthcare" (149). Both terms, focused on individual self-advocacy, call attention to the fact that decision-making in medical contexts is always a matter of various rhetorical factors such as power, perceived credibility, expert knowledge, listening, and presumptions about the appropriate communicative roles of patient and medical professionals. A strategic leading question, then, is a rhetorical device that can help doctors and patients reach concordance and promotes patient empowerment by enlisting the help of a doula-rhetor. As a rhetorical listener, a doula-rhetor engages in what Krista Ratcliffe calls "eavesdropping," or a form of active listening that tunes into "conversations in which eavesdroppers are not directly addressed" (91). In this scenario, a doula-rhetor assists in negotiating the rhetorical dynamics of giving birth even if they are not explicitly addressed by a healthcare worker or even the birthing person. The purpose of eavesdropping as a rhetorical tactic is to enable "hearing over the edges of our own knowing, for thinking what is commonly unthinkable within our own logics" (90–91). As the Pitocin example above illustrates, a birthing person may face extreme rhetorical constraints in actively engaging with the birthing process, moving from "object" to rhetorical agent. My concept of a strategic leading question as a rhetorical device aligns with and extends Ratcliffe's concept of eavesdropping as "positioning oneself to overhear both oneself and others, listening to learn, and being careful (that is, full of care) not to overstep another's boundaries or interrupt the agency of another's discourse" (91). In other words, a doula's eavesdropping involves interpreting a rhetorical situation as it unfolds in real time, listening not only to a medical provider but to a birthing person's previously expressed *and* in-the-moment wishes, and determining how to effectively interrupt the rhetorical situation so as to help the birthing person understand and use their rhetorical agency to the extent of those wishes, even if this means overstepping a medical provider's command. At the same time, strategic leading questions remain questions—interruptions that center the birthing person's desires, needs, and emotions without allowing the doula to take over or center themselves as the primary rhetorical agent in the situation.

Strategic leading questions are pieced together within a dynamic medical space. They are like rhetorical questions in that they are used, in part, for the purpose of teaching or informing the audience. However, with strategic leading questions, the answer is necessary and ideally informative to the childbirth process/experience. Strategic leading questions are supportive of the person giving birth. In this case, strategic leading questions are like leading questions, in that a specific response is intended from the patient/"object." However, unlike a leading question, which is traditionally used to manipulate an "object" to answer in a way that supports the purpose of the subject, the strategic question builds a rhetorical exchange for the purpose of supporting the goals of the birthing person answering the question. This approach helps facilitate a dialogue, a conversation, and a discussion—a process that usually helps the patient better understand and feel more in control and to arrive at concordance within the exchange. The strategic leading question is small "a" assembled in that it is always created within a given situation, using previously stated keywords or phrases stated in the spoken exchange, and it is large "A" Assembled in that it is also aware of larger sociopolitical forces at play within a setting (Deleuze and Guattari).

Calling for Systemic Change: Advocating for Free Rhetor-Doulas

Studies consistently show that hiring a doula decreases negative birth experiences (Gruber et al.). Since women of color, poor women, trans men, non-binary people, incarcerated people, young people, and others are particularly at risk for negative birth experiences, free doula programs, rhetorical devices, and sharing experiences might all be supportive of more positive birth experiences and can therefore promote reproductive social justice in the childbirth setting. At the same time, such free services could contribute to the trend in which the state depends on volunteer efforts as a primary response to birth injustice instead of providing resources to address this need (Nash, "Birthing" 40). However, free volunteer doula programs are not common. Some medical professionals dislike working with doulas, and some hospitals work to limit the role of doula support. (This limitation is especially common in surgery settings.) Furthermore, doulas deserve to be paid for their labor, and so the onus should be on the institution to provide financial support if they work to build and then boast a free doula program.

Volunteer doula programs, and doulas in general, serve people during childbirth, when patients in hospitalized settings are most vulnerable to birth violence and violations of consent. Advocating for oneself and navigating sometimes very complex medical scenarios can be difficult. Engaging self-advocacy while also being a member of a vulnerable population and also while physically in labor is even more challenging—even life threatening, as Adele N. Nichols's chapter in this collection attests. Yet, these challenging scenarios play out day in and day out as people give birth. All birthing people, and especially people of color, poor women, trans men, non-binary people, incarcerated people, and young people, are all too vulnerable in the current system.

Access to doulas is uneven across the population. While the use of doulas during childbirth is on the rise, because doulas can be expensive (women routinely pay upwards of a few thousand dollars for doula services), they are often, though not exclusively, utilized by highly affluent populations. This has not always been the case. In previous decades poor women, who had less access to medicalized care, frequently used doulas (or a doula equivalent) during childbirth, along with family members, midwives, and others with childbirth experience. In more recent times, having access to, education about, and even valuing doulas has been a mostly privileged enterprise. Also, "predominantly white midwifery programs and professional organizations have had a history of racial exclusiveness" (Ross and Solinger 262). Oftentimes, this means wealthy white women use doulas, and that there has been, in recent decades, a problematically low percentage of doulas (and midwives) of color. In many cases, the women who use doula services are those who tend to have access to family planning options, fertility treatment, education, time, money, and other resources, all of which are supportive of a more positive and empowered childbirth experience. Recently, however, unregulated and unpaid birth work by women of color has been invoked publicly and politically as a solution to a crisis in Black maternal health. Such work has been figured as "the touchstone of reproductive justice and as precisely the birthing innovation that will save Black women and children's lives" (Nash, "'In the Room'" 26:23–26:34).

This response to inequity is potentially complicated. Hospitals can make available volunteer doula services, and/or the state can support efforts to improve birth outcomes. This effort might be leveraged to actively dismantle the obstacles standing in the way of people of color being professional doulas, because those with professional status usually receive remuneration for services rendered and are certified through known organizations. Solutions could also come through state-based strategies for recognizing paraprofessional doulas, who are trained in various ways and who may or may not advocate for hospital births. In these differing ways, institutions could "support" doula communities and extend the range of culturally appropriate doula availability. DONA has made a call for more inclusive doula practices as well. In a September 2020 open letter to doulas, DONA leaders wrote that they are "committed to identifying and eliminating processes, practices and perspectives that perpetuate racism and discrimination within our organization and the broader birthing community." They continued, "While we have made progress toward that end, we still have a long way to go" ("Open"). It is important to recognize that doula training that happens in the US and especially in nonwhite communities can have corporate (that is, more standardized) or community (that is, less standardized) approaches. A corporate approach typically means that a doula is paid and has less autonomy in their work, while a community approach is more likely to involve unpaid or underpaid work with greater autonomy (Nash, "Birthing" 36–37). Considering how the "state has increasingly relied on to doulas as the solution to the problem of black maternal and infant death," Nash encourages people to question "why the state has outsourced black maternal and infant health care to underpaid and often minimally trained workers" ("Birthing" 40).

When free doula services exist, are replicated in other communities, are widely used, and are populated with well-trained doulas from various communities advocating for people giving birth, birth experiences may improve for most people. As Davis notes, "Supporting women through pregnancy, labor, and birth is a way to navigate structures of oppression within the medical environment and to shift the ways that care is provided" (195). This service must be accessible, and usually that means "free," in order to help those who need it most. While such support might look like the volunteer doula program I have described, it might also mean different types of programs in different communities or hospitals. For instance, such a "free" program might not charge birthing people but may offer Medicaid reimbursement for doula work ("Doula Medicaid"). The idea of free doula services in hospital settings at this time also raises additional and important structural questions of reproductive justice, ones that a doula-rhetor can consider.

- Can a free doula program balance standardization of services while also allowing for doula practice to respond to immediate or local needs?
- How might a free, hospital-based doula program address the reality that for some people, especially people of color, hospitals—even ones with a doula program, potentially—are unsafe spaces?

- What rhetorical and material practices would support this broader concept of birth work, especially if it happens in a hospital? Can a hospital-based free doula program provide birthing support *and* life work, that supports related issues, such as food insecurity and police violence, as some Black birth workers currently model in places like Chicago?
- How might a free doula program in a hospital serve as a way for those in power to both address birth injustice and, at the same time, contribute to other injustice (such as the economic injustice of relying on volunteers to respond to a systemic problem)?
- On a more individual level, how might white doula-rhetors with privilege approach their work as part of the systems of oppression in birth work within the contemporary US?

These questions demonstrate how important doulas can be but also how complicated the role can be for different people and in multiple contexts. These questions could be useful for volunteers working in a free doula program as well as for people advocating for the creation of a free volunteer doula program in a hospital. Importantly, doulas working within these systems and other childbirth attendants can be further trained to utilize rhetorical strategies, such as storytelling and strategic leading questions, for improving communication in the childbirth setting. As I have suggested throughout this chapter, doula-rhetors function as activists, while supporting the doula's mission to provide physical, emotional, and informational support during childbirth. These rhetorical strategies, whether in a specific birthing situation or applied structurally (e.g., in the negotiation for free doula services in a hospital or community) are supportive of the larger goal of improving reproductive justice, which should help improve the childbirth experience and outcomes for babies and for people giving birth.

Works Cited

"Benefits of a Doula." *DONA International*. https://www.dona.org/what-is-a-doula/benefits-of-a-doula/. Accessed 10 May 2020.

Davis, Dána-Ain. *Reproductive Injustice: Racism, Pregnancy, and Premature Birth*. New York UP, 2019.

Dean, Marleah. "You Have to Be Your Own Advocate: Patient Self-Advocacy as a Coping Mechanism for Hereditary Breast and Ovarian Cancer Risk."

Women's Health Advocacy: Rhetorical Ingenuity for the 21st Century, edited by Jamie White-Farnham, Bryna Siegel Finer, and Cathryn Molloy, Routledge, 2020. pp. 148–62.

Deleuze, Gilles, and Félix Guattari. *A Thousand Plateaus: Capitalism and Schizophrenia*. U of Minnesota P, 1987.

"Doula Medicaid Project." *National Health Law Program*. https://healthlaw.org/doulamedicaidproject/. Accessed 8 Mar. 2021.

Ehrenreich, Barbara. *The American Health Empire: Power, Profits, and Politics*. Vintage, 1971.

Gaskin, Ina May. *Ina May's Guide to Childbirth*. Bantam Books, 2003.

Glenn, Amy Wright. *Birth, Breath, and Death: Meditations on Motherhood, Chaplaincy, and Life as a Doula*. Amy Wright Glenn, 2013.

Gruber, Kenneth J., et al. "Impact of Doulas on Healthy Birth Outcomes." *The Journal of Perinatal Education*, vol. 22, no. 1, 2013, pp. 49–58.

hooks, bell. *Ain't I A Woman: Black Women and Feminism*. South End Press, 1981.

"Kimberly Turbin's Forced Episiotomy Case: The Resolution." *Improving Birth*. https://improvingbirth.org/2017/03/kimberlys-case-the-resolution/. Accessed 16 Mar. 2017.

Lay, Mary M. *The Rhetoric of Midwifery: Gender, Knowledge, and Power*. Rutgers UP, 2000.

Mayer, Gordon. "Increase Power, Improve Health Outcomes, Amani Says." *HealthConnect One*. healthconnectone.org. Accessed 18 Nov. 2020.

Nash, Jennifer C. "Birthing Black Mothers: Birth Work and the Making of Black Maternal Political Subjects." *WSQ: Women's Studies Quarterly*, vol. 47, no. 3 & 4, 2019, pp. 29–50.

—. "'In the Room': Women of Color Birth-Work in a State of Emergency." *YouTube*, uploaded by Center for Social Science Scholarship, 5 Mar. 2021, www.youtube.com/watch?v=Y86TnXxtCHw.

Olsen, Caroline. "Birthworkers Are on the Front Lines of Chicago's Maternal Health Crisis." *Chicago Magazine*, 16 July 2019, www.chicagomag.com/city-life/July-2019/Chicagos-Maternal-Health-Crisis/. Accessed 13 April 2021.

"Open Letter to DONA Members Regarding Antiracism Efforts." *DONA International*. https://www.dona.org/antiracism/. Accessed 8 March 2021.

Owens, Kim Hensley. *Writing Childbirth: Women's Rhetorical Agency in Labor and Online*. Southern Illinois UP, 2015.

Ratcliffe, Krista. "Eavesdropping as Rhetorical Tactic: History, Whiteness, Rhetoric." *JAC*, vol. 20, no. 1, 2000, pp. 87–119.

Ross, Loretta J., and Rickie Solinger. *Reproductive Justice: An Introduction*. U of California P, 2017.

Ross, Loretta J., Lynn Roberts, Erika Derkas, Whitney Peoples, and Pamela Bridgewater Toure, editors. Introduction. *Radical Reproductive Justice: Foundations, Theory, Practice, Critique*, edited by Loretta J. Ross, Lynn

Roberts, Erika Derkas, Whitney Peoples, and Pamela Bridgewater Toure. Feminist P, 2017, pp. 11-31.

Segal, Judy Z. *Health and the Rhetoric of Medicine.* Southern Illinois UP. 2008.

United States, Supreme Court. *Dobbs, State Health Officer of the Mississippi Department of Health, et al. v. Jackson Women's Health Organization, et al.* 24 June 2022. *Supremecourt.gov,* https://www.supremecourt.gov/opinions/21pdf/19–1392_6j37.pdf.

"What Is a Doula?" *DONA International.* www.dona.org/what-is-a-doula/. Accessed 10 May 2020.

"What Is a Doula?" *WebMD.* www.webmd.com/baby/what-is-a-doula. Accessed 10 May 2020.

Yam, Shui-yin Sharon. "Birth Images on *Instagram*: The Disruptive Visuality of Birthing Bodies." *Women's Studies in Communication*, vol. 42, no. 1, Feb. 2019, pp. 80–100.

—. "Complicating Acts of Advocacy: Tactics in the Birthing Room." *Reflections,* vol. 20, no. 2, Fall/Winter 2020, pp. 198–218.

—. "Visualizing Birth Stories from the Margin: Toward a Reproductive Justice Model of Rhetorical Analysis." *Rhetoric Society Quarterly*, vol. 50, no. 1, 2020, pp. 19–34.

Afterword—Scaling Up and Out: Co-Creating a Future for Reproductive Justice

Shui-yin Sharon Yam and Natalie Fixmer-Oraiz

We write this afterword in a moment replete with intense trauma and upheaval. A global pandemic. Shuttered economies and schools. Vaccine distribution inequities and healthcare systems on the brink of collapse. White supremacy and authoritarianism rising. State censorship of educational curricula pertaining to social justice and the brutal, uneven silencing of dissent worldwide, in places like China, the United States, and Russia.

The precarity of sexual and reproductive rights proves no exception. In the US, the Supreme Court of the United States (SCOTUS) has overturned the landmark 1973 decision *Roe v. Wade,* which has emboldened states to criminalize abortion across the country. Just over half of US states have since put in place criminal and civil laws that prohibit abortions. Sixteen of them restrict nearly all forms of abortions (Perley Masling et. al.). Legal experts have noted that, because Justice Samuel Alito's leaked document proved accurate, the decision reaches far beyond abortion care access, with devastating implications for contraception, marriage equality, and transgender health and rights. And the systemic reproductive abuse of the most vulnerable among us—those detained and incarcerated by the state—was on clear and devastating display when Dawn Wooten, a nurse working in an ICE detention facility in Georgia, filed a whistleblower complaint that detailed forced sterilizations of detained immigrant women (Narea; Project South: Institute for the Elimination of Poverty & Genocide). On a global scale, as Sophia Sadinsky, Zara Ahmed, and Lauren Cross write: "The COVID-19 pandemic has exposed and exacerbated a global gender equality crisis, provoking alarming increases in gender-based violence, a sharp decrease in women participating in the workforce, and new challenges in access to contraception, abortion and other essential health care." They urge the adoption of feminist public policy in response to global human rights challenges.

We echo and extend their call with a plea for radical rhetorical reproductive justice now. We do so in no small part because the chaos of now is of immense consequence, the nature of which is—as of yet—undetermined. Naomi Klein has written extensively on "the brutal tactic of using the public's disorientation following a collective shock—wars, coups, terrorist attacks, market crashes or natural disasters—to push through radical pro-corporate measures" ("How Power Profits"). As Klein noted in the early months of the COVID-19 pandemic: "In times of crisis, seemingly impossible ideas suddenly become possible. But whose ideas? Sensible, fair ones, designed to keep as many people as possible safe, secure and healthy? Or predatory ideas, designed to further enrich the already unimaginably wealthy while leaving the most vulnerable further exposed?" ("*Coronavirus Capitalism*"). In short, Klein reminds us that chaos is rife with possibility. If we fail to seize this moment, those in power will.

Rhetoricians of color have illuminated the ways in which marginalized communities challenge the status quo, specifically in moments of crisis (e.g. Baniya; Soto Vega). More importantly, marginalized communities have been redefining crisis on their own terms. Drawing on Black feminist Brittney Cooper, Tamika Carey argues that Black women have been engaging in acts of "rhetorical impatience" to disrupt what she calls "temporal hegemony" dictated by a system of white supremacy (270). Rather than abiding by the temporality of whiteness that dismisses the severity and urgency of Black women's concerns, Black women rhetors have historically deployed "time-based arguments" and performed "instructional and discursive" urgency to disrupt misogynoir (270). In other words, rather than waiting for the dominant institution to acknowledge their marginalization and suffering, they generate rhetorical moments of disruption to make clear that the time to act against systemic oppression is now.

Black women and grassroots activists' prowess in harnessing moments of crisis becomes all the more important during the pandemic, and at a time when human rights are under assault. On May 2, 2022, after the draft SCOTUS majority opinion on *Roe v. Wade* was leaked, Black woman activist Brittney Packnett Cunningham tweeted, "The long game to dismantle any rights that are not 'deeply rooted in the nation's history and tradition' is white supremacist patriarchy that will never stop at abortion. This moment will either invoke despair or revolution. The choice is ours" ([@MsPackyetti]). It is no small thing that amidst so much personal suffering and political oppression we bear witness nonetheless to extraordinary collective resilience, courage, and grassroots mobilization. We have seen the radical made possible in the US as states have tripled unemployment benefits, eliminated bail, released prisoners, and banned utility shutoffs and evictions (Cohen). But policy shifts are preceded by people. And people have been making their voices heard—they have organized in their communities and stood in solidarity with one another in unprecedented ways. In the US, for example, widespread outrage over the murder of George Floyd by former police officer Derrick Chauvin catalyzed a season of widespread social unrest as millions of people flooded streets across the country demanding racial justice and an end to state-sanctioned anti-Black racial terror. Led by Black feminists and Black mothers, Black Lives Matter has since been declared the largest movement in US history—while it has met with predictable backlash, it has unequivocally elevated awareness of race and racism in public consciousness, prompted policy changes at various levels of government, and assembled a historic multiracial coalition for Black lives and liberation (Buchanan et al.). Consider another illustration of this point: in the midst of racial uprising, anti-authoritarianism protests, and the pandemic, people around the world have witnessed how state governments fail to respond ethically and effectively to crises—at times, as Dean Spade points out, governments have even engineered such crises. In response, people have been enacting alternative forms of care and support through mutual aid networks in the US, and in places like Hong Kong, China, Myanmar, and Lebanon (Chestnut et al.; "Interview"; "Mutual Aid Myanmar"; Spade). These allied movements organizing under extraordinary pressures underscore indeterminacy as the linchpin of the now—that out of disaster, something new will invariably emerge to order our world. Intersectional grassroots movements are key in determining that future.

Thus, in this moment of rupture, reproductive justice—as a framework, movement, and "rhetorical mindset" (Adams and Myers)—has much to offer. For instance, it offers incisive structural critique of the material conditions that have been exacerbated by COVID. COVID has heightened visibility surrounding various forms of reproductive injustice: gendered segregation in low-wage, essential labor; the caregiving responsibilities shouldered primarily by women and femmes, and especially poor women of color; the impacts of intensified policing and surveillance against marginalized communities under the guise of public health; and the transnational logics of white supremacy and racial capitalism that target poor people of color across the globe (Lausan Collective et al.; Powell; Yam, "Why Hong Kong's Covid-19 Policies"). Articulated and enacted by people who are multiply oppressed, reproductive justice's focus on intersectionality and coalition politics reminds us that these phenomena are interconnected. We cannot achieve reproductive and sexual freedom without combatting racism, authoritarianism, and economic violence. As such, reproductive justice offers us the conceptual tools and organizing strategies to chart another path forward. As the editors point out in their introduction, a rhetorical mindset is attuned to "the agency-oriented possibilities of rhetorical movement." In confluence, the reproductive justice framework and a rhetorical approach allow us to not only notice and critique systemic injustice produced by networked ideologies and arguments, but also to invent rhetorical acts that could challenge the system.

Possibilities and Rhetorical World-Making

If we will permit it, if we insist on it, reproductive justice might frame our response in ways that would transform our discursive frameworks, materialities, and infrastructure to create a more just future. Indeed, the essays in this collection are engaging in what we see as a rhetorical worldmaking that is built upon four key moves: a deep understanding of critical histories, a refusal to accept the status quo, an eagerness to identify and cultivate coalitions with different stakeholders and communities, and finally, a robust critique of hegemonic discourse and institutions.

First, rhetorical worldmaking pivots on an intimacy with shared and disparate histories, on our capacity to curate a usable past. For example, in tracing the complex entanglements of eugenics and birth control within the mid-nineteenth century Oneida Community, Michelle C. Smith clarifies the stubborn biopolitical residue of the rhetoric of reproductive "choice" in contemporary contexts. As Smith's historiography complicates the connection between individual "choice" and reproductive freedom, Melissa Stone and Zachary Beare's analysis of Nurx extends this interrogation by examining how Nurx, a telehealth medicine platform, renders reproductive and sexual healthcare more accessible to privileged people, while reinforcing neoliberal values that ultimately reinscribes the harmful affect of shame. Taken together, these two chapters remind us that barriers towards reproductive freedom traverse across time, despite different circumstances. Addressing contemporary challenges demands deep attunement to these critical histories and struggles.

Second, in order to challenge the status quo, scholars and activists must actively call into question deeply ingrained narratives and ideologies that threaten reproductive freedom and sovereignty. Thus, essays in this volume deploy reproductive justice as a critical rhetorical heuristic to critique dominant narratives and imagine alternatives. For example, Jenna Vinson's analysis of vasectomy in popular US culture reveals how these representations reify "white supremacist patriarchal gender roles" and put the onus once again on women to manage fertility and reproduction. Writing against the grain of mythic norms that position young women's childbearing as pathological and in need of redress, Meta Henty's chapter on #NoTeenShame elucidates how activists deploy alternative rhetorical practices in digital spaces to assert young people's right to have children and to parent them in an inclusive environment. By amplifying how #NoTeenShame proliferates a discursive framework that returns agency to young parents while refusing co-optation and silencing by more established organizations, Henty uplifts a model of reproductive justice discourse and mindset that is often sidelined even in reproductive advocacy. In another example, James D. Warwood's chapter explores how storytelling in the groundbreaking podcast *Masculine Birth Ritual* expands the scope of reproduction and family formation beyond a cisheteronormative framework. The stories centered in this space challenge dominant exclusionary discourse on pregnancy and birth in ways that recognize and affirm masculine-of-center birthing people. In these chapters, authors interrogate dominant assumptions about reproduction and amplify historically marginalized experiences; in so doing, they highlight how reproductive justice can serve as a method of rhetorical analysis and mindset.

Other essays expand on this use of rhetoric to promote reproductive justice with an eye toward coalition building across communities and stakeholders. As Adele N. Nichols connects "systemic racialized maternal abuse (SRMA)" to the African rhetorical concept *nommo,* "the generative power of spoken word" (Hamlet 27), she also makes clear the intimate tie between reproductive justice and rhetoric. In this case, the accurate naming of SRMA allows Black birthing people and activists to connect the medical racism they experience with the histories of reproductive violence against Black women in the nineteenth and twentieth centuries. As Nichols' work clarifies, having the language to describe and connect intergenerational trauma and systemic violence is crucial in imagining and creating a more just present and future. In another chapter that is similarly centered on obstetric violence (Davis), Sheri Rysdam reflects on her experience as a volunteer doula and rhetor as she works with marginalized birthing people. As Rysdam points out, doulas often serve as "activist rhetors" who advocate for and with the birthing person. Rysdam's essay illustrates the rhetorical tactics doulas deploy to challenge dominant medical scripts and practices, so as to help the birthing person achieve their ideal birth process and outcome.

Finally, many of these essays engage in a politics of refusal by challenging the legitimacy of dominant discourse and the hegemony of established institutions and frameworks (McGranahan). In so doing, these authors imagine and enact new subjectivities outside of the confines of oppressive ideologies and histories, attending to rhetorics of reproductive justice with an eye toward coalition building across communities and stakeholders. In Jill Swiencicki's chapter, she examines Wendy Davis's filibustering through the lens of "reproductive justice brokering," illustrating how reproductive justice activists leverage their multi-membership in different communities to amplify marginalized voices and build solidarities. Hannah Dudley-Shotwell traces the history of the US women gynecological self-help movement in the 1970s-1990s, elucidating how the legacy of the movement, while empowering for some, perpetuates cisnormativity. Turning toward contemporary feminist attempts to redress transgender and nonbinary exclusions, Dudley-Shotwell examines more inclusive clinic languages. This work offers a critical praxis for reproductive-justice-centered healthcare and underscores the significance of knowing our histories in order to build a more inclusive future.

In concert, these essays offer a powerful articulation of rhetorical worldmaking in the spirit of reproductive justice. Focused on alliance, practice, and suggested possibility, here we encounter stories of struggle and perseverance that offer us equipment for living—legacies from which we might assemble alternative futures and more just ways of being in the world. Tracing these alignments—in all of their specificity, complexity, and nuance—is a critical dimension of realizing the power of reproductive justice on a global scale.

Scaling Up and Out: Transnationalism and Reproductive Justice

We hold that it is crucial also for reproductive justice scholars to continue to identify coalitional potential and grounds for solidarity with different stakeholders. Thinking through transnational feminist social movements and discourse, Ashwini Tambe and Millie Thayer remind us that our current context calls for "'scaling out' across social and ideological boundaries, as well as 'scaling up' across geographical ones" (6). For Tambe and Thayer, it is insufficient to pay attention to singular domestic issues without attending their intersections with other systems of oppression in a transnational context. While "scaling out" reminds us to look for ways in which individuals across ideological and social divides are interpellated by the same issue, "scaling up" calls for us to examine how seemingly domestic exigences generate activism, collaborations, and solidarities across national boundaries. As both of us (Fixmer-Oraiz; Yam, "The City of Tears"), along with intersectional feminist scholars such as Sophie Lewis, Jallicia Jolly, and Alison Bailey, have argued elsewhere, reproductive justice is a useful framework to critique and combat transnational systems of power and oppression.

In this anthology, tracing past transnational collaborations between reproductive justice activists in the US and reproductive rights organizers in Latin America, Fabiola Carrión articulates both the need for and histories of solidarity across national borders. Observing the similar struggles faced by women of color in the US and Latin American reproductive activists, Carrión asks: "I realized that reproductive justice is not necessarily a novel framework for Latin American advocates because it mirrors modes of resistance to oppressions that exist among women of color in the US and among women who live South of the US border. . . . Why is it that these connections are not part of our common and shared knowledge?" As an intersectional framework that emphasizes coalition building across difference, reproductive justice can be harnessed to cultivate different kinds of cross-border solidarities. As Zakiya Luna points out, prior to the 1995 Fourth World Conference on Women in Beijing, reproductive justice activists from the US agreed that "greater attention to more effective linkages between the grass roots and national and international NGOs is required . . . the lessons learned and strategies shared through the international process need to be more effectively disseminated to women organizing in their local communities, while local strategies need to be more effectively amplified at the transnational level" (73). The US Women of Color Delegation to the Beijing Conference also articulated the interconnectedness between US domestic and international policies and the material conditions of marginalized women in developing countries (Luna). Loretta Ross, one of the founding mothers of the Reproductive Justice Movement, was wary of the population control discourse proffered in these two conferences (Starkey and Seager). Touted as a developmental goal for the Global South, the global politics of population control enforces stratified reproduction while eclipsing structural causes of poverty, environmental degradation, and women's disempowerment (Hartmann). As Development Studies scholar Betsy Hartmann posits, the Reproductive Justice Movement and framework is useful in resisting dominant narratives about population control enforced by Western countries and the intergovernmental organizations they dominate. Activists in the Reproductive Justice Movement have been resisting population control policies in a transnational arena, advocating instead for accessible healthcare, education, and economic opportunities for marginalized women so that they could make informed decisions about their fertility (Hartmann; Ross and Solinger). Reproductive justice activists, in other words, have long articulated an intersectional and transnational orientation towards organizing across borders (Ross and Solinger).

In addition to borders that demarcate nation-state boundaries, there are also borders that prevent coalitional work across communities and interest groups. As Ross and Rickie Solinger make clear, "The reproductive justice framework is defined by coalition politics and cannot achieve its human rights goals without building coalitions" (77). To enact coalition politics in an expansive way, we must first map out how oppressions and systems of power are interconnected both in and outside of the United States. As we understand the US as a node rather than the center of a transnational network, we see that the three pillars of reproductive justice encompass the rights of *all* marginalized people, and not just people in the US, who are affected by transnational racial capitalism, white supremacy, authoritarianism, and other forms of systemic oppression. In the face of police brutality and state-sanctioned violence against migrants, reproductive justice activists and scholars in the US have scaled out by connecting with migrant justice advocates and abolitionists (Hofmann-Kuroda; Murillo and Fixmer-Oraiz; Olivera). Transnationally, we may also scale up by identifying shared struggles across contexts and by advocating alongside activists from countries outside of the US. For example, as reproductive justice activists fight against anti-transgender bills proposed in a number of US states, they join those who have recently successfully advocated for the rights of transgender and nonbinary people in Australia, Canada, Chile, Colombia, Costa Rica, and Pakistan (Chiam et al.).

And as reproductive justice scholars and activists in the US critique police violence against Black people as a form of reproductive injustice, we can observe and cultivate the coalitional potential between abolitionist and reproductive justice activists in the US and those in other countries—such as Hong Kong, Chile, and Nigeria—who are resisting similar kinds of state and police violence. As we advocate for detained migrant women and incarcerated women in the US who were forcibly sterilized, we must attend to the reproductive abuses of Uyghur women in Xinjiang at the hands of the Chinese government (Graham-Harrison and Kuo). While these instances are all uniquely situated, they are also intimately connected, as state powers and systems of oppression are linked across borders. The US, for instance, has helped train the police force in Hong Kong and provided military resources to Israel, which were used in part to dispossess Palestinians (Abdelfatah et al.; Chan). The Chinese government's dehumanizing narratives and policies against the Uyghur people in Xinjiang drew on transnational Islamophobia and anti-Muslim racism the US's War on Terror post-9/11 (Byler). The separation of families and state-sponsored reproductive injustices in Xinjiang echo the human rights violations committed against migrants and asylum seekers at the US border, albeit different by degree. In both cases, racialized bodies are rendered less valuable by state powers that operate on logics of disposability.

Given these intricate transnational connections, reproductive justice research and activism becomes a more powerful tool of resistance when it attends simultaneously to specific local contexts and transnational systems of power. This observation has several implications for rhetorical scholars and scholar-activists in reproductive justice. First, in our research and activism, we need to be attentive towards scale: how seemingly local events and matters of concern are connected to transnational systems and forces that are affecting others in similar but different ways outside of our immediate context. Offering ways to examine interconnected systems of oppression and circulation, scholarship in transnational rhetorics provides a sound foundation that could enhance our research orientation (Dingo et al.). Second, as we scale out and up in our research on reproductive justice, we will likely encounter movement artifacts, interlocutors, and rhetorical performances that do not fit neatly into our preconceptions. As Luna has rightly pointed out, writing about social movements as they continue to evolve is a complex act, as it entails understanding the different and sometimes conflicting ideologies and visions people hold. Since our research is always political, we have an obligation to deeply contextualize, triangulate, and engage with materials and interlocutors even when they complicate our existing worldviews and frameworks. Finally, by engaging in ethical collaboration with scholars and activists from communities that are not our own, we will be better able to cultivate and enact sustainable coalitions that take into account the shared struggles and differential oppression different groups face. By collaborating with others who have different lived experiences and epistemic privileges from us, we can coproduce a body of knowledge that reflects the diverse but intersecting experiences of marginalization and resistance.

Works Cited

. [@MsPackyetti]. "This Draft Decision Is Evil. The Long Game to Dismantle Any Rights That Are Not 'Deeply Rooted in the Nation's History and Tradition' Is White Supremacist Patriarchy That Will Never Stop at Abortion. This Moment Will Either Invoke Despair or Revolution. The Choice Is Ours. Https://T.Co/5hCCN0uMEn." Tweet. *Twitter*, May 3, 2022. www.twitter.com/MsPackyetti/status/1521462983200808961.

Abdelfatah, Rund, et al. *How Settlements and Displacements Are Part of the Gaza Conflict*. www.npr.org/2021/05/25/1000247156/palestine. Accessed 14 June 2021.

Bailey, Alison. "Reconceiving Surrogacy: Toward a Reproductive Justice Account of Indian Surrogacy." *Hypatia*, vol. 26, no. 4, Oct. 2011, pp. 715–41.

Baniya, Sweta. "Managing Environmental Risks in the Age of Climate Change: Rhetorical Agency and Ecological Literacies of Transnational Women During the April 2015 Nepal Earthquake | Enculturation." *Enculturation: A Journal of Rhetoric, Writing, and Culture*, no. 32, 2020, www.enculturation.net/managing_environmental.

Buchanan, Larry, et al. "Black Lives Matter May Be the Largest Movement in US History—The New York Times." *The New York Times*, 3 July 2020, www.nytimes.com/interactive/2020/07/03/us/george-floyd-protests-crowd-size.html.

Byler, Darren. "How China's 'Xinjiang Mode' Draws from US, British, and Israeli Counterinsurgency Strategy." *Lausan*, Oct. 2020, www.lausan.hk/2020/chinas-xinjiang-mode-counterinsurgency-strategy/.

Carey, Tamika L. "Necessary Adjustments: Black Women's Rhetorical Impatience." *Rhetoric Review*, vol. 39, no. 3, July 2020, pp. 269–86. *Taylor and Francis+NEJM*, https://doi.org/10.1080/07350198.2020.1764745.

Chan, Wilfred. "Trump's Executive Order Confirms US State Department Has Trained the Hong Kong Police." *Lausan*, 15 July 2020, www.lausan.hk/2020/state-department-train-hong-kong-police/.

Chestnut, et al. "Mutual Aid and the Rebuilding of Chinese Society—Part 1." *Lausan*, July 2020, www.lausan.hk/2020/mutual-aid-and-the-rebuilding-of-chinese-society-part-1/.

Chiam, Zhan, et al. *Trans Legal Mapping Report 2019: Recognition before the Law*. ILGA World, 2020, pp. 1–244, www.ilga.org/downloads/ILGA_World_Trans_Legal_Mapping_Report_2019_EN.pdf.

Cohen, Rachel M. "Opinion: The Coronavirus Made the Radical Possible." *The New York Times*, 11 Mar. 2021. *NYTimes.com*, www.nytimes.com/2021/03/11/opinion/covid-eviction-prison-internet-policy.html.

Davis, Dána-Ain. *Reproductive Injustice*. New York UP, 2019.

Dingo, Rebecca, et al. "Toward a Cogent Analysis of Power: Transnational Rhetorical Studies." *JAC*, vol. 33, no. 3/4, JAC, 2013, pp. 517–28. JSTOR.

Fixmer-Oraiz, Natalie. "Speaking of Solidarity: Transnational Gestational Surrogacy and the Rhetorics of Reproductive (In)Justice." *Frontiers: A Journal of Women Studies*, vol. 34, no. 3, 2013, p. 126–63. *Crossref*, doi:10.5250/fronjwomestud.34.3.0126.

Graham-Harrison, Emma, and Lily Kuo. "Uighur Muslim Teacher Tells of Forced Sterilisation in Xinjiang." *The Guardian*, 4 Sept. 2020, www.theguardian.com/world/2020/sep/04/muslim-minority-teacher-50-tells-of-forced-sterilisation-in-xinjiang-china.

Hamlet, Janice D. "Word! The African American Oral Tradition and Its Rhetorical Impact on American Popular Culture." *Black History Bulletin*, vol. 74, no. 1, Association for the Study of African American Life and History, 2011, pp. 27–31.

Hartmann, Betsy. *Reproductive Rights and Wrongs: The Global Politics of Population Control*. 2016.

Hofmann-Kuroda, Lisa. "Prison Abolition Is a Key Component of Reproductive Freedom." *Wear Your Voice*, June 2019, www.wearyourvoicemag.com/prison-abolition-reproductive-care/.

"Interview: Mutual Aid in Lebanon in the Wake of Disaster." *Freedom News*, Aug. 2020, www.freedomnews.org.uk/2020/08/10/interview-mutual-aid-in-lebanon-in-the-wake-of-disaster/.

Jolly, Jallicia. "On Forbidden Wombs and Transnational Reproductive Justice." *Meridians: Feminism, Race, Transnationalism*, vol. 15, no. 1, 2016, pp. 166–88.

Klein, Naomi. *"Coronavirus Capitalism": Naomi Klein's Case for Transformative Change Amid Coronavirus Pandemic*. Interview by Amy Goodman, 19 Mar. 2020, www.democracynow.org/2020/3/19/naomi_klein_coronavirus_capitalism.

—. "How Power Profits from Disaster." *The Guardian*, 6 July 2017, www.theguardian.com/us-news/2017/jul/06/naomi-klein-how-power-profits-from-disaster.

Lausan Collective. "Asian Leftists Challenging Global Racial Capitalism in the Time of COVID-19." *Lausan*, May 2020, www.lausan.hk/2020/asian-leftists-challenging-global-racial-capitalism-in-the-time-of-covid/.

Lewis, Sophie. *Full Surrogacy Now: Feminism Against Family*. Verso, 2019.

Luna, Zakiya. *Reproductive Rights as Human Rights: Women of Color and the Fight for Reproductive Justice*. New York UP, 2020.

McGranahan, Carole. "Theorizing Refusal: An Introduction." *Cultural Anthropology*, vol. 31, no. 3, 3 Aug. 2016, pp. 319–25. *journal.culanth.org*, doi: 10.14506/ca31.3.01.

Murillo, Lina-Maria, and Natalie Fixmer-Oraiz. "Reproductive Justice in the Heartland: Mothering, Maternal Care, and Race in 21st Century Iowa." *Maternal Theory: Essential Readings*, edited by Andrea O'Reilly, 2nd edition, Demeter P, 2021, pp. 745–60.

"Mutual Aid Myanmar." *Mutual Aid Myanmar*, www.mutualaidmyanmar.org. Accessed 16 June 2021.

Narea, Nicole. "The Outcry over ICE and Hysterectomies, Explained." *Vox*, 15 Sept. 2020, www.vox.com/policy-and-politics/2020/9/15/21437805/whistle blower-hysterectomies-nurse-irwin-ice.

Olivera, Katherine. "Immigration Is a Reproductive Justice Issue." *International Women's Health Coalition*, 3 Aug. 2018, www.iwhc.org/2018/08/immi gration-is-a-reproductive-justice-issue/.

Perley Masling, Sharon, et al. "Evolving Laws and Litigation Post–Dobbs: The State of Reproductive Rights as of January 2023." *Morgan Lewis*, 5 Jan. 2023, www.morganlewis.com/pubs/2023/01/evolving-laws-and-litigation-post-dobbs-the-state-of-reproductive-rights-as-of-january-2023.

Powell, Catherine. "The Color and Gender of COVID: Essential Workers, Not Disposable People." *Council on Foreign Relations*, June 2020, www.thinkglobalhealth.org/article/color-and-gender-covid-essential-workers-not-disposable-people.

Project South: Institute for the Elimination of Poverty & Genocide. *Re: Lack of Medical Care, Unsafe Work Practices, and Absence of Adequate Protection Against COVID-19 for Detained Immigrants and Employees Alike at the Ir-*

win County Detention Center. 14 Sept. 2020, www.projectsouth.org/wp-content/uploads/2020/09/OIG-ICDC-Complaint-1.pdf.

Ross, Loretta, and Rickie Solinger. *Reproductive Justice: An Introduction*. First edition, U of California P, 2017.

Sadinsky, Sophia, et al. "Here's Why Sexual and Reproductive Rights Must Be the Linchpin of Feminist Foreign Policy." *Guttmacher Institute*, 27 May 2021, www.guttmacher.org/article/2021/06/heres-why-sexual-and-reproductive-rights-must-be-linchpin-feminist-foreign-policy.

Soto Vega, Karrieann. "Colonial Causes and Consequences: Climate Change and Climate Chaos in Puerto Rico." *Enculturation: A Journal of Rhetoric, Writing, and Culture*, no. 32, 2020, www.enculturation.net/colonial_causes_consequences.

Spade, Dean. *Mutual Aid: Building Solidarity During This Crisis*. Verso, 2020.

Starkey, Marian, and John Seager. "Loretta Ross: Reproductive Justice Pioneer - PopConnect." *Population Connection*, www.populationconnection.org/article/loretta-ross/. Accessed 16 June 2021.

Tambe, Ashwini, and Millie Thayer, editors. *Transnational Feminist Itineraries: Situating Theory and Activist Practice*. Duke UP, 2021.

Yam, Shui-yin Sharon. "The City of Tears: Reproductive Justice and Community Resistance in Hong Kong's Anti-ELAB Movement." *Feminist Formations*, vol. 33, no. 2, 2021, pp. 1–24.

—. "Why Hong Kong's Covid-19 Policies Are Racist to the Core." *Hong Kong Free Press HKFP*, 4 May 2021, www.hongkongfp.com/2021/05/04/why-hong-kongs-covid-19-policies-are-racist-to-the-core/.

Contributors

Zachary Beare is an associate professor of English, the director of first-year writing, and a core faculty member of the Communication, Rhetoric, and Digital Media (CRDM) program at North Carolina State University. His research and teaching focus on composition pedagogy, queer and feminist rhetorics, affect and emotion, and digital culture. He is especially interested in how identity and emotion mediate rhetorical activity. His work has appeared in *College Composition and Communication*, *College English*, *Composition Studies*, the *Journal of Cultural Research*, *Reflections: A Journal of Community-Engaged Writing and Rhetoric*, *Writing on the Edge*, and in various edited collections.

Fabiola Carrión is the Director of Reproductive and Sexual Health at the National Health Law Program, where she works to expand access to reproductive health care services in public and private health programs. Carrión graduated with high honors from University of California Berkeley in Latin American Studies and Political Science and has law degrees from American University in Washington, DC, and La Universidad Alfonso X in Madrid, Spain. Earlier in her career, Carrión was an advocacy program officer at Planned Parenthood Global, where she designed, developed, and oversaw projects on sexual and reproductive rights in Latin America. She was also the director of government relations at Planned Parenthood of New York City and a policy advisor for a network of state legislators and advocates from across the United States. She is on the boards of various reproductive justice and health organizations. Her work has been featured in *Rewire*, *TruthOut*, and *Cosmopolitan*. Her 2015 piece, "How Women's Organizations are Changing the Legal Landscape of Reproductive Rights in Latin America," was published in *CUNY Law Review*.

Hannah Dudley-Shotwell is a historian in the Cormier Honors College at Longwood University in Farmville, VA. She teaches courses on US, women's, and queer history; the intersections of bodies and citizenship; and reproductive justice. Dudley-Shotwell earned her BA in history and English at the College of William and Mary and her PhD in United States history (with a post-baccalaureate certificate in women's and gender studies) from the University of North Carolina Greensboro. She is the author of *Revolutionizing Women's Healthcare: The Feminist Self-Help Movement in America* (2020), which won the Western Association of Women Historians' Frances Richardson Keller-Sierra Prize. Her current work investigates the influence of late-twentieth century lesbian separatist theory on the rise of trans-exclusionary radical feminist (TERF) ideology. Her scholarship is informed in particular by her work establishing both the Race and Ethnic Studies minor and the Lavender Graduation Ceremony at Longwood.

Natalie Fixmer-Oraiz is F. Wendell Miller Associate Professor of Communication Studies and Gender, Women's and Sexuality Studies at the University of Iowa. She is the author of *Homeland Maternity: US Security Culture and the New Reproductive Regime* (University of Illinois Press, 2019), an award-winning book that examines the policing of pregnancy and parenting in the United States from a rhetorical perspective. She has published numerous essays on feminism, rhetoric, and reproductive justice and is currently at work on two book projects that grapple with the politics and possibilities of queer family formation. Her scholarship and teaching emerge from a combination of academic training alongside more than fifteen years of experience in reproductive politics as a community organizer and advocate in a number of local and regional contexts.

Meta Henty is a lecturer in the department of English and Creative Writing at Stephen F. Austin State University. She teaches courses in literature, rhetoric, and composition. She received her PhD in English (with a graduate certificate in women's and gender studies) from Texas Christian University, where she studied American literature and women's rhetorics. Her scholarship lies at the intersection of rhetorical, gender, and cultural studies. Her 2019 dissertation analyzes #NoTeenShame and the stars of MTV's *Teen Mom* to explore how teen mothers employ rhetoric to claim agency over their own narratives and effect change.

Adele N. Nichols is a pre-nursing student at the Community College of Baltimore County, an independent researcher, and a freelance editor. She received two masters degrees from Towson University, one in professional writing with a focus on qualitative research design, rhetorical theory, and composition, and a second in women and gender studies with a focus on Black maternal health. Her scholarly interests are Black feminist theory and praxis, Womanism, Black maternal health, and interdisciplinary studies. In May 2018, she presented her research "Reclaiming the Tradition: Black Women Need Traditional Birth and Postpartum Doula Services to be Included as Essential Health Care Benefits" at the Re-Imagining Black Girls' and Women's Health Symposium.

Sheri Rysdam is an associate professor in the Department of English/Writing and director of the writing center at Eastern Oregon University. Her PhD is in rhetoric and composition from Washington State University. Her scholarly work is on responding to student writing, nonviolent response, rhetorics of political economy, and reproductive rhetorics, especially related to doula work and advocacy for women during childbirth. Her writing is informed, in part, by her own experience as a mother and her work as a volunteer doula.

Michelle C. Smith is an associate professor of English at Clemson University. She earned her PhD in rhetoric and composition from Penn State University. Her teaching and research interests include feminist rhetorics, rhetorical theory, and historiography, with a particular focus on rhetorics of gendered labor. Her writing has appeared in *College English, Rhetoric Society Quarterly*, and *Peitho*, as well as other journals and edited collections. She is the author of *Utopian Genderscapes: Rhetorics of Women's Work in the Early Industrial Age*, which offers an ecological reading of domestic, professional, and reproductive labor in three mid-nineteenth century utopian communities.

Melissa Stone is an assistant professor of English in the Writing, Rhetoric, and Technical Communication program at Appalachian State University in North Carolina. Stone's research focuses on rhetorical studies and technical communication with an emphasis on reproductive justice. Her solo and co-authored published works have appeared in *Rhetoric of Health and Medicine, Peitho, MAI: Feminism & Visual Culture,* and *Reflections: A Journal of Community-Engaged Writing and Rhetoric.*

Jill Swiencicki is an associate professor of English at St. John Fisher University in Rochester, New York. She teaches courses in rhetoric, writing, and feminist studies. Her research focuses on the rhetoric of social justice and civil rights movements, feminist activism, and writing studies. Her work appears in such journals as *Women's Studies in Communication, College English, Peitho, Liberal Education,* and *Prompt,* as well as the edited collections *Feminist Connections, Going Public,* and *Rhetorical*

Education in America. Since 2015 Swiencicki has been a talk line volunteer at Connect and Breathe, the only secular, nonjudgmental talk line in the United States for people to process their feelings after abortion.

Jenna Vinson is an associate professor of English at the University of Massachusetts Lowell. She specializes in feminist rhetorical studies and rhetorics of reproductive injustice. Her book, *Embodying the Problem: The Persuasive Power of the Teen Mother* (2017), challenges the pathologizing discourses of teenage pregnancy prevention and investigates the creative strategies young mothering women use to resist negative representations of their lives. Her articles have appeared in journals such as *Feminist Formations*, the *Journal of Multimodal Rhetorics, Kairos, Present Tense, Reflections*, and *Sexuality Research and Social Policy*.

James D. Warwood is a PhD candidate in the composition and rhetoric program at the University of Wisconsin-Madison. Their dissertation project explores trans and embodied rhetorics as a means of worldmaking and creating trans joy.

Shui-yin Sharon Yam is an associate professor of Writing, Rhetoric, and Digital Studies, and a faculty affiliate of Gender and Women Studies and the Center for Equality and Social Justice at the University of Kentucky. Her research focuses on citizenship, affect, race, and reproductive justice. Her public scholarship can be found in *Foreign Policy,* the *New York Times, The Diplomat,* and *Hong Kong Free Press.* She was the winner of the 2021 Rhetoric Society of America Fellows' Early Career Award. Yam's work has been published in journals such as the *Quarterly Journal of Speech, Rhetoric Society Quarterly, Women's Studies in Communication*, and *Feminist Formations*. Her article, "Visualizing Birth Stories from the Margin: Toward a Reproductive Justice Model of Rhetorical Analysis" received the 2021 Association for the Rhetoric of Science, Technology, and Medicine's Article of the Year Award. Her book *Inconvenient Strangers: Transnational Subjects and the Politics of Citizenship* was the winner of the 2021 CCCC Outstanding Book Award and was shortlisted for the RSA 2019 Book Award.

Index

About the Editors

Heather Brook Adams is an associate professor of English and a cross-appointed faculty member in the Women's, Gender, and Sexuality Studies program at the University of North Carolina Greensboro. She teaches graduate and undergraduate courses on contemporary rhetoric, rhetorics of health and medicine, advocacy and argumentation, and feminist pedagogy. Her research investigates discourses of gender, reproduction, and shame as well as intersectional methodologies and undergraduate research as a writing practice. Her book *Enduring Shame: A Recent History of Unwed Pregnancy and Righteous Reproduction*, was published by the University of South Carolina Press. Adams's work has appeared in journals including *Quarterly Journal of Speech, Rhetoric of Health and Medicine, Rhetoric Review, Women's Studies in Communication, Peitho, Computers and Composition,* and *Pedagogy* as well as in several edited collections.

Nancy Myers is an associate professor of English at the University of North Carolina Greensboro, where she teaches rhetorical theory and history, composition, and linguistics and is cross-appointed faculty in the Women's, Gender, and Sexuality Studies program. Her more recent feminist rhetorical scholarship includes essays in *Nineteenth-Century American Activist Rhetorics, Women at Work: Rhetorics of Gender and Labor, Remembering Differently: Recollecting Women's Rhetorical Narratives, In the Archives of Composition*, and *Rhetoric, History, and Women's Oratorical Education*. She is coeditor with Kathleen J. Ryan and Rebecca Jones of *Rethinking Ethos* and was coeditor with Edward P.J. Corbett and Gary Tate of the third and fourth editions of *The Writing Teacher's Sourcebook*. Myers served from 2010 to 2012 as president of the Coalition of Feminist Scholars in the History of Rhetoric and Composition.

www.ingramcontent.com/pod-product-compliance
Lightning Source LLC
Chambersburg PA
CBHW031413270326
41929CB00010BA/1444

* 9 7 8 1 6 4 3 1 7 4 2 4 2 *